THE GREAT CAMPAIGNS:

Reform and War in America, 1900-1928

Otis L. Graham, Jr.

THE
GREAT
CAMPAIGNS:
Reform and War
in America, 1900-1928

ROBERT E. KRIEGER PUBLISHING COMPANY
MALABAR, FLORIDA
1987

Original Edition 1971
Abbreviated Edition 1987

Printed and Published by
ROBERT E. KRIEGER PUBLISHING COMPANY, INC.
KRIEGER DRIVE
MALABAR, FLORIDA 32950

Copyright © 1971, Prentice-Hall, Inc.
Transferred to Otis L. Graham, Jr. May 1979
Printed by Arrangement

Printed in the United States of America.

Library of Congress Cataloging-in-Publication Data

Graham, Otis L.
    The great campaigns.

    Bibliography: p.
    Includes index.
    1. Progressivism (United States politics)   2. United States—Politics
and government—1901-1953.   3. United States—Foreign relations—
1865-1921.   I. Title.
E743.G72   1987   973.91   86-33741
ISBN 0-89464-204-9

contents

foreword

The opening of the twentieth century seemed an appropriate time for self-congratulation. If some doubted the extent of American ingenuity and technological progress, they had only to attend the Pan-American Exposition at Buffalo, New York, and marvel over the new wonders of electric lighting. The United States had just emerged from a popular war with Spain, and with spoils which included the Philippine Islands and a semi-protectorate over Cuba. (There was no need to linger over the costly and brutal suppression of the Filipino insurgents, whose principal crime had been to demand independence rather than Anglo-Saxon tutelage.) The prosperity which the Republican Party had promised was now apparently at hand—it was sufficiently impressive, at least, to turn the heads of commercial farmers from notions of free silver and third parties to business ledgers, business organization, and pressure politics. The labor wars of Homestead and Pullman, and that ugly spectacle of a march of the unemployed on Washington, D.C., were all but forgotten; indeed, it seemed almost certain that the "labor agitator" was on his way to becoming an extinct species. And, best of all, William McKinley was President of the United States. His very face and demeanor suggested a nation at peace with itself. "I can no longer be called the President of a party," he proclaimed in 1900. "I am now the President of the whole people." That he was—surely the most popular President since Abraham Lincoln. The new Vice-President, Theodore Roosevelt, reconciled himself to four years as "a dignified nonentity." But Leon Czolgosz, a self-professed anarchist, decided otherwise. On September 6, 1901, he shot and mortally wounded the President. "It is God's way," McKinley murmured. "His will, not ours, be done." It was an ominous note on which to usher in the new century.

There was good reason to be concerned about the health, the moral integrity, and the destiny of the American Republic, whatever the outward signs of equanimity and the apparent prosperity. The danger was sufficiently obvious: a growing fragmentation of American society, made urgent by an accelerated and unregulated industrialization and urbanization, and the distinct possibility that a brutalized and radicalized proleteriat would fulfill Jack London's apočalyptic vision in *The Iron Heel*. Yet, Americans remained confident that their society was sufficiently durable, flexible, and liberal to handle any social crisis. What emerged in the early years of the twentieth century was "a wave of reform, the mounting of a thousand campaigns of all shapes and sizes to intervene, to bring under control and redirect, the forces that were at work with such alarming result in modernizing America." This is the central concern of Otis Graham's *The Great Campaigns*. To explain the nature of that movement called Progressivism, to comprehend the varied and often contradictory banners which it unfurled, is no easy task. It demands inquiries into motivation—the kinds of impulses that moved men and women from a state of apathy and indifference to become indignant Christian crusaders. "Progressives liked to run under the flag of generosity and conscience," Graham argues, "but what they were usually about was something quite legitimate but less angelic, group economic and cultural self-interest. This should not make progressivism the less interesting. Indeed, it makes it more interesting because it becomes thereby believable."

To study the Progressive Era is not simply to explore political clashes, legislative debates, political personalities (though Roosevelt and Wilson afford a veritable bonanza for the amateur psychologist), or the various doings at city hall and the state house. This is the stuff of which most textbook accounts are made, but it fails to illuminate the diverse forces at work in this period. It tells us little, for example, about the crucial role of business and professional groups in reform activities, the kinds of attitudes which infused the Progressive mentality, the obsessions with "efficiency," "rationalization," and "orderly procedure." We have reached a point in historical scholarship, Graham states, when "we need no longer rely upon rhetorical evidence in reconstructing what was being proposed and done by whom to whom in this tumultuous period." These are precisely the kinds of issues that he sets out to clarify.

It is customary to view World War I as a chapter in American diplomacy and as the bridge between the reformist Progressive Era and the conservative, complacent Twenties. But the War was also a significant and suggestive chapter in the history of Progressive reform—indeed, in some ways, its finest hour. This is not to argue that Progressives had an affinity for war. Graham rejects this notion. But the ways in which Progressives mobilized for the War, the kind of unity they sought to impose on American society, the rhetoric they used in the prosecution of the War, and the wartime lessons in business-government cooperation are most instructive for an understanding of this many-sided movement. The War, for example, perverted the idea of the regulatory state and virtually crippled the humanitarian side of reform. "No historian," Graham writes, "has described this process in full detail, for it involves matters of mood and spirit as well as the traditional pull and haul of politics." Although protest was by no means absent in the Twenties, the dominant spirit was clear enough, and wartime Progressivism was to reap a rather strange harvest—prohibition, Americanization, immigration restriction, and white supremacy. This "triumph of the reactionary spirit," Graham notes, was not the result of a sinister plot hatched in Wall Street. It was eminently American—"a national phenomenon expressing the ultimate decision of the great bulk of the American people that they would not tolerate any further disturbance or uncertainty, and were in no mood for idealism." It reached its apogee, in fact, in the very home of American reform, when the State of Massachusetts executed two

Italian aliens and anarchists, Nicola Sacco and Bartolomeo Vanzetti, on the most circumstantial kind of evidence.

What Otis Graham has described so well is essentially the American reform mentality—its changing moods, aberrations, triumphs, and far-reaching consequences. That his analysis departs from some traditional views of Progressivism is abundantly clear. "We see social control where older histories described liberation, we attribute reform measures to professional and commercial elites rather than the indignant rhetoricians of Congress, pulpit, and magazines, and we describe the goal as the rationalization and centralization, not the democratization, of American society." Graham's Progressivism may not be the Progressivism described in most textbooks but it becomes more believable, precisely because it is so characteristically American.

The objective of each volume in The History of the American People series is to encourage the student to think critically about how we got to where we are. There is no attempt to be definitive—that is, to treat every aspect of American society in its historical development or to describe every legislative act and presidential election. Each of the participating authors will make his own choice of emphasis, seeking thereby to illuminate what is most significant about a particular historical period. The documentary and photographic sections are essays in themselves. They are intended not as appendices but as integral and essential portions of the author's total presentation. They are aimed, too, at involving the student in the mood and spirit of the period. There is no conscious attempt in this series to present either "Revisionist" or "Counter-Revisionist" history. We have simply invited some thoughtful, critical, and skeptical minds to address themselves to the history of American society. And it is precisely to that kind of audience that we dedicate these volumes.

Leon F. Litwack

preface

Leon Litwack and Robert Fenyo spoke to me about this volume some three years ago. Just about that time I was feeling more than usually tentative about the things I was telling students about the reform experience at the beginning of this century, and I welcomed the opportunity to rethink the period and its problems. If one is interested in liberal reform, I discovered, one is lured into the war years and the 1920s. The design of this book reflects that discovery. The decision to end the study at the eve of the Depression was not made on historical grounds. My interest remained, and there was more to the story, but the book began to encroach on another in this series.

Readers will note the critical attention paid to the work of four men—Samuel P. Hays, Richard Hofstadter, Gabriel Kolko, and Robert Wiebe. It was these men (Hofstadter in the 1950s, the others in the 1960s) who unsettled my settled views and finally left me no alternative but to attempt a synthesis of my own.

Some of my extensive debts to other authors are acknowledged in the Bibliographic Essay. Citations to direct quotations are also included in this essay, which takes the form of a running bibliographic commentary on the text. It could easily be four times as long, for the shelves are full of indispensable studies.

Special thanks go to Leon Litwack, Henry Adams, Barton J. Bernstein, David Burner, W. Elliott Brownlee, A. Russell Buchanan, Maurice Conway, George Dangerfield, Alexander DeConde, Carroll Pursell, and Roger Williams for critical readings. Samuel and Sherrill Wells went to unusual lengths to talk me out of some of my errors, as did my brother, Hugh D. Graham. All of these scholars deserve the thanks of myself and my readers, and must not be blamed for flaws of style or content. My greatest debt is to my best friend, to whom I dedicate this book.

Otis L. Graham, Jr.

THE GREAT CAMPAIGNS:

Reform and War in America, 1900-1928

part one

REFORM: 1900-1916

I.

In that melancholy, fascinating, inconclusive book, *The Education of Henry Adams* (1906), a weary descendant of the nineteenth century's greatest American family brooded his way into the new century, trying to perceive what lay ahead for his country. Henry Adams was personally inclined toward a strong sense of the apocalypse, but his feeling that the nation was in a unique crisis was shared by many thoughtful people. The turn of a century naturally produces a good deal of introspection, but well before 1900 American intellectuals began to express a growing consensus that the United States, if not the entire Western world, was entering a time of unprecedented peril and opportunity. Josiah Strong's popular book *Our Country* (1886) judged the end of the nineteenth century to be a time in human affairs second in importance only to the time of the birth of Christ, a "fateful moment" of fluidity in which the national destiny was being shaped by forces only half understood.

The air of crisis was a compound of confidence and foreboding. The signs of the times were mixed, and individuals came to varying conclusions about the future. There were grounds, of course, for that well-entrenched American confidence. The war with Spain was successfully concluded, the flag had been planted in Puerto Rico, Hawaii, and the Philippines, and the threat of Bryan and his angry millions seemed well in hand. The country was in the middle of a fabulous economic expansion, with the national wealth nearly doubling between 1890 and 1900. New marvels were appearing yearly, among them electric lights and trolleys, X-rays, wireless transmitters, autos, and even rumors of flying machines. With such sure signs of progress there were many whose rising excitement at the turn of the century was untroubled by serious doubts. "Laws are becoming more just," orated the Reverend Newell Hillis in 1900, "rulers humane; music is becoming sweeter and books wiser; homes are happier, and the individual heart becoming at once more just and more gentle." The popular novels of the day, such as Gene Stratton Porter's *Freckles,* Charles Major's *When Knighthood Was in Flower,* or John Fox, Jr.'s *The Little Shepherd of Kingdom Come,* while they were not untouched by the general excitement and sense of big things impending, reflected a remarkable absence of any feeling that what was going on in the Western world at the turn of the century might disturb the verities of God, home, family, neighborliness, and a safe return on investments. In addition to clergymen of sunny disposition and those novelists who were in touch with the mood of middle-class ladies, others here and there in the social structure greeted the new century with considerable confidence. A biographer of J. P. Morgan wrote of him in 1900: "His married children and grandchildren were all well and happy...his friends were near by. The people in his social world were of his own kind. ... New York was a friendly, neighborly city. ... He was looking forward with the eagerness of a much younger man to the great possibilities of the century that was about to begin."

But for many contemporaries the dynamic epoch just ahead was awaited with a good deal of anxiety. The novel may have been largely immune to pessimism until the eve of the World War, but many general books at the juncture of the centuries expressed fears that the times were out of joint—Strong's *Our Country,* Henry Demarest Lloyd's *Wealth Against Commonwealth* (1894), William T. Stead's *If Christ Came to Chicago* (1894), Walter Rauschenbusch's *Christianity and the Social Crisis* (1907), Homer Lea's *The Valor of Ignorance* (1900). Journalist Mark Sullivan, surveying the popular mood in his *Our Times: The Turn of the Century,* found a prevailing "irritation," a feeling that "some force or other was "crowding" the average man, that he was "being circumscribed in a tightening ring."

The grounds for such a volume of pessimistic thoughts, unprecedented since the dark, doubtful days of the 1780s and 1790s, were everywhere to see. The 1890s had been a frightful decade. Contemporaries noticed that immigration of undesirable ethnic groups from Europe had mounted alarmingly, and were further shaken by the news, extrapolated from the Census of 1890, that the supply of free land was on its way to exhaustion and that a continuous frontier line no longer existed. Agrarian radicalism had been massing ominously even before the economic slump of the mid 1890s, and the depression produced a high level of industrial disorder, of which the most visible episodes were the Homestead strike of 1892, the Pullman strike of 1894, and the march of Coxey's rabble in the same year.

By 1900, it is true, a returning prosperity had at least for the moment removed the threat of actual armed uprisings by the labor force. But other problems had appeared and intensified. Shortly after the turn of the century the volume of social criticism and warning reached a point where contemporaries recognized that a national movement of self-criticism was under way, and they called it, in Theodore Roosevelt's term, muckraking. The exposure movement in journalism cannot be accounted for without mention of the new mass audience hungry for both shock and a more personalized news; a new class of publishers unhampered by the old literary tastes; and the arrival in the ranks of journalists of a class of ambitious, moralistic, and talented college graduates. But it was grounded in real and mounting social problems, and reflected the widespread social uneasiness at the opening of the twentieth century. From this muckraking literature, supplemented by autobiographical material and the record of corrective action, we can reconstruct the leading concerns of that vocal segment of the public which had detected disturbing developments and tendencies in the dynamic society that was *fin de siècle* America.

II.

Lord Bryce had said in 1888 that the governing of cities was the United States's most conspicuous failure. Contemporaries understood without consulting a sociologist that the country was industrializing, that industrialization meant urbanization, and that the cities, and in and around them the factories, were attracting and using people too fast for decent standards to be maintained. Too many people moved to the cities, and too many different kinds of people, straining urban public services, the peace of the streets, and the older residents' peace of mind. We are at the core of the matter when we know, for example, that Seattle had a population of 80,000 in 1900 but 237,000 in 1910, that as many as 50,000 people tried to settle in Chicago every twelve months through the 1890s, that between 1880 and 1910 the total of urban-dwellers in the nation trebled. These masses came to urban centers not only because employers offered good money to those who would man the lathes and looms, carry and cook, draft and file; they came also because young men (and women, although they were less mobile) wished to be where the action was, and defined this more broadly than merely economic opportunity. Commercial schemes and new pleasures beckoned, limitless and undreamed-of vistas opened to farm-born boys who were tired of the tempo of Iowa afternoons.

As a result of this population shift, governmental problems proliferated in America's bulging cities, taking familiar forms of waste and inefficiency, ineptitude, and outright scandal. Municipal governments in those days did not have extensive duties, but where they functioned—providing police services, granting utility franchises, cleaning the streets—they did not seem to function according to reasonable standards of honesty and efficiency, according to the best magazines. Readers learned that in virtually every large city the city government was more or less openly bought and sold by the "interests" which their few functions affected. This situation was objectionable because it was expensive and immoral—and, quite probably, in that order. The classic account of these conditions, Lincoln Steffens's report on six cities in his series, "The Shame of the Cities," appeared in *McClures' Magazine* in 1904 and 1905. At this distance it is too easy to shrug at the "bit of graft" that seems to have been the central feature of the misgovernment that aroused Steffens and his upper-middle class readership, but for one thing we forget the size of the stakes. The franchises granted to the public service corporations in New York City in 1903, although appraised at 235 million dollars, were actually worth half again as much, and returns on this investment were not taxed. This untaxed local monopoly engaged the cupidity of enterprising men who thought little of purchasing a city council or board of aldermen for what Cleveland reformer Fred Howe called "a possession fairly regal in its proportions."

State governments were equally susceptible to purchase because the functions they shouldered—granting urban charters, corporate charters, franchises, permits in resource management, and deciding who should and should not be taxed—had to do with allocating advantages of a very lucrative sort. Naturally, men with much at stake did not leave such things to chance. Frank Norris's novel *The Octopus* described a simple case: the government of California at Sacramento was owned outright by the Southern Pacific Railroad. In a state like LaFollette's Wisconsin, a number of interests—railroads, lumber, and mining companies—had always used the state government as the pathway to public lands and untaxed franchises. What was new at the turn of the century was not the increased occurrence of such arrangements, although there may have been some of that as industry expanded, but the spreading awareness that such lavish attention to private interests did not automatically forward the public interest.

These functions and malfunctions had to do with spending the public's money and with dispensing rights to the public domain, not with any question of the range of public services. Misgovernment in the former areas was objectionable enough, but was probably insufficient to generate a sustained, nationwide protest. Yet the same process of industrialization and urbanization that brought city and state governments to such venal arrangements created additional problems of a different type. Misgovernment that took the form of fiscal dishonesty or subservience to a few transit corporations and extractive industries came about primarily because the scale of operations of these quasi-utilities had grown so great that the interests involved felt it both necessary and possible to purchase their host governments in order to gain security and stability. But industrialism did more than place strains upon elected officials, strains that, in a newly impersonal environment, usually proved too much for their integrity. It affected the conditions of life and work for millions in the cities, and affected them in a way that added to the sense of wrong that was growing in the country.

Conditions of life and work for most of humanity, even in America, had always been hard and unattractive; but as Americans packed into cities and around factories in the years after the Civil War the human price of modernization ran very high. While the farm population showed some increase, the cities grew three times as fast. Most of that growth reflected immigration from rural America, but the most visible part of it in the largest cities came off the boats from Europe. Nearly nine million immigrants entered between 1900 and 1910, until a city like New York recorded 76 percent of its population (in 1910) as foreign born or their children, and even the small cities off the seaboard averaged one-third immigrants or first generation Americans. Whatever the combination, the cities choked on the numbers. Wards in New York and Chicago groaned under a greater mass of humanity than the center of Bombay, India, and millions packed into tenements if they were lucky, into rows of shanties if they were not. Basic municipal services, inadequate at the beginning of the period, could not cope with the growth. Two-thirds of Chicago's streets in 1900 were mud; cities like Rochester and Pittsburgh were at best half sewer and half privy, and Baltimore and New Orleans had no sewers at all. Water, both in quantity and quality, was everywhere a problem. In Washington, D.C., the water pressure was so low in the eastern portion of the city that half the city schools had no operative toilets at all.

Some could buy relief from such conditions, but a sea of people could not. America, even then the world's wealthiest society, was a poor country. Robert Hunter estimated in 1904 (in his book *Poverty*) that ten million Americans were so poor that they were slowly starving to death, and his estimate excluded the entire agricultural population, for whom figures were nonexistent. Wages for the American worker were in a slow ascent, as they had been since the Civil War, but still pressed close to the subsistence level: track hands on Southern railroads earned 47.5 cents a day, unskilled packinghouse workers averaged $7.40 a week in the seasons when they worked, and the Triangle Shirtwaist Fire investigation revealed that the girls worked seventy hours a week at top speed to earn $4–5. The nutritional level permitted by such earnings, added to the abominable housing available in the industrial centers, meant staggering health problems, of which tuberculosis and anemia were the most common, with typhoid and bubonic plague not unheard of. Occupational diseases such as lead poisoning, respiratory diseases among miners, "Phossy Jaw," and so on, were largely uncompensated, as were the industrial accidents that statistician Frederick Hoffman estimated at 1,664,000 (fatal or near-fatal) in 1900. The strains and hazards of industrial labor broke the health of many adults, and widespread child labor brought the most vulnerable class of employables into brutal contact with the factory regimen. And the human beings who endured these social arrangements for such meager rewards now lived without the supports of community life, largely unknown to employer and fellow-employee alike. Those who could not keep up, the old, the blind, the injured, the epileptic, the orphaned, the feeble-minded, or merely the unemployed, had previously found some small havens in the interstices of community—family, church, neighborhood. The industrial order, harsh for even the healthy wage earner, had no use at all for the others. Woodrow Wilson provided an apt summary in his first inaugural address: The nation was too busy becoming an industrial power to

> count the cost of lives snuffed out, of energies overtaxed and broken, the fearful physical and spiritual cost of the men and women and children upon whom the dead weight and burden of it all has fallen pitilessly the years through.

These accompaniments of industrialism were of concern not only to those who endured them but also to the middle class, who narrowly escaped the worst of them. For the American who did not directly experience such conditions of life, they were deplorable not only because they made for the degradation and unhappiness of those on the bottom, but also for what they threatened to provoke. Men who were subjected to such torments might, like the barbarians within the gates of the city, rise up and destroy the comfortable folk around them either by riot or by plague.

The threat of riot has received the greater attention. And one is struck by the frequency, in both the public addresses and private remarks of men of that generation, of expressions of fear of a radicalized lower class. The industrial unrest of the 1880s and 1890s continued only slightly abated in the new century, and more ominous than strikes was the jump in union membership, from 800,000 in 1900 to over 2,000,000 in 1904, and the Socialist Party's steady growth after its founding in 1901. While some concerned middle-class people dallied with socialism, most of them, like Theodore Roosevelt, became sympathetic to reform so that a way might be found to preserve the system against the twin horribles of plutocratic revolution and socialist revolution. T.R. equated his reformism with antisocialism many times in public and more often in private, and he has been frequently quoted. Editor Joseph Pulitzer said it just as well in a letter in 1907, in which he praised Roosevelt's efforts to bring corporations into line: "The greatest breeder of discontent and socialism is lack of confidence in the justice of the law, the popular belief that the law is one thing for the rich another for the poor."

This concern with the political threat constituted by a depressed urban lower class is familiar to any student of this period. But it seems to me after reviewing the literature on urban reform, and urban biographies in general, that we have too often undervalued the fear of the unsanitary impact of the urban mass—what today most educated people would call the urban ecological problem. When urban reformers like Charles Loring Brace called the slum dwellers "the dangerous classes" they had in mind the problems of germs and sewage fully as much as muggings or socialist assemblymen. James Crooks, in his biography of Baltimore during this era, for example, reminds us that extensive efforts in that city from 1895 to 1911 to improve public health, to revise housing codes, and to enlarge recreation facilities were motivated at least as much by fear of disease among the poor, packed into their reeking, dank quarters in an unsewered part of town, at they were by humanitarianism or civic pride. The rhetorical evidence from other cities and the pattern of urban reforms suggest that Crooks's judgment has broad validity. Urban citizens from the middle and upper walks of life developed in large numbers a broad sense of social urgency over these issues, and whether they thought of the working class as suffering or threatening or both, they were adopting a broad view of society which might move them to action in matters beyond immediate and accustomed interests and formerly left to Fate.

This same generation of Americans also became aware of a menace that transcended state lines and that had developed at the apex rather than the bottom of the social order. The consolidation movement in industry was a long-term trend, but a burst of mergers from 1897 to 1904 more than tripled the number of so-called trusts, establishing effective control of the market in a number of areas, among them sugar, tobacco, oil, steel, and railways. A similar centralization took place in investment banking. While we now know that the concentration movement was brought to a monopolistic conclusion only in certain areas and that continuing invention and new entries into the market kept competition fierce in most sectors of the economy, contemporaries took the revelations of monopoly such as those of Ida Tarbell on Standard Oil, Charles Edward Russell on the beef trust, or Louis Brandeis on the financial empires of Wall Street as accurate descriptions of a general process that was overtaking and revolutionizing American life.

The average citizen could think of any number of reasons to dread the continuation of this trend. Monopoly closed off economic opportunity, stifled the spirit of new enterprise, and threatened to end the social mobility which had been America's chief appeal. Another and more immediately visible result of economic concentration was the production of huge fortunes, opening an intolerable gulf between the classes. Andrew Carnegie earned 23 million dollars making and selling steel in 1900 (tax free), while the girls at the Triangle Shirtwaist Company were working six days for their five dollars a week. The largest American fortune, estimated to be about one billion dollars, was equal to the savings of the poorest 2.5 million people; the top 2 percent of the population held 60 precent of the country's wealth. The fortunes piling up in the hands of a few men and families represented immense power, and America had no defense against it comparable to the constitutional defenses erected by the Founders against political power. But the threat to liberty posed by economic monopoly went beyond the creation of limitless private fortunes. The owners and managers of the corporations that had eliminated the chastening force of competition in their economic area held important powers that were quite beyond challenge. They could force consumers to eat beef that was in too large part made up of suspect portions of cows and other mammals (including the immigrants who worked about the vats); their only alternative was not to eat canned meat at all. Most important, they could force consumers of staples like sugar and steel to pay prices that had no relation to costs—except the costs of maintaining the captains of industry and their wives and daughters in their fullest opulence. Pricing power was the mightiest weapon of all, the key to national economic health, the arbiter of every man's consumer decisions. Men trusted such a power only to the impartial and invisible hand of the marketplace, and were appalled to see it fall into the grasp of a few men selected not for their wisdom but for their ambition and cunning. A general inflation from 1897 to 1913 supported suspicions that pricing power was in fact in such hands and was being used to exploit the consuming public in the most shameless way. And if quality deterioration and price-fixing were not enough, economic monopoly permitted unrestrained entrepreneurs in the extractive industries to scar the earth, poison the air and water, and waste the treasure of the planet, passing on to future generations a part of the price of their present enjoyment.

There were a number of other social ills that darkened the new century, such as the use of liquor, prostitution, the inferior legal and social position of women (too few worried about blacks for this to be listed as a general concern), expensive armaments and the threat of war, poor public education, and so on. But the leading concerns were as we have reviewed them: misgovernment; the state of life of the' urban lower classes, their uncontrolled increase and political instability; economic concentration and all forms of unfair economic advantage. The contemporary sources are clear enough on these matters. But of the larger, overarching fear they contain only hints, multitudinous but nowhere fully developed. This might be stated as a fear that the social order was breaking apart, that the binding commonalities could no longer be sure of mastering the centrifugal, disintegrative forces which were lately gathering momentum.

Of course, America had always been an unruly, individualistic society, perhaps especially in the nineteenth century, and patriots long dead—Hamilton, Emerson, Hawthorne, Lincoln—had worried about its divisive tendencies. But there had always seemed to be enough cultural consensus, enough common purpose in expansion and physical survival, to hold the society together. It was only toward the end of the nineteenth century that anxiety about the very existence of the social order became widespread, and it served as the common denominator of the various maladies that beset modernizing América at the hinge of the centuries.

The concern over social cohesion was far from unwarranted. The sources of authority that had held the nation together were visibly eroding. Any contemporary conservative could have catalogued the problems of order: neither God, the family, the ethical prohibitions of the Protestant clergy, nor the social constraints of respectable community opinion were holding their own against the doubts, heresies, and temptations of modernism. As these loyalties of a village culture began to dissolve in the acids of science, geographical mobility, and that school of cultural relativism, the city, there was exposed to view the lack of national institutions for social integration. There was no national church, nor any consensus really on the value of religion, let alone the true denomination; there were no national universities, no national media, an enfeebled army and navy with thin traditions, and only poorly connected local elites to pose as a national aristocracy. There was little sense, either, of a national cultural inheritance, In place of a historic and viable national literature, art, music, or drama, there were only ethnic and regional survivals from European cultures, and on the whole a society too busy to define itself in cultural terms.

Most important, there was only a tiny, feeble national government, without the means and without the inclination to offer authority, vision, direction. Lord Bryce devoted one of his chapters in *The American Commonwealth* to the subject, "Why the Best Men Do Not Go Into Politics," describing for his English audience how the American national government, enervated by laissez-faire doctrines and the absence of constitutional power, adequate revenues, and a trained and aggressive civil service, was quite rightly not regarded in the late nineteenth century as a proper place for young men of energy and promise. Why should the best men have served the public? Government had no mandate to play a large role, and if it had, it did not possess the resources for sustained management. The executive staff at the White House in the 1890s numbered ten people, of whom four were bookkeepers and messengers. The president had access to no economists, no statisticians, no planning staff for either foreign or domestic questions. The secretary of agriculture complained in 1900 that more men worked for George Vanderbilt on his North Carolina estate than worked for the entire Department of Agriculture. When the European scholar M. I. Ostrogorski published his observations of American government in 1902 (*Democracy and the Organization of Political Parties*), he summed up the relation between American government and the larger society:

> From one end of the scale to the other, the constituted authorities are unequal to their duty; they prove incapable of ensuring the protection of the general interest, or even place the power which has been entrusted to them by the community at the disposal of private interests. The spring of government is weakened or warped everywhere.

"The weakened spring of government"—an incisive description of the frailty of national institutions of social cohesion at the end of the nine-

teenth century. And just at the time that the exuberances of industrialism and urbanism began their historic and apparently permanent
undermining of the authorities of community life, which in the absence
of strong national institutions provided all of the bonds between individuals in a fiercely competitive society, the forces of division began to
be augmented. The tide of immigrants from eastern and southern
Europe, the steady northward migration year after year of 10,000 or
more blacks from their invisible existences south of the Potomac,
threatened to fragment what seemed a homogeneous Yankee culture
into a babel of tongues, colors, and customs. The increase of tensions
between economic classes projected a disintegration of another sort,
probably more violent and lethal than the cultural conflicts which
were intensifying between nativists and others. "The present assault
upon capital," spoke the gloomy Justice Stephen J. Field, "is but the
beginning. It will be but the stepping-stone to others, larger and more
sweeping, till our political contests will become a war of the poor
against the rich; a war constantly growing in intensity and bitterness."

It was only natural that as men began to suspect that social antagonisms were multiplying beyond the capacities of the old processes of
reconciliation, they would begin to sense total disorder in the wings.
And so we detect beyond their fears of ethnic and class conflict a
general fear of forces building off somewhere in the surly ranks of
labor, among ruthless industrialists with continental schemes and un-
limited capital, in the laboratories of scientists with their revolutionary
probes into matter and energy. "The shadow of force lay over the
period," wrote Alfred Kazin, and while he knew this by reading the
novels of Jack London, Theodore Dreiser, Frank Norris, and many
others, we find it everywhere in the written record. Contemporaries felt
themselves entering an age of power—not restrained power, but uncoordinated aggregations of power in a setting of deep social antagonisms. In the words of Henry Adams:

> The citizens were crying, in every accent of anger and alarm, that
> the new forces must at any cost be brought under control. . . . Prosperity
> never before imagined, power never yet wielded by man, speed never
> reached by anything but a meteor, had made the world irritable,
> nervous, querulous, unreasonable, and afraid.

The response of others was more ambiguous, since the rising level of
tension and the new concentrations and techniques of power engen-
dered in younger men a sense of zest and excitement as well as forebod-

ing. But the foreboding went deep. It was not power alone which so set the nerves on edge, but the feeling that power seemed no longer harnessed toward a common vision, that it was instead hoarded by unseen men in whom one had no trust, for some deadly thrust against the rights of citizens. Power massed, not where the community willed it, but in private, irresponsible hands. Social change accelerated, out of control.

Such a catalogue of worries might have sent an older society into fatalism and a scramble for private sanctuary. But America in 1900 felt herself a young nation, bursting with energy and an instinctive confidence. Even though men doubted the future, almost none of them doubted that the future was worth a fight. The big news of the inter-war period (1898–1917), therefore, was the emergence of a wave of reform, the mounting of a thousand campaigns of all shapes and sizes to intervene, to bring under control and redirect, the forces that were at work with such alarming result in modernizing America. Were her cities foul, their governments inept and criminal? This was intolerable; they must be cleansed. Were her people suffering, brooding upon foreign ideologies? They must be uplifted, given hope in the American system. Was the society being pulled apart by the mounting pressures of materialism, distrust of strangers, the unpredictable and selfish conduct of irresponsible private groups? Then we must at once discover effective principles and techniques of order, and a strengthening of our common purpose. Just at the beginning of the century, but near the end of his life, Henry Adams wondered if he could come back in 1938, on the one hundredth anniversary of his birth, and, "for the first time since man began his education among the carnivores, . . . find a world that sensitive and timid natures could regard without a shudder." Even as he wrote, young men and women were stirring themselves for the efforts necessary to answer his question in a proud affirmative.

III.

Mere hardship and accelerating social change, of course, do not always produce a reform movement. Men must not only become collectively aware of social troubles, but do so in a spirit of indignation, which means imagining that things could and should be better than they are. It is well to remind inhabitants of a dissident, reformist, even revolutionary century, that such social activism is not typical of human life. Docility and privatization have been more general, interrupted occasionally by outbursts of dissatisfaction, which have been brief and atypical. The emergence of social protest is what must be accounted for, not apathy, and it makes a fascinating study. The problem may be approached in the aggregate, asking what group or groups are making an uprising and for what ends, or it may be approached individually. In the latter case it becomes the problem of accounting for the making of a reformer, of learning how a man came to hear the fire bell of progressivism in the night, when those around him slept. The approaches are complementary: biography is also history.

Earlier writers did not always think this a difficult or particularly interesting problem. The task was to account for the awakening of altruism and enlightened self-interest—in that order. The answer seemed obvious, especially to readers of progressive manifestos, speeches, and autobiographies. First, social conditions had worsened abruptly, and then a few talented and sensitive souls saw what was happening around them. They were the early theorists and the muckrakers, and they awakened the nation. The nation—or a large part of it—become converted to social concern and reform because these persuasive writers touched its conscience and alerted its sense of self-interest.

But how were these early harbingers themselves shaken from lethargy? It seems that the prime incubator was the chaotic city of turn-of-the-century America, with its sweaty ghettos, its crime and unhealthiness, and its feeling of being out of control. Most of the muckrakers were from small-town environments, and the city shocked them by contrast to the neighborly, orderly world they had known. They were too spirited and principled to witness these social conditions with anything but sustained indignation, and it was to be they who alerted the millions who could not witness urban social problems firsthand, either because they still lived in little New England or Midwestern towns, or because their urban careers—unlike those of journalists—did not take them on the other side of the tracks and did not encourage social observation. Thus we account for the muckrakers and early writers, and they account for the others.

There is vast evidence in autobiographical accounts to support the claim that progressivism was launched by a few mighty books. Countless reformers report that they were transformed originally by one of the early indignant classics of progressivism, books like Edward Bellamy's *Looking Backward* (1888), William T. Stead's *If Christ Came to Chicago* (1894), Jacob Riis' *How the Other Half Lives* (1890), Charles Sheldon's *In His Steps* (1896), or a book that made more reformers than any other since *Uncle Tom's Cabin,* Henry George's *Progress and Poverty* (1886).Tom Johnson, for example, the great reform Mayor of Cleveland (1901–09), was converted from the aggressive pursuit of wealth to the sacrifices of the reform effort (which cost him his health and his fortune) by reading *Progress and Poverty* on a train to New York. Johnson returned to Cleveland and a life of reform when a lawyer he hired for the purpose could not prove to him that George was wrong. Once converted, men like Johnson, and Chicago's John Peter Altgeld, Wisconsin's Robert LaFollette, and especially Theodore Roosevelt and Woodrow Wilson, men of charismatic power whose lives were dedicated to a cause beyond self, turned thousands of young men to reform by the power of their personalities and their rhetoric.

One of the problems with the account just offered is its heavy reliance upon altruism. Once aroused, reformers spoke of justice, of sacrifice, of duty, of service. Their literature is saturated with such terms, and with an intensely moralistic temper. This is because that generation was a religious—primarily a Protestant—generation, and the only language they knew to express their aroused feelings was the hortatory language of the Gospel—Uplift, Redemption, Conversion, Battles for the Lord, Forces of Evil, Crusades, and so on. Not only was their language drawn straight from the pulpit (to which most of them had been subjected two or three times a week since early youth, unlike our own generation), but most of their campaigns resembled revivals. In 1912 the Progressive Party of Theodore Roosevelt, with some of the most advanced and sophisticated minds of the era in the auditorium, stood and sang without reserve "We Stand at Armageddon and We Battle for the Lord."

While some of the leading ideas of progressivism were in the long run hostile to both Puritanism and Christianity, the great bulk of the movement was unaware of these ideas or at least of their implications, and confronted the problems of the era with the familiar mental attitudes and rhetoric of the Puritan tradition. Historians by the nature of their work have reread this rhetoric and have usually allowed themselves to believe that all of this language drawn from the Gospel of the prophet of love suggests that progressivism was chiefly about altruism. But they were misled by more than language. There was an element within progressivism for which altruism is the only appropriate descriptive term: the social work and social settlement element, supplemented by the Social Gospel clergy (some of them), and a few general intellectuals or professional reformers—one hardly knows what to call them—who worked, not just talked, for the underdog..

But altruism thins out quickly when one moves from these circles outward to areas of progressive effort that were far more typical. The language, admittedly, was the same. But when progressives outside these small groups used the word "justice," its primary meaning had to do not with benevolence or with wrongs done by society to its helpless victims. Most of those in hot pursuit of justice were calling for more advantages for themselves and less for their economic competitors. This is not a question of "sincerity" but of determining exactly what people meant by certain terms. Actually, some measure of justice and equity was often involved when a group in revolt sought to advance its own ends, but such motivation should not be confused with altruism. Few movements of any size are ever mounted by men disturbed primarily by the plight of others—and progressivism was a large, complex, national movement. As we shall see, most progressives were brought to rebellion by pain experienced directly, by some setback to their own interest. Aware that his taxes were high, a citizen joined the Municipal Voter's League of Chicage to eliminate graft and put the city on a more frugal footing. Angry at what seemed to be exorbitant rates for shipping goods to market, a farmer or grain shipper would work for a state regulatory commission or a strengthening of the Interstate Commerce Commission. Shocked by Upton Sinclair's description (in *The Jungle,* 1906) of what he had thought was good, clean ham, a citizen become a T.R. supporter in the fight for federal regulation of meatpacking. Such motivation was thoroughly American, quite proper and natural, and often actually coincided with the broader public interest. It was the motivation behind the vast bulk of progressive pressures. Progressives liked to run under the flag of generosity and conscience, but what they were usually about was something quite legitimate but less angelic, group economic and cultural self-interest. This should not make progressivism the less interesting. Indeed, it makes it more interesting because it becomes thereby believable.

Those not of a speculative turn of mind may doubt the value of inquiries into motivation, especially in view of its complexities. That would be a mistake. The most entertaining argument in recent years was started by a man who was dissatisfied not only with suggestions of the motivating power of sheer altruism, but was also skeptical that the force of ideas was a sufficient cause of a man becoming a reformer. Ideas, of course, are indispensable to any reform movement, and we have the testimony of innumerable progressives that they were transformed by a book, a speech, a sermon. But what accounts for the selective effect of ideas—for their striking sparks in some who encounter them, and not in others? In *The Age of Reform* (1955), Richard Hofstadter noted evidence gathered by other investigators indicating that progressives were drawn inordinately from a special segment of society, essentially the young, well-to-do, and well-educated sons and daughters of the older American families that some like to call WASPs. They and their fathers generally belonged to social and occupational groups—clergy, small-town lawyers, doctors, merchants, and small manufacturers—who were not quite so prestigious at the turn of the century as they had formerly been, for a number of complicated reasons. Hofstadter suggested that the thunderbolt of reform struck most frequently where certain relative (not absolute) losses in personal status had begun to irritate, preparing the ground for great exertions which would be somewhat misleadingly labeled as aimed at improving others' lives.

This thesis, widely acclaimed, has also been widely resented. To some, Hofstadter seemed to be saying that progressives only *thought* they were awakened by the condition of the country and the plight of disadvantaged groups, and only *thought* they pursued altruistic ends. Actually they were awakened by personal discomforts having nothing or little to do with trusts or poverty, and they pursued psychic relief. Hofstadter was not saying exactly this. His argument was complex, comprehensive, and brilliantly stated, and ought to be sampled in the original—but to some readers who knew *they* were altruists he seemed to be excessively cynical. Such readers might well have cited Jane Addams on this point: "It is natural to feed the hungry and care for the sick, it is certainly natural to give pleasure to the young, comfort the aged, and to minister to the deep-seated craving for social intercourse that all men feel."

Thus it has been felt by some that the study of motivation is risky ground for historians; and historians like Hofstadter and Christopher Lasch (*The New Radicalism in America,* 1965) who wrote about what motivated the modern reformer, and others like David Donald who wrote about the motivations of the abolitionists, have not been universally welcomed. The critics are correct about the risks, since psychology and sociology are inexact sciences, especially when the people under study are no longer alive. But historians of reform movements that parade under the banner of crusades for altruistic goals must and will critically compare the announced aims of such reform movements with any evidence, sociological or psychological, they can find. This is so because it is decidedly *not* natural, Jane Addams notwithstanding, for most people to go beyond their minimal and convenient philanthropies and sacrifices.

I do not mention the Hofstadter book because the thesis has proven "true," for some damage has recently been done to it by historical investigation, and the argument is far from resolved. The most important result of this controversy has been the stimulation of dozens of studies of the sociological profile of progressivism. Such studies provide a broad range of data on who the reformers were in the various areas of activity, and some attention has also been paid to the "conservatives." Such studies are invaluable. We need no longer rely upon rhetorical evidence in reconstructing what was being proposed and done by whom to whom in this tumultuous period.

IV.

However it came about, indignation replaced complacency in the minds of thousands of Americans around the turn of the century, and prospects began to brighten for some sort of disturbance of the status quo. But even with social maladjustments identified and condemned as scandalous and intolerable, there still remained intellectual barriers to corrective action. One was a traditional laissez-faire attitude which, while often violated in practice, had been greatly talked of as a virtue, especially after the Civil War. Its constitutional counterpart, strict construction, in the hands of skilled judges like Stephen J. Field, had drawn a tight circle around political power in order to leave unfettered such "natural" forces as the acquisitive geniuses of John D. Rockefeller, Henry Clay Frick, Judge Elbert Gary, "Buck" Reynolds, and their like. A scientific version of laissez-faire, "social" or "hard" Darwinism, was imported from England and adapted to American conditions by men such as William Graham Summer. They saw it as Nature's way that some should visit morally invigorating but often fatal hardships upon others so that Nature could at length locate those she shouldn't have created in the first place and repair her error by eliminating them. These were the major intellectual barriers to reform, and a man could hardly move from indignation to action without first removing them, for they were widely held ideas. A few recent immigrants, due to their defective European educations, held none of these theories and could proceed to collective action at once, but this was thoughtless in more than one sense of the word. Had everybody behaved so without premeditation and soul-searching as did the simple socialists from Europe, the very livelihood and certainly the joys of the American intellectual historian would be in jeopardy.

The process of reeducating a generation is an interesting one to follow, especially for those who enjoy books and ideas as much as the progressives themselves enjoyed them. What was needed to liberate men from laissez-faire and social Darwinism, with their view of the social system as some sort of natural machine that men should not tamper with since they had not built it, was a general skepticism about the sanctity of current relationships, a confidence in the tinkering impulse, and a social theory that made social control no violation of some cosmic law. The skepticism was provided by any number of irreverent thinkers, the most effective being Thorstein Veblen (*The Theory of the Leisure Class*, 1899; and *The Theory of Business Enterprise*, 1904), and two professional satirists who are less appreciated by historians, Mark Twain and Peter Finley Dunne. The confidence in deliberate, rational manipulation of a complex social order, always latent in the American character, was given powerful expression by William James and John Dewey, who provided philosophical arguments why men should trust more in their intelligence—trained, scientific intelligence, not hunches—than in traditional wisdom or habit. The social theory that rebutted Sumner's reading of Darwin was also the work of many hands, among them the economist Richard T. Ely, who found no economic law prohibiting economic reform, and religious thinkers like Washington Gladden, John A. Ryan, and Walter Rauschenbusch, who testified as theologians that God had no objection if men did not meekly accept their temporal fate. The most comprehensive rebuttal of social Darwinism came at the hand of the sociologist Lester Frank Ward (*Dynamic Sociology*, 1883), who proved to all but the most hardened readers that Herbert Spencer and Sumner were wrong to assume that progress for human society could best be achieved by abdicating the directional function to fate. Ward was emphatic that fate was in no way superior to the guidance of intelligent men, and that anyway the control of social change had never been left to fate but had always been exercised by men—currently the more aggressive industrialists and financiers.

Men who were ready to act found the new theories persuasive and unshackled themselves from the old. This was not simply done; men cherished their old ideas more fondly than their wives, and discarded them with a good deal more anguish than any divorce. Among all the old theories that delayed and obstructed reform, undoubtedly the most hampering—because it was institutionalized—was a body of jurisprudence built up laboriously during the nineteenth century and designed to defend the rights of property from competing claims such as humanity, mercy, or the public good. That jurisprudence was intricate and in its way fascinating. It was also infuriating to Populists, Grangers, and progressives of all types who from time to time tried to expand the police powers of the state or build on the general welfare clause of the Constitution. Such efforts were almost invariably struck down or circumscribed by some canon of conservative jurisprudence—usually the due process clause of the fifth and fourteenth Amendments, or, when conservative judges were tired of being confined to constitutional language and were in a sporting mood, "freedom of contract."

What was needed to dissolve the bonds of conservative legal theory was another legal theory that emphasized the necessity for the law to be alert to changing circumstances and also to the fallibility of judges, indeed the fallibility of the Constitution makers themselves. Such a new view of the law was provided by Oliver Wendell Holmes, Jr., an activist in trying to get the Court to adopt a more passive role toward legislative experimentation. Holmes was inclined toward judicial self-restraint even though he usually thought the laws of reform-minded legislatures to be socially misguided, and he was skeptical of many of the "constitutional principles" that his brethren on the Supreme Court had discovered in and between the lines of the Constitution. He once rendered his judicial philosophy as follow: "Long ago I decided I was not God. When a state came in here and wanted to build a slaughter house, I looked at the Constitution and if I couldn't find anything in there that said a state couldn't build a slaughter house I said to myself, if they want to build a slaughter house, God-damnit, let them build it." In 1918 the Supreme Court struck down the Keating-Owen Child Labor Law on the ground that among the vital Fifth Amendment liberties was "freedom of contract," in this case the solemn right of eight-year-old Homer Dagenhart of North Carolina to either agree or not agree to work twelve hours a day. "When my brethren talk of 'freedom of contract'," Holmes said philosophically, "I compose my mind by thinking of all the beautiful women I have known." Holmes' doctrine of judicial self-restraint, along with Louis D. Brandeis' insistence that judges examine not only the law but the facts of social life (see his "Brandeis Brief" in *Muller* v. *Oregon,* 1908), helped squeeze a few modest reform measures past hostile courts. The work of these judicial thinkers, along with Charles A. Beard's *An Economic Interpretation of the Constitution of the United States* (1913), a history of the writing of the Constitution that painted the warts of self-interest on the faces of the Founders themselves, helped to inform and justify a popular suspicion of the courts, where conservatives were accustomed to take up their last stand.

These were the liberating theories of what Eric Goldman calls "Reform Darwinism," acting as corrosives of established belief and practice and as encouragement to innovation. They were warmly welcomed by men tired of the incantations of their elders, but still men of an essential conservatism despite their new plans, who wished first of all to assure themselves that they did not break some rule of the universe before they went about their renovations. Such theories put into the hands of a generation about to undertake collective action against existing arrangements the intellectual tools they needed to denounce things as they are, to discredit the idea that "things as they are" are as they have to be, and to justify rearrangements in social affairs based on reason, science, justice. The central features of these new modes of thought were a passion for the concrete, a confidence in human nature, human reason, and an aroused majority. They were formidable convictions. History was to treat them roughly. It was also to reveal significant differences and variations, among reformers themselves, in the weight given to democratic participation as against scientific expertise. But this is to anticipate the story.

V.

While it is true that the chief significance of progressivism is undoubtedly the resort to the state for a number of purposes, from arranging a different distribution of economic rewards and burdens to enforcing correct moral behavior, a large part of the reform effort took nonpolitical forms. Though scholars have a tendency to skip over these forms in order to get to the political battles, the nonpolitical aspects of reform deserve careful attention. Socially concerned people today believe in the efficacy of going down to Mississippi delta shacks and Chicago slums to share the situation of the poor and try to improve it. The progressive counterpart was settlement work. Modeled on London's Toynbee Hall, the first American settlement houses were established in the 1880s—Neighborhood Guild in New York, Hull House in Chicago—and at the turn of the century there were over a hundred. The intent of the settlement was to "fill the gap" that was opening between the urban lower class and the rest of society. Settlement workers did not think of themselves as simply uplifting the poor, although this was unquestionably involved. The best of them saw settlement work as a chance for the sons and daughters of comfortable, old-stock families to take advantage of contact with peoples whose culture had a number of things to offer. The spirit of the settlements, unlike the earlier charities movement, was not paternalistic; individual improvement in standards of behavior seemed less important than a pragmatic concern for improvement in standards of living. The routines were roughly similar in all the settlements; they may be followed in Jane Addams' *Twenty Years at Hull House* (1910), in Mary Simkhovitch's *Neighborhood: My Story of Greenwich House* (1938), or in Lillian Wald's *The House on Henry Street* (1915). They included day nurseries, counseling, clinics and visiting nurses, classes in hygiene, cooking, and spelling, the formation of clubs for all ages around interests such as athletics or Great Books or singing, the establishment of art museums and libraries, the serving of meals at all hours of day and night.

There has never been a satisfactory attempt to measure the effect of the settlement. Without doubt the settlement movement, like the Peace

Corps currently, had more beneficial effects upon those who came to serve than on those who received the attention of these lay missionaries. After observing the social roots of poverty, a few settlement workers left the settlement and stormed city hall, demanding better housing, sewage and sanitation, and factory laws. But although the settlements contributed people and ideas to the political wars of progressivism, the heart of the work was nonpolitical, the work of volunteers, people-to-people, in the ghetto.

The social ills that produced the progressive revolt, especially the problems of economic concentration and the problems of social inefficiency and disorder, suggested another nonpolitical remedy to reformers. This was functional organization, the organization of one's occupational interest against competitors or potential intruders. Actually, the word should be counterorganization, since those Americans who federated along functional lines in the progressive years saw themselves as driven to it by the prior organization of enormous corporate interests.

Railroads were consolidating, or being consolidated by financiers, until by 1900 six large systems controlled 95 percent of the nation's mileage; therefore, belatedly and indignantly, shippers organized to seek some control of rates affecting their region, usually in businessmen's leagues, chambers of commerce, or farmers' commodity groups and cooperatives. The same process went forward in professional circles, where rising occupational groups vital to the new technology combined in associations to improve salaries, upgrade standards, regulate entry into the field, and improve public relations. The labor force continued its slow self-organization after the depression of the 1890s had interrupted unionization, with union membership jumping from 868,500 in 1900 to 2,000,000 in 1904. Employers, alarmed at any workforce organization and exaggerating its extent (union membership grew very slowly after 1904, and was only about 2.5 million when the war began), formed hundreds of local employer organizations and three national groups, the National Association of Manufacturers (1895), the National Civic Federation (1896) and the Citizens' Industrial Association (1903).

This wave of counterorganization which followed the industrial combinations of the 1880s and 1890s may be sketched by consulting the *National Organizations of the United States* (Encyclopedia of Associa-

tions vol. 1.) : The Farmers Union, 1902; The International Brother-
hood of Teamsters, 1903; The American Astronomical Society, 1899;
The American Association of Agricultural Engineers, 1907; The Federal Council of Churches, 1908; The American Federation of Teachers,
1905; The American Association of State Highway Officials, 1914;
The New England Fish Exchange, 1908; The American Landscape
Architects Association, 1899; The Society of Automotive Engineers,
1905; The Anti-Defamation League of B'Nai B'rith, 1913; The American Institute of Chemical Engineers, 1908; The American Association
of Petroleum Geologists, 1917; The American Chamber of Commerce,
1912. Admittedly many such organizations learned to exert political
pressure when the need arose, but they were founded primarily to gain
group ends through economic pressure upon larger power blocs, or by
controlling entry into the field of their activity. A secondary interest,
especially among the professional groups like doctors, architects,
engineers, and the like, was to secure some control over group standards
and practices by consolidating to control the licensing process.

Some years ago this development would not have been seen as a part
of progressivism, since the formation of trade and professional organizations had nothing to do with elections and was not conspicuously
altruistic. And indeed I am not arguing that the simple fact of organization was a sign of progressivism; voluntary organization long predated the progressive era. What we perceive as distinctive in this period
is not the fact of organization but the scale and frequency of it. Americans of that generation, in numbers which allow us to speak of a mass
movement, turned to group organization to defend themselves against
economic rivals, rationalize disorderly and unpredictable business and
professional practices, and pursue a vision of an expanded role in
society. And while there were exceptions, there was about much of this
organizing binge a fervor and a sense of social responsibility which are
a second distinctive feature of the group life of the prewar years. Of
course this was true of the civic groups, the ministerial associations, and
the charity organization societies. Their purpose was altruistic, and we
expect them to talk like saints and go on crusades, which they did. A
familiar part of the progressive movement were the voluntary organizations formed to advance the consumer interest. They were not many
and they were never powerful; but to some the consumer seemed the
truly forgotten man of a period when every other conceivable interest
was being protected by federation; organizing the consumer allowed

full play to the progressive preference for activities that could be designated as in the public interest. The best known of the consumer organizations was the National Consumer's League, established by Florence Kelley in 1899 as a federation of state leagues. But other groups established at that time also adopted the consumer interest as part of their charge—for example the People's Lobby, formed by Samuel Merwin of *Success* magazine in 1906, and the American Home Economic Association, established in 1909.

While such groups have always been recognized as signs of progressivism, voluntary organization of a distinctly progressive cast was taking place among commercial and professional groups not normally thought of as participating in, for want of a better term at this point, uplift movements. The rhetoric that accompanied much of this organization marks it as sharing not only the era but also the spirit of progressive reform. In conventions and meetings among engineers, doctors, architects, and others, the talk, after the middle nineties and especially between 1910 and 1916, was likely to be not only about strength of materials and medicine and design, but also about the social crisis and the social responsibility of men whose considerable talents had previously served only self. The engineering profession, to take only one example, had organized into its four Founder Societies in the 1870s and 1880s in order to upgrade standards and regulate practices. But the rise of a sense of group responsibility occurred in the early twentieth century, appearing in the presidential addresses delivered at annual conventions of the Founder Societies (American Institute of Mining and Metallurgical Engineers, American Society of Mechanical Engineers, American Institute of Electrical Engineers, American Society of Civil Engineers), in the establishment by Morris L. Cooke and others of the Committee on Public Relations of the ASME in 1910, in the founding in 1917 of the Engineering Council, a federation of engineers interested in social action. Here in the organizational life of a commercial group one finds a part of the story of progressivism—not only a wave of organization so that control might be imposed on some area of confusion and waste in the economy, but the high-minded language of social responsibility. Admittedly, everybody talkin' 'bout Heaven ain't goin' there. Progressive engineers hoped to achieve the good society by running industry the way it should be run, namely, to produce goods, not profits; but the bankers and managers whom circumstances had regrettably placed in charge of the productive system proved too dull to see the logic of this. In the end, progressivism in the engineering profession produced some elevated language (such as the statement by President E. D. Meier of ASME in 1912, "the golden rule will be put in practice through the slide rule"), energetic subcommittees which framed denunciations of financiers and mono-polies, and a study, *Waste in Industry,* published in 1921. But whatever the accomplishments of reformers in this area, no account of progres-sivism is complete if it examines only City Hall and the halls of Con-gress and ignores the group life of many commercial groups and virtually all of the professions in the years between the Spanish-American War and World War I.

One could extend the mention of areas outside politics where the progressive spirit stirred. All three major faiths in America, Protestant, Catholic, Jewish, experienced internal questioning and a realignment toward a greater sense of social relevance, at least in the urban areas and among religious writers and thinkers. Painting and literature reflected social themes, often critically. Legal and Constitutional thought developed a strong interest in social facts, relied less on prece-dent. Old professions such as medicine, engineering, and the law reverberated with calls to duty, to social activism, to community as well as client service. New professions sprang up—social work, city planning, public health—where young people could prepare technical solutions to pressing moral problems. Psychotherapy emerged within psychiatry, behavioralism within psychology, and attacked their enervated parent disciplines for their lack of fervor, their lack of interest in improved human behavior, their lack of appreciation of the malleability of man and his future.

The most quickened profession, the most altered social institution outside politics, was surely education. Citizens and administrators banded together for more schools and better teachers. Progressive edu-cators sought the improvement of society by sweeping aside the old, rigid, classical curriculum in favor of an education relevant to life and directed toward freeing the creative potentialities of the student. Think-ing of education in a broader sense, virtually the entire muckraking literature, most of the general books written by reformers from Edward Bellamy to Herbert Croly, and all of the sermons preached by the reform-oriented clergy of the Social Gospel were efforts to solve the social crisis by educating and exhorting the public. It is with good reason that Rush Welter, in *Popular Education and Democratic Thought* (1963), sees progressivism primarily as an effort in public education, not in political action. Many men thought that it would be enough to speak out, breaking the silence that concealed the social crisis; individual enlightenment would follow, and wrongs would be voluntarily corrected. Many a progressive novel showed that all that was needed was the conversion of some wealthy but unenlightened factory owner who would then with a word eliminate all the selfish practices that had grown up while his conscience unaccountably slept. Such writers had no intuition that the state and its coercive powers would play such a large role in the action that followed their exposures.

VI.

Much, doubtlessly, was accomplished by these nonpolitical activities, especially if one's goals were modest. But it is a characteristic of modern life that before long every issue becomes politicized, and in due time the progressives found, if they had not realized it at the beginning, that the changes they wished could best, or only, be achieved through a resort to government. The power of law was quicker than education, more permanent and reliable than group counterpressures.

The first resort was usually to the most immediate level, municipal government. The progressive movement really began there, in a series of battles that are the skirmish line of a long war—Chicago, 1896; Toledo, 1897; Detroit, 1899; Cleveland 1901; then too many to count. While municipal reform involved reformers of quite diverse origins and aims, the predominant type was the Good Government progressive, a citizen from the comfortable classes who dropped his law practice or took time off from his business in order to sweep the grafters out of city hall. The "Goo Goos" resented the waste and inefficiency of the typical ward-based machines, whose careless ways seemed not only immoral but inadequate to the governance of booming cities. So these civic reformers counterattacked to restore—or to secure for the first time—both honesty and rationally organized government.

The pattern was similar from city to city. First came the formation of a City Club or Municipal Voters' League, then the launching of a campaign to replace the existing Irish mayor with a son of one of the better families.[1] Subsequently, seeing the need for structural rather than personnel changes, there would be a remodeling of city government, encompassing perhaps the city manager or commission from, and a new city charter allowing the city to own its utilities and exercise broader functions in a number of areas. And always there was the establishment of new agencies staffed with engineers, city planners, statisticians and other professionals to administer the vital health, crime prevention, and welfare functions of the metropolis. Great rhetorical efforts accompanied all these innovations, identifying reform with Democracy, The People, and so on. But the few close studies we have indicate that these municipal reformers were usually drawn from a narrow segment of society, the upper-middle business and professional classes. As Samuel P. Hays writes, they were "a small elite segment of society," businessmen whose interests were not focused in the street corner but were city-wide, and the lawyers who saw things as did the broader-visioned businessmen.[2] Since the groups they ousted were representative of social classes lower on the economic and social scale, municipal reform, according to the most recent and best evidence, should be seen as a shift of power upward in the social pyramid. This is not the only time in this century when the word *democracy* was borrowed by a movement that the unbiased observer might see as elitist.

The foregoing summary of the activities of municipal reformers slights the excitement, color, and difficulty of these crusades. The Goo Goos must have been making some headway, since in every case the "machine" and its allied business interests (usually the existing franchise holders in utilities) fought back as if capitalism itself were at stake. It was not safe to be a municipal reformer: Francis Heney was shot in the head in San Francisco and Fremont Older was kidnapped,

---

[1] While there was usually one large "Citizens' " alliance formed to guide the city's reform energies, when the moment finally came for a city-wide political campaign, American cities in the progressive era fairly teemed with businessmen's leagues, women's groups, and other organizations formed to advance the civic good. Zane Miller tells us that in Cincinnati in 1909 there were 40 civic groups, all tugging and talking Cincinnati upward.

[2] S. P. Hays, "The Shame of the Cities Revisited: The Case of Pittsburgh," in *The Muckrakers and American Society,* ed. Herbert Shapiro (1968). Hays found the opponents of reform to be small businessmen, white-collar workers and skilled workers, and other middle and lower-middle class elements. Less than a quarter (24 percent) of these "ins" (conservatives would be the wrong word) were drawn from the larger business and professional groups, whereas *all* of the reformers were from this elite.

and in Chicago Raymond Robins was brutally beaten by hired thugs.[3] Politics, as Mr. Dooley reminded onlookers, "ain't beanbag." The risks the municipal reformers took, their herculean exertions, their appealing rhetoric, these earned them the acclaim of subsequent writers. But in recent years we have not thought entirely well of this type of reformer. Some of this shift of opinion came when it became understood that the "bosses" usually came back after a few years, bringing the bad old days back to city hall. But a more basic critique has emerged, in part stimulated by the discovery of exactly which classes the Goo Goos represented. The civic reformer was property oriented, and typically offered greater efficiency in government and a stricter accounting for the public monies. But honesty is a less valuable virtue than compassion, which the old machines actually possessed in large degree. Although there was graft in the unreformed system, it made some efforts to minister to the needs of the lower classes, while the reformers were trying chiefly to reduce the taxes paid by property.

In this sort of reassessment the hazards are romanticizing the old machines on the one hand and regarding too lightly the improvements in the way of efficiency on the other. But when the right balance is struck, it seems that the gains of efficiency were made at the expense of removing government a few steps from the more needful and numerous people of the city and turning it over to the experts. The 1960s have sharpened the realization that such a shift is not entirely beneficial. The current mood seems to favor the compassionate local democracy, with its easy standards and sticky fingers, to the efficiency experts in city hall.

But municipal reformers were not all honesty-oriented. Some of them were services-oriented, and some of these had a lower-class bias even though they were usually themselves of upper-middle class origin. Of course there were municipal services that benefitted all classes, such as an aggressive public health service, prompt collection of garbage, smoke abatement, and lower water and electricity rates. But many progressives also worked for services of special benefit to the

---

3 Of course, there are forms of retaliation more dread than violence—excommunication, for example. Melvin Holli tells us (in his *Reform in Detroit: Hazen S. Pingree* and *Urban Politics* (1969)) that after Mayor Pingree's attack on the transit interests he was deprived of his pew in the Woodward Avenue Baptist Church.

crowded, working-class sectors—parks and recreation areas, lower streetcar fares subsidized by general taxation, humane criminal treatment, free or low-cost clinics, tenement inspection, and the like. Where these functions were successfully pursued by a reform administration, as in New York City, it generally meant that the Goo Goos had been joined in their insurgency by elements from the immigrant or working-class community. But whether the municipal reformers' efforts benefitted their own class or the one beneath it, at their best they followed a vision that combined the interests of all—a vision of a beautiful city on a hill, the twentieth century embodiment of that refuge envisioned by the Puritans who crossed the Atlantic to the new world.

VII.

At about the time that urban reform movements were increasing and becoming commonplace, progressives opened a second front at the state level. This order was no accident. In the nature of things, urban reform drew attention to inadequacies in state constitutions and administrations. Urban experimenters were everywhere hampered by state constitutions and codes, and it soon appeared that the way could not be cleared for thorough urban housecleaning without some preliminary renovation at Sacramento, Columbus, or Albany. At first the urban reformers' demand was merely for greater home rule, but the difficulty in achieving this at the capital brought them to see the need for substantial changes in the personnel and structure of state government. State legal arrangements not only fastened impotence upon the cities, but state governments were if anything more venal than city governments—they were found to be veritable Sodoms and Gomorrahs of lobbyists and graft, machines, cliques, and indifference behind which a few vested interests looted undisturbed.

When this was learned by urban reformers the progressive movement broadened to the state level, and a series of "honest" governors led angry citizens' movements in state after state. Here were produced some of the great figures of progressivism, men like Robert LaFollette, Hiram Johnson, Charles Evans Hughes, and Woodrow Wilson. The pattern of housecleaning was standard: after the election of a Peoples' Governor, there would be procedural reforms to sweep away the electoral arrangements that had been so complicated and slow that they had encouraged voter apathy—the most familiar of these reforms being the initiative, referendum, and recall, the direct election of senators, the short ballot, direct primaries, shorter terms for elective officials, and the like. Government was brought closer to the "public" and parties were diminished in power. The virtue of such changes of course depended upon the willingness of the public to exercise such powers as had been wrested in their behalf from the party apparatus, public officials, and the judiciary. The public was to disappoint its self-appointed champions, but the dearly-won victories of the Direct Democracy reformers were an important experiment and one that had to be tried.

As with urban reform, state progressivism was a coalition of diverse callings. The middle-class reformer described in George Mowry's study of California progressives was called by duty to the purgation and democratization of state politics, and he saw his role largely in negative terms. He would take the government away from the railroads and other special interests and return it to "the people," or, as he sometimes put it, "set it free." But there were other types jostling in the ranks of state reform. Many had something substantive to achieve once government was in purer hands. They were of two general types, the champions of their own group interests and the champions of the unrepresented and the disadvantaged. Both of these took up when and where the Goo Goos left off. They had lent a hand when the fight was being made for direct primaries and the other Direct Democracy measures, but such changes of the electoral rules were to them only preliminary.

The best-reported of the "positive" accomplishments of state reform were the social justice measures. In this category came the child labor laws, the statues regulating hours and wages, factory working conditions, and the like. While measures of this sort were secured in some cases with the self-interested help of organized labor, most of the pressure came from middle-class groups like the American Association for Labor Legislation, the National Consumers' League, or the General Federation of Women's Clubs. Cooperation between such groups and the representatives of organized labor was never extensive, and this was only partially because Sam Gompers preferred not to divert labor's attention from collective bargaining by allowing these costly and wearying forays for some small legislative advantage. It was also because middle-class reformers did not enjoy working with the representatives of labor, whom they found materialistic, unrefined, and hopelessly mired in a very narrow social perspective. In a book like Irwin Yellowitz' *Labor and the Progressive Movement in New York State, 1897–1916* (1965), for example, one sees these hostilities at work in a period and place of considerable class tension and can understand why a labor-progressive coalition for social legislation rarely became more than a theoretical possibility.

The entire body of child labor law passed in the South, for example, was secured by pressure from middle-class reformers in the child labor leagues, interested clergy (the head of the child labor movement was the Reverend A. J. McKelway), women's clubs, and the PTA. For such a coalition based primarily upon altruism, the passage of child labor laws in thirty-one states, of minimum wage laws (for women) in fifteen states and maximum hours (for women) in thirty-nine states, was a remarkable display of the power of appeals to conscience, factual studies, and sheer persistence. Most of these laws were watered down in passage and the funds appropriated for their enforcement were invariably skimpy, but advocates could ignore these things in their enthusiasm for the precedents they were setting.

But the social justice forces accounted for only a part of those enlarged state functions resulting from progressive pressure. Among the legislation-minded newcomers to the state capitals were angry businessmen of various sorts. Usually they were producers or shippers with freight rate grievances against the railroad, and they hoped to replace the intractable railroad traffic manager with a state rate commission. In small states like New Hampshire progressivism was a businessman's revolt against a railroad, and little else. Even in California, which ultimately produced a comprehensive reform experience including labor legislation and conservation measures, the origin of the movement was in an uprising of businessmen and publishers against the Southern Pacific Railroad. Other businessmen demanding state reform legislation were industrialists who had found the costs and uncertainties of the employers' liability system burdensome, and who saw in workmen's compensation a way to make the costs of industrial accident more predictable. Workmen's compensation laws have been taken to be a part of the social justice side of progressivism, but their chief support came from the manufacturers (through the National Association of Manufacturers especially) and insurance companies, who wished, in Roy Lubove's words, "to substitute a fixed, but limited charge for a variable, potentially ruinous one."

To be sure, the professional altruists of the social welfare camp also worked for workmen's compensation, but the laws bore the stamp of their business sponsors. In three out of four instances the laws provided that reserve funds be held by private insurance companies rather than by the state, and in the central matter of the level of compensation the victory of the employers was graphic in the meager extent of benefits. But whether employer or employee benefitted most, these laws were the embodiment of progressivism—passed in the teeth of apathy and indifference, designed to secure through state power some measure of predictability and control over the costs of industrialism.

VIII.

Even before progressivism at the state level had reached its apogee, reformers began to think of Washington. Note the grievances that required federal action. Only national legislation could satisfy the businessmen of the South and Midwest, who hoped to break the grip of eastern interests by tariff reduction and national banking reform. Only federal action could remove the constitutional barrier against a graduated income tax. Only the national government could effectively "do something about the trusts." Only the federal government could curb local pressures on the public domain and inaugurate satisfactory conservation policies. Only in Washington could those businessmen whose national interests and aspirations were blocked by confusing and overlapping state laws secure sensible and safe regulation of industrial enterprise. Only in Washington could farmers secure adequate credit for their seasonal needs, and only there could those determined ladies who wished to vote in federal elections secure their inalienable rights.

All of these goals—tariff reform, banking and industrial regulation, effective antitrust action, an income tax, conservation—required national legislation. A number of other reforms might be secured piecemeal through the states, such as woman suffrage, child labor reform, or wage and hour laws. But in the case of the labor legislation especially, the forces behind them were weak, and their progress through the states was retarded by the reluctance of individual states to raise the operating costs of industry while neighboring states did not. Such considerations led these social justice reformers with their chronically weak constituencies to turn their eyes toward Washington where the assistance of an enlightened president might enable them to win the measures their numbers could hardly hope to secure. Prohibition and woman suffrage were also for a time pushed in the individual states, but a federal solution was seen to be quicker, and these reforms also were brought to Washington for fulfillment.

Thus reform rose to the national level primarily because certain tasks could best, and in some cases only, be accomplished there. There was, too, the allure of national action. Men of ambition and energy could see no reason why the entire nation should not share in their enlightened leadership. Out of this complex field of hundreds of progressive groups and interests, there emerged in a little over a decade an altered and enlarged national state that bridged the years between laissez-faire and the welfare state of Franklin Roosevelt.

The legislative landmarks of national progressivism are familiar enough, but the story of who was actually getting what is only now becoming clear. Progressivism came to Washington in the days, and some say in the person, of Theodore Roosevelt, and we remember a number of events that appear as battles between the forces of reform and the forces of standpat-ism. These battles seem to have eventuated in victories for T.R. and his followers, usually in victories over business. One of the early signs of a new spirit at the apex of government was the antitrust prosecution of the Northern Securities Company (1902–4). This was clear evidence of a zeal for antitrust that previous administrations had conspicuously lacked, and reformers were heartened when the government secured a dissolution decree in the case. But this opening gun of the progressive antitrust campaign was one of the last moments of unanimity among reformers. Although the balance of the national progressive experience had largely to do with federal action involving large business enterprise, nothing was ever very clear again. What should be done about monopoly, and when something finally was done, who had done what to whom? The Northern Securities Company case heralded a reform administration, but it gave no clues as to the complexities inherent in the relation of large industrial operations to justice, the public interest, or the reasonable demands of interested parties in the world of commerce.

On this question, T.R., searching for what was politically safe before he decided what was morally right, pursued several lines at once.

His attorney general instituted a few suits against conspicuous trusts, such as Standard Oil and the meat-packing combine. But the courts had no clear notion of what was wise or of the precise meaning of the Sherman Act (they thought about it in that order), and these cases dragged out past T.R.'s departure from office with no clear result. While the president thought dissolution of large corporations was indicated in some cases, he leaned toward regulation of practices and standards in others. Leading examples of the latter were the meat-packing industry and the food and drug industries, where the administration sought regulatory power. That power was conferred in 1906 after two bitter legislative battles, and most accounts give the impression that Roosevelt had forced the public interest upon reluctant packers, processors, and drug manufacturers.

Such was not the case. The packers themselves were eager for stricter federal regulation (cursory inspection had been begun in 1891) to reassure their European buyers. The mere passage of the meat inspection act was no sign that the industry had been reformed, at least as T.R. and his supporters used that word. It might, on the contrary, be a sign that the government was being used. Everything depends upon a comparison of what the industry wanted in such an act, what was wanted by the advocates of regulation who had the public rather than the industry good in view, and what the legislation eventually provided. There was indeed an uproar from the industry as the government moved toward some sort of resolution of the matter in early 1906, but the uproar was largely against further exposures like those of Upton Sinclair (*The Jungle,* 1906) and of T.R.'s two investigators, Neill and Reynolds. The packers favored regulation, but protested agitation and the threat of the wrong kind of regulation. With regard to the important issues on which there was dispute, Senator Beveridge and other reformers argued that the cost of regulation should be placed upon the packers, insuring a stable source of funds for administration and enforcement. If the funds did not come from such a levy on the industry, Beveridge pointed out, Congress might emasculate any law by making piddling appropriations. He was perhaps recalling that the Congress had appropriated *no money* to enforce the Sherman Act during the first twelve years after its passage.

The packers opposed carrying this charge, and they won. The president and the reformers wished to date the cans; the packers had this stricken from the bill. T.R. also resisted close court supervision of Department of Agriculture orders issued under the law, and the result here was a draw. In summary, the meat-packing law of 1906 was a law the packers shaped to a large degree, and with which they were content. As Senator McCumber, a friend of strict regulation, commented: "We have met the enemy and we are theirs." The industry could easily live with the degree of federal supervision the law entailed, and all it really yielded to T.R. was the principle that the meat-packing industry was affected with the public interest and that the guardian of this interest was the federal government. Little was changed in the processing of canned meat; certainly nothing was changed for the workers, about whom Upton Sinclair had been most concerned.

This same general assessment holds also for the Pure Food and Drug Act of 1906, banning misbranded or adulterated food and drugs. Its leading advocate, Dr. Harvey Wiley of the Department of Agriculture, saw the struggle for regulation as one between Good and Evil, but it is more accurate to see it as a struggle between some food and drug interests and others. True, the strongest opposition to the law of 1906 came from food and drug companies, either patent medicine firms or canners and packagers whose interests would be hurt if certain preservatives were banned. And the General Federation of Women's Clubs, the public-spirited doctors of the young American Medical Association, and the implacable bureaucrats from the state food and dairy departments led by Edwin F. Ladd of North Dakota and Robert M. Allen of Kentucky composed the noisy, resourceful lobby for the public that colored the bill a bit pink. But decisive support and influence came from businesses that would be subject to regulation under a new federal law—established firms with an interest in stability and good public relations, which looked with more than mild approval upon a law that drove their unscrupulous, fly-by-night competition to the wall. The president of the Proprietary Association, a patent medicine group that helped shape the law after an early opposition, said in 1928: "Many of us remember the days when the business was laughed at. Today it is a most substantial, firmly established, constantly growing industry." And it was this Association, according to a trade journal, that deserved primary credit for having secured the law of 1906.

The popularity of that law among drug companies is easier to understand when one observes how a combination of weak provisions and lax enforcement diluted its effect. Enforcement was hampered by small appropriations and extensive court review, and even when convictions were obtained the penalties were low. The maximum fine under the act was $300, and the average fine levied from 1907 to 1933 was only $66. The first case brought by the Bureau of Chemistry under the 1906 law was an expensive, carefully drawn indictment of a company producing Cuforhedake Brane-Fude. The government won the case, and by a combination of fines was able to relieve a Mr. Harper, one of America's truly brilliant captains of industry, of the sum of $700. Lest the modern reader either laugh at the nomenclature of the medicine involved or take satisfaction at the victory of the watchdogs of the public health, it should be pointed out that Mr. Harper merely subtracted the $700 from the $2 million a leading scholar estimates as having been his take from sales of Brane-Fude. A firm determined to bottle and sell such questionable potions could afford to regard such a sum, which was rarely imposed anyway, as a virtual licensing fee. The bottling, advertising, and selling of useless and even poisonous substances continued, as Americans were to learn in the early 1930s when a small revival of muckraking searchlighted the food and drug industries.

T.R.'s leadership had been important in getting any law at all through a divided Congress, but he had inherited reform pressures in both meat-packing and food and drugs that went back almost twenty years. Similar pressures had been building since the 1880s to take the power of rate-making out of the hands of railroad traffic managers. Rail transportation was often a monopoly, with no effective competition from rival roads or water transport to discipline those who made the rates. Theodore Roosevelt put himself at the head of forces who wished to reform the making of rates, bringing them under public control. The Hepburn Act of 1906 seemed to bring the reformers victory over the railroads. Certainly the battle was hard enough, with the parliamentary maneuvering against Senator Aldrich and the "conservatives" consuming over eighteen months and taking all Roosevelt's skill. But again it is enlightening to look closely at the details.

The Interstate Commerce Commission, established in 1887, had been ineffective from the start. The Supreme Court ruled in a series of cases that the ICC could only *invalidate* rates through a tortuously slow process, but could not set binding ones. The Court also held that the legal basis for "long–short haul" equalization and rebate control was inadequate. The Hepburn Act was the centerpiece in a set of four reform laws that finally gave the ICC effective power to control the rate-making process. The Elkins Act of 1903 outlawed rebates, the Hepburn Act of 1906 conferred power to set maximum rates; and a major weakness of that act—that the courts could choose between ICC and railroad judgments as to what was a fair or an unfair rate—was remedied by the Physical Valuation Act of 1913, allowing the ICC's estimate of a fair return to prevail. Power to overrule long–short haul differentials came with the Mann-Elkins Act of 1910. The Hepburn Act may properly stand as a symbol of this legislative record, representing the substitution of public for private control over a vital service—rail transportation.

But public control, of course, is not synonymous with democracy, justice, or the public interest—although it *is* reform. What the progressives had done with regard to the railroads was to make a procedural change whereby an area of important decision-making was regularized, rationalized, and opened to the political pressures of more of the affected groups (but not all or even most of them). The changes were urged not by "the people" but by shippers from geographical areas whose natural economic advantages were nullified by the basing-point system, or by shippers of commodities in economic difficulties who attributed this to high rates on the only railroad available, or by railroad managers themselves who preferred predictability to the rate wars and ill-feelings of private rate-making. Where was the public interest in all this? Neither the Congress nor the ICC could discover it, and they have not to this day. How was one to set rates so as to advance the public interest? Often a long haul to centers of population received lower rates than shipments to closer points, but this was because of the economies of heavy traffic. A rate system that charged strictly by the mile might seem fairer to short-haul shippers, but its effect would be to eliminate the advantages of heavily populated areas and to decentralize industry. The South and rural areas generally would gain, but at the expense of efficiency. The South would also gain if the basing-point system were overturned by the ICC, but in this case the result would probably be *more* efficiency. What is clear is that the existing rate structure that the newly empowered ICC inherited, with its built-in differentials, rewarded established economic advantage and penalized aspiring competitors. But it required the wisdom of Solomon to discern where in these questions lay the general good.

Another divisive question had to do with a fair return. Presumably a fair return—and no more—was in the public interest, and years of litigation had placed a "fair return" at somewhere between 6 percent and 8 percent of invested capital. But who was to assess the physical worth of the sprawling railroad empires? These were questions of the most technical nature, and in the process of considering them it was impossible to keep clearly in mind the good, beautiful, and true. But there *was* a solution, and the progressive generation found it. The Congress, pressed by angry groups of shippers and by the railroad men themselves, passed these impossible questions on to a commission. Machinery was evolved to somewhat stabilize a situation that was chaotic. Experts now decided in an atmosphere charged with political pressure what railroad rate-makers had decided in an atmosphere of economic pressure. The process was more open than in the days when John D. Rockefeller powered his way to a favorable rate, and it allowed the consultation of more interests before a decision was reached. No man can demonstrate with exactitude that justice was the end result of the progressive regulation of railroads, but regularity of procedure was accomplished, and this was close to the heart of progressivism. And when formerly private decisions are politicized, whether aggrieved groups actually improve their position or not, the new procedure reduces the feeling of powerlessness among the unconsulted, which is a clear gain for any democratic society.

These were the leading progressive achievements of T.R.'s two terms: the establishment of regulatory agencies in the areas of rail transportation, meat-packing, food and drugs, and a reputation for antitrust action. One recalls the T.R. years also for conservation, another area where The People are supposed to have mastered The Interests, and another area where this was not at all the case. Progressive conservationists were primarily scientifically oriented men, like the forester Gifford Pinchot or the geologist W J McGee, who wished to bring rationality and a national perspective to resource exploitation. To such men a scientific use of America's resources required an immediate control over access to and disposition of these resources, a control that could only be exercised by men such as themselves. In addition to far-sighted and ambitious federal bureaucrats, such a program appealed to those larger extractive industries already on the resource site. It tended to infuriate small operators and those contemplating entry into the public domain, who felt they could

not control the remote eastern bureaucracies under Pinchot and
Roosevelt, and could not stand to have their costs raised by any shift
to "scientific management." The conservation movement was thus
primarily the promotion of an elite of scientists, their few sympathizers
in Congress, and the larger corporations involved in resource exploitation. The "little people" at the grass roots in the West and
elsewhere were more often than not suspicious and opposed to the
centralization that conservation implied.

These general remarks do not do justice to the complexities of the
conservation movement. Conservation involved forests, mineral reserves, irrigation and water rights, grazing, flood control, and recreation. No single legislative battle clarified the issues. The only significant
legislation was the Newlands Act of 1902 establishing the Bureau of
Reclamation, and the Weeks Act of 1911 providing federal grants
for fire prevention in the forests, and neither act caused major debate
or produced major consequences. The story of conservation in the
progressive era may be a simple story of good and evil in T.R.'s
speeches, but behind the rhetoric the story was one of obscure
bureaucratic struggles to control the policy of one or more of the
twenty-six government agencies having cognizance over public resources. Some of these struggles—most notably the Ballinger-Pinchot
contest of 1910—were invested with the usual the-people-vs.-the-inter-
ests rhetoric, but the progressive conservation movement could not
be accurately described by the progressives' own words, certainly not
by the word *democracy*.

If anything, conservation was antidemocratic in that it sought to
gather "rights" from thousands of private hands—from miners, lum-
bermen, ranchers—and centralize them in the hands of experts in
Washington. That the movement was not democratic in the simple
sense of the word should not discredit it, since the little people fully
intended to continue to rape the land in the way they always had.
Those who wished to put access to resources on a scientific basis
may perhaps be seen as the trustees for the many unborn, a silent
majority. They claimed, at any rate, to be acting in the interests of
some larger public when they overrode the wishes of a majority of
local resource users. Whatever they claimed, they usually lost. The
story of progressive conservation efforts is the story of a wave of
general publicity and a few specific proposals like the Inland Waterways Commission Report of 1907, all followed by legislative inaction

or outright hostility. Congress refused to set up the permanent Inland Waterways Commission through which Pinchot and T.R. hoped to establish multiple-purpose resource planning, and when T.R. asked for funds to continue his National Conservation Commission, that request, too, was refused.

Another aspect of conservation was preservation, itself a minority movement and quite antithetical to Pinchot's emphasis upon scientific use. But the prophetic dreamers of the preservation movement, men like John Muir, were if anything less successful than the elite that wanted scientific control over exploitation. Their chief effort came in the fight to save Hetch Hetchy valley for aesthetic enjoyment, and they lost the valley to San Francisco's water needs in 1913. Presumably some public education was accomplished by both wings of the progressive conservation movement. But both were disappointed in their immediate goals, since the destructive exploitation of both the wilderness and of cultivated land went on, as the brown cargo of the Mississippi River attested daily, and the dust storms and floods of the 1930s were to prove dramatically and conclusively.

IX.

While the national progressivism of the T.R. years primarily involved efforts to bring order and rationality to certain sectors of the economy, pressures for direct democracy measures and for labor legislation were gathering strength. Roosevelt's last Annual Message (1908) spoke of the unfinished business ahead: improved regulation of industry, abolition of child labor, shorter hours for all labor, a federal workmen's compensation act, a progressive inheritance tax, an inland waterways commission, and perhaps even old-age insurance. He was never given the chance he sought in 1912 to advance toward these goals. Some well-informed people have doubted that he would have achieved much along these lines, or that he really wanted to. Certainly his priorities after 1912 were weighted toward national unity, and social justice measures were divisive issues. But Roosevelt's accomplishment by 1908 was not negligible, and it satisfied his sense of what was possible. Those who were in sympathy with the man who was the American President from 1961 to 1963 will appreciate T.R.'s largest achievement: a young president with style and ideas came into office, bringing fresh vistas and attracting young and talented people into public service, all in contrast to an earlier, more sluggish leadership. Of course, as with John F. Kennedy, nothing much happened along the lines laid down in the speeches. But who can say that such revivals of simple faith in national leadership, faith that forces are being brought under the control of decent men, are not in certain circumstances worth more than the scornful radical ever imagines?

But the animation died under Taft, and a sense of being thwarted returned to those who wished to master their environment. Actually, Taft was as honest as any reformer, and more interested in antitrust and efficient government than most. Yet he did not like movement and change, and was soon on good terms only with the conservatives. The pressures for additional federal action grew on a number of fronts, and were strong enough to produce a few victories even if Taft would not lead. The thrust for direct democracy brought on a successful fight to curb the powers of Speaker of the House Joseph Cannon, and secured the Seventeenth Amendment requiring senators to stand for election before the registered voters rather than before state legislatures. Foes of the existing pattern of economic advantages worked for a lower tariff, and while they were unable to reduce it noticeably in the Payne-Aldrich Tariff of 1909, they got out of the effort a sense of solidarity and a momentum toward further change. Conservationists brought about the removal of Secretary of the Interior Richard Ballinger, suspected (unfairly, it now appears) of granting excessive rights in the public domain to corporate interests that rewarded him personally. The trust issue was still unresolved. Some men still seemed to be getting too rich by methods that were questionable. Women and children still worked under inhumane conditions for unhealthful periods. By the beginning of the second decade of the century virtually all intellectuals, many preachers, undetermined numbers of businessmen and lawyers, and large blocs of Congressmen were in an urgent, indignant mood. The year 1912 saw a skirmish for positions, an alignment of the heterogeneous forces of reform behind presidential candidates, and the stage was set for the culminating surge of national progressivism.

It appeared from the talk of the central figures that the many elements of progressivism had fused into two coherent schools in

1912.[4] The leading question seemed to be what to do about the Trusts. The second question was what would be the relation of government to disadvantaged groups. Behind T.R. one could see gathered those who felt that industrial concentration ought to be welcomed but regulated, and that it was now the responsibility of government to intervene on behalf of those social groups too weak to defend themselves under the new conditions. T.R.'s New Nationalism further held that no narrow construction of the Constitution, no property claims, ought to stand in the way of federal power as it coerced entrenched oligarchies and unified the nation. Behind Woodrow Wilson were to be found those who trusted to a vigorous antitrust policy and a lowered tariff to make such a medding state unnecessary.

Had Roosevelt won, it would have been discovered that his following was as varied and contradictory as progressivism itself. Grouped uneasily under his banner were big industrialists like George Perkins and Dan Hanna, for whom Roosevelt's attitude toward size in business had a welcome and enlightened ring; social workers who had a number of specific tasks to suggest for T.R.'s active and humanitarian state; antitrusters like Amos Pinchot and George Record, who were either confused (they should have been with Wilson on doctrinal grounds) or would not relinquish their faith that T.R. was still the trustbuster of 1902; and an assortment of "out" politicians, admirers of T.R., and anti-Taft Republicans. Some theoretical unity was imposed by T.R.'s campaign speeches, in which the New Nationalism was reasonably coherent, but his talk only papered over serious divisions in program and emphasis not only in the Bull Moose party but also in T.R.'s mind itself. Progressivism contained innumerable faiths, and even under the campaign pressures of 1912 it could not be fused into only two schools.

Wilson's following had somewhat more theoretical unanimity. His New Freedom speeches represented fairly well the things his party believed to be true at the end of their intellectually sterilizing sixteen years

---

[4] A small number of progressives preferred the Socialist candidate Eugene Debs in 1912, but it simplifies matters to ignore both these and that small group that voted for Taft. Whether one judges by numbers or by doctrine, Wilson and Roosevelt spoke for progressivism in 1912.

out of power. But the results of his administration were also to show how many voices were raised in the tents of reform. Wilson's following included agrarians who, while far from being advocates of big government, hankered after the special favors which the New Nationalism had promised. Agrarian pressures were among those that drove Wilson from the negativism of the New Freedom in the transitional year of 1915.

But for a time the new Democratic administration acted as it had talked. Both tariff reduction by the Underwood Tariff of 1913 and the Federal Reserve Act of the same year were plainly legislative products of the New Freedom philosophy, which enjoined the removal of barriers rather than compensatory favors. To reduce privilege by bringing down the tariff was a first priority among many reformers but especially among Democrats, and the Underwood Act brought rates down from an average of 40 percent to an average of 29 percent. Enough populism remained in the Democratic Party to produce a move to add a progressive income tax to the tariff bill, and conservatives saw revolution in such taxation. In fact, the Democratic progressives passed the tax not to redistribute income but to make up for revenue lost by a lower tariff. They were out to balance the budget, not to soak the rich. The rates ran from 1 percent to a towering maximum of 7 percent. Nonetheless the battle for tariff and tax reform had been hard, with the intervention of Wilson himself required to defeat the swarms of lobbyists who resented losing control of the government on this issue for the first time since the 1870s.

The antimonopoly bent of Wilson's party also suggested action to break the "money trust" discovered in the Pujo investigations, and Wilson's political skills were adequate to that task, gaining the Federal Reserve Act after a fierce congressional struggle in 1913. Democratic rhetoric and many accounts have called the act a victory for The People over the bankers. It was not that, and it was very nearly the reverse. Bankers small and large had hoped for banking "reform" since the panic of 1907. The existing banking system (or lack of system) permitted no fluid reserves to cover local crises, provided for no national currency, no coordinated check clearance. These deficiencies needed to be remedied, but they had nothing to do with democracy or social justice, only with efficient banking. Some bankers and the few reformers who understood banking also wished central control over the supply of money (essentially, control over credit), a useful power that might or might not advance the public good. Western and southern commercial and agricultural interests simply wished credit decentralized so that they might have more of it than Wall Street had been willing to supply. Out of these conflicting pressures came the Federal Reserve Act of 1913, the first national banking reform since Lincoln's day.

Who had done what to whom? The New York bankers had offered the Aldrich bill, which would centralize credit controls in the hands of a committee of bankers. Wilson stood firmly for the principle (he later lost sight of the substance) of public control of the supply of money. His supporters divided between those who wished public control lodged in Washington, and those provincial supporters who wished a more decentralized, "democratic" system allowing each region of the country to control its own monetary destiny. The form of the Federal Reserve Act suggested a victory for the latter interests, for it set up twelve reserve districts, which were empowered to pursue independent credit policies up to a point, and it was expected that each district—governed largely by locally appointed businessmen and bankers—would be responsive to local needs. A Federal Reserve Board in Washington retained some monetary powers and was appointed by the President. This paper decentralization represented a legislative victory for western and southern voices (some of them bankers' voices) over the eastern money managers, and a symbolic victory for public control of banking. Both victories soon proved illusory. The New York Reserve Bank (one of the twelve) came quickly to dominate the system, giving New York bankers more power than they had possessed before 1913. The nonbanking interests which were supposedly built into the Federal Reserve Board simply never emerged. The Federal Reserve Board appointments of Wilson and subsequent presidents were men subservient to the eastern banking community and without much vision or courage. Anyway, the board's powers were not extensive. Oddly enough, the New York branch under Benjamin Strong in the 1920s (until Strong's death in 1928) more effectively pursued policies that conduced to the public interest than those favored either by the parochial bankers in the other eleven branches or by the Federal Reserve Board in Washington.

That the bill did not actually democratize the important banking decisions in America, despite its twelve districts, turns out in retrospect to have been no disaster. To bring more bankers into the decision-making process would not have produced wiser policies. Monetary powers should certainly be in public hands, and the Federal Reserve Act was a small step in that direction, but a very, very small step. Even had Wilson not staffed the Board with ex-bankers and conservative economists, there was in the country little understanding of what a banking policy in the public interest might be.[5] Had that understanding existed, the Board possessed insufficient powers to pursue it and what was worse, insufficient will. The collapse of 1929 demonstrated this, and the search for both went on in the 1930s. Like most other progressive regulatory measures, the banking reform of 1913 replaced uncoordinated strivings with an orderly, more centralized apparatus very friendly to the industry it was mandated to guide. The gain for efficiency was immediate, but the gain for other social goals took years and a different climate to materialize.

On the final issue on the New Freedom agenda, the trusts, there was the most embarrassing confusion. Progressivism had never spoken clearly or in one voice on the issue. Mr. Dooley expressed the prevailing ambivalence from his saloon on Halstead Street: "Th' trusts, . . . are heejous monsthers built up be th' inlightened enterprise iv th' men that have done so much to advance progress in our beloved country. . . . On wan hand I wud stamp thim under fut; on th' other hand not so fast." While all reformers were sure something ought to be done, only a few—like Senator Gilbert Hitchcock from Nebraska, where there were few trusts—wanted the courts to accept the literal line of the Sherman Act, making illegal all combinations or firms large enough to exercise market control, or in the law's words, to "restrain trade." Yet the Court, left without further guidance after the law of 1890, had decided by 1911 in the Standard Oil case that restraint of trade had to be "undue" restraint, the word *undue* inviting the

---

[5] It is quite clear from the brief congressional debate on the bill and from the accounts of the few interested and economically competent contemporaries that Congressman Glass and Senator Owen were probably the only men in the 531-member U.S. Congress who understood either the problem or the Federal Reserve bill, and one has doubts about Glass. One clue to the confusion of that body, a confusion that is thoroughly understandable, lies in the final vote in the Senate—the bill passed on 22 December, 1913 by a vote of 43–25. Since all 25 Nays were cast by Republicans, it is clear that the Senators were doing what they always do when the technical details of a matter are obscure, i.e., repairing to the firm ground of partisanship.

judges to refer to their own "standard of reason." In concrete cases, this meant that the Sherman law would be construed generously in favor of the corporations before the dock. Rather than leave the trusts to friendly judges, progressives produced innumerable proposals designed to create firm legal and moral ground somewhere between dissolution of all industrial combinations and the leniency of the Court. Before Wilson had time to clear up his thinking on the matter the congressional hoppers were full of proposals, and his own Attorney General, James McReynolds, had boldly added a drastic one of his own.

Wilson, in addition to being pledged to act on the monopoly question, was not a man who enjoyed confusion, and he set himself to think the matter through during a vacation in December, 1913. Of course he was not alone in wishing clarification. While a few businessmen felt comfortable with the issue in the hands of the Court, most did not like to pursue their schemes for expansion in a state of legal uncertainty. Administrations came and went, attorneys general came and went even more often, and no businessmen could be sure what would be thought reasonable and legal at any given time. This uncertainty inclined such men to prefer either a governmental commission to advise them in advance as to disputed portions of the law, or additional legislation spelling out what was permitted and what was proscribed.

But more than legal uncertainty brought businessmen into the camp of those wishing something done about the monopoly question. Despite the competitive ideal, the business community itself had for years spawned ingenious plans for avoiding "destructive" competition —competition that disordered the market and prevented anyone from planning intelligently. The "Gary dinners" were only the most civilized of these. Inevitably, a legal remedy appeared most appealing. The Congress could formulate a law specifying unfair practices in business, thus making illegal those forms of competition that disrupted plans and shortened tempers—and presumably making legal all those things businessmen wished to do toward bringing the market under control.

Wilson ultimately agreed with those, whether businessmen or aroused reformers, who counseled action rather than delay. He thought for a time that a law could be drafted explicitly prohibiting wrong ways of doing business, and the Clayton bill introduced in April, 1914, was his chief proposal. But it soon became clear that it was permanently unclear what was legal and what was not, since no law could keep abreast of entrepreneurial inventiveness. Congressmen closest to the question, the members of the Senate Interstate Commerce Committee, were cool to the idea of writing a permanent list of Thou-Shalt-Nots, and they pressed Wilson to drop the Clayton approach. Seeing no way to frame a law whose language alone would forever demarcate monopoly from legitimate interfirm cooperation and planning, Wilson allowed himself to be persuaded by Brandeis, the lawyer George Rublee, and a number of senators that the problem was best passed on to a strong commission with a broad congressional mandate. The commission could then search for the elusive public interest and punish transgressors. Ignoring the New Freedom philosophy he had articulated with such clarity, he cut the Clayton bill adrift and placed his faith in regulation.

Once again, the progressives turned to the experts. The Federal Trade Commission was established in September, 1914, and was thought by business generally to have been a happy inspiration. There was now an agency to advise businessmen what was legal and what was not, before their (to them) well-meaning efforts landed them in an expensive lawsuit. It was important to them that the commission be staffed with men of large experience (in business) and friendly disposition. They were not disappointed in Wilson's appointments, nor in the spirit of the Federal Trade Commission and Justice Department regulation during the war years and the 1920s. There were some disgruntled New Freedom progressives who muttered about having voted for Wilson and instead getting Roosevelt's New Nationalism, but it was equally fair to say that the New Freedom philosophy had never been adequate and that Wilson had been flexible enough to see it. The important question was, had Wilson capitulated to the interests of large business or had he provided the machinery by which the national interest would henceforth prevail? As events were to work out—many of them, such as the war, beyond Wilson's control—the suspicions of the jilted New Freedomites were amply justified. Wilson spoke the truth when he declared, after signing the bill establishing the FTC, that "the road at last lies clear and firm before business."

After years of ambivalence and confusion over the issue of business combination, the progressive generation had reached a decision of sorts. The government would permit that stabilization that established business interests sought, but it was pledged to police the game so that flagrant collusion was not allowed to anesthetize the market. Experts were hired to look after a matter that had proven too intricate for the representatives of the public. A predictable commission replaced a variable Department of Justice and changeable Congress, a gain for order but not necessarily for the competitive ideal or the claims of small business. As to the public interest, there was no agreement on what had become of it or into whose hands it had been delivered. But since much of progressivism had to do with imposing order on confusion, this third achievement of Woodrow Wilson's first administration was one of the culminating moments of progressivism.

The hard fight for these measures occupied an exhausting eighteen months, and Wilson declared the end of progressivism in a letter to McAdoo in November, 1914. A business recession of that year reinforced his feelings that enough had been done to clear the road and that clearing the road was enough. Wilson announced his contentment with the reformed status quo. Legislation to aid special groups was not progressivism to him, and in 1914–15 Wilson killed long-range agricultural credits, fought off organized labor's demands for exemption from the antitrust laws, resisted a national child labor bill and a Constitutional amendment permitting women to vote in federal elections. He continued to ignore the few reformers such as Oswald Garrison Villard, who pressed the cause of the American Negro on him, and his administration extended racial segregation in the federal services.

But a number of pressures, about which historians disagree, forced Wilson to gradually abandon his principled objection to an active, paternalistic role for the government. He signed the LaFollette Seaman's Act in March of 1915, although it obviously conferred upon one sector of the citizenry a boon denied to others, a precedent sure to excite a clamor from other aggrieved groups. He had breached his New Freedom position again, just as in the struggle for a monopoly law, and moved further toward the New Nationalism. The approach of the election of 1916 finished his education in the virtues of a more active government. Proving himself more a political leader than an ideologue, Wilson moved to befriend those groups who stood to make his reelection possible.

Historians have called this 1916 burst a radical phase, and in some sense it was. Wilson appointed the liberal Jew, Louis D. Brandeis, to the Supreme Court, an act that sent fear and fury through those Arthur Link calls "the masters of capital." Their dismay was understandable, as the high court had always belonged not only to Anglo-Saxons but to conservative ones. A system of federal farm loan banks was established with Wilson's blessing in 1916 to provide the long-sought rural credit. Wilson now supported a workman's compensation bill for federal workers and the Keating-Owen child labor bill, and both were enacted. He signed into law a measure establishing the U.S. Shipping Board, an agency empowered to build or charter vessels and to regulate rates on the ocean. Social Justice progressives were sure their hour had come.

But the hour was only partially allotted to them. The decision to commit the government to the aid of pressing special interests was not radical. It seemed so because some of these groups were underdogs, and to aid them appeared to force justice upon the system. But the willingness to pass special legislation was neither radical nor conservative. Everything depended upon the groups aided. Count as evidence of radicalism, or at least advanced progressivism, the prohibition of child labor, workman's compensation for federal workers, and perhaps —some argument is possible—the rural credits bill. The Adamson Act granting an eight-hour day to railroad workers is hard to categorize, since with the help of the ICC the costs were passed on to consumers. But now that the government was answering to pressures there were sure to be gains for those already strong. Wilson backed a tariff commission that would be friendlier to protection than the Congress (Wilson's biographer Arthur Link called the Tariff Commission "a victory for protectionists"), an emergency tariff protection for chemical industries threatened by German dumping, legislation allowing firms in the export trade to violate the antitrust laws and a businessman's advisory group to establish early control over the imminent mobilization process.

True, 1916 was a big year for reform forces, for the Democratic Party had jettisoned its Constitutional scruples. But it was also a big year for those already wealthy and powerful, for they could do as well—even better—in an open struggle for governmental benefits as the do-gooders on leave from Hull House. The progressive era by 1916 had brought an active, intervening government. Which groups this government would favor remained still a matter of pressure, luck, and politics. As much as advanced Social Justice progressives complained about Wilson's capitulations to businessmen, it was clear from the way they voted in 1916 that the president was thought to have a leaning toward using government for afflicting the comfortable and comforting the afflicted, all things being equal. In this they read his mind correctly, to his eternal credit. But a war he did not seek diverted Wilson from this phase of advanced progressivism toward another type of reform—the remaking of international relations. In the process—and it was a complicated process—most of the progressive hopes of 1916 were rudely disappointed.

part two

WAR: 1914-1918

On 4 August, 1914, a war started in Europe, and before it was over on 11 November, 1918, men had shot, stabbed, gassed, and drowned each other, finally killing 8–10 million of each other—the bulk of the young, educated elites in each participating country. The survivors carried away memories of months and years of mud, boils, diarrhea, fear, and mutiny. It was a performance for which it was hard to devise proper adjectives, owing to the inadequacies of words like *insane, barbaric, meaningless,* and so on. For the first three years the war was almost entirely a European affair, and it raised some fundamental doubts about Europeans, about mankind, indeed about God himself. Americans could make little sense of it at all and almost unanimously assumed that such an irrational orgy had nothing to do with their country, where life was going forward so satisfactorily.

Their newspapers invented euphemisms like "fronts," "advances," "barrages," utilized maps and arrows, and in these forms provided the reading public with a minimal dose of information about the situation. Belligerent propaganda services attempted to supplement this with pictures of actual violence and indecently graphic stories of the crimes of soldiers, but these glimpses of the horror of Europe produced no widespread feeling that the war had any meaning for neutral America. We had nothing to do with such things. In the words of the American President, Woodrow Wilson, America must be "neutral in fact as well as in name...impartial in thought as well as in action."

Thirty-two months after the carnage had begun, on 2 April, 1917, this man went before a joint session of Congress and asked the nation to join in the war. Of some, more would be asked than of others. It was "a message," he frankly admitted to a friend, "of death for our young men." Within the week the Congress sent a war declaration to the president for his signature. For the country at large, this meant that the U. S. government would over the next eighteen months require the bodily service of 5 million men, would requisition some $33 billion of the national wealth, would exercise the right to allocate resources, fix prices, wages, and standards, and imprison men for improper speech and publication. For some 130,000 young males, the demands of our foreign policy were translated into a very compact sacrifice. The burdens of national defense are always distributed unevenly. Walter Hines Page, age 60 in 1914, and American Ambassador to Great Britain, wanted very much for "his country" to join the war against Germany. On 25 June, 1918, his nephew Allison Page was shot dead in a scrubby forest near the French village of Belleau.

Early death is always thought provoking. Young Page's curiosity about the ends to which he was being put, if he was ever curious, ended in a ditch in northern France. And there were some, including his uncle, who never doubted the worth of this and other sacrifices distributed somewhat unevenly among the people. But a great disillusionment set in after the war. Perhaps such sacrifices had been in vain. This note was strong in postwar literature, as for example in George Santayana's *The Last Puritan:*

> I should be glad to die now, if I could find something to die for. These poor recruits are told that they are dying for their country. That's sheer cant. Nobody knows whether he's doing his country any

good by dying for it, or whether his country is better worth dying for than any other. And what is one's country, anyhow? A piece of land? How is a piece of land in danger? Institutions and ideas? But institutions and ideas are always changing; by dying to preserve one set you will be creating another.... It's a blind current that sweeps us on, we don't know for how long or to what issue.

Historians, naturally, were more specific. Many of them in the 1920s and 1930s became revisionists, critical of the decisions reached by American leadership in the neutrality period. They piled up a literature of condemnation, told a story of unofficial selfishness and official folly. The years, however, have brought a new attitude. We have no more taste for angry condemnation. Problems of policy-makers seem staggering. Having seen no president shape an entirely successful foreign policy, our standards are more realistic. It now appears to many scholars that we would do better to understand the interplay of events and the process of decision-making than to search for fools. In the words of Ernest May, Harvard's respected diplomatic historian, one leaves the study of American policy in the years 1914–17 with "a sense that it could not have ended otherwise."

A strong note of historical determinism seems just the antidote for the runaway indignation of revisionists, who, through no fault of their own, were not yet educated by the unfolding years of unmanageable foreign relations and the enormous pressures for a broader American involvement in world affairs. But surely policy-makers in the 1914–17 period had some choices. If so, and if, after choosing, their hopes were disappointed, then possibly their choices were wrong. Granting this, the study of such errors might help reduce disappointment and social cost in the future. John F. Kennedy was of this mind when he tried to apply what he had learned from reading Barbara Tuchman's *The Guns of August* to the Cuban crisis of the autumn of 1962. Secretary of State Dean Rusk reflected on the Munich Agreement of 1938, and it led him to advise the commitment of American troops in Vietnam. I do not cite these applications of historical study with uniform approval, but one must approve of the effort to discipline the decision-making faculties through a thoughtful study of the past. And if historians will not help, busy public figures will do it for themselves.

Such a purpose for historical study involves a dispassionate attempt to understand how things happen (and, as Lewis Namier said, how

they don't happen), but also implies that one look hard for errors as
well as success. But it is no invitation to unrestrained moralists. Let
them find their therapy elsewhere. It constitutes a legitimate and
valuable effort, methodologically imperfect and usually futile, to fend
off tomorrow's disasters.

In August, 1914, there seemed to be no chance that any American
would be a combatant in the war. Indeed, most English and German
boys had reason to expect to miss the thrill of combat, as a short war
was universally predicted. Modern armies were irresistible, and they
were also so expensive that the struggle could not be supported for
more than a few months. In addition to the short life expectancy of
this European quarrel, American males who were over seventeen and
under forty were protected from any involvement by the broad agreement in the country that the war and its outcome were no concern
of ours, and—there were a few dissenters here—that war was
repugnant and pointless wherever it occurred. As a final comfort to
those who might have worried about American life and limb, the
American president, whose Constitutional and traditional powers
over foreign policy had over the years become almost total, was a
near-pacifist whose considerable personal talents were enlisted squarely
behind the maintenance of neutrality.

Despite these conditions, the peace of the nation, if one looked
quite closely, stood in a certain jeopardy. The country was in large
cultural and ethnic debt to Great Britain, and a strong undercurrent
of sympathy for the Allies soon developed and was sure to complicate
the government's desire to be officially neutral. As for the government,
where foreign policy is concerned the word refers to the president
and those officials in a position by function, political power, or
friendship, to influence or advise him. The composition of this part of
the United States government, the decision-making part of it in the
field of foreign policy, cast a slight and at that time unsuspected
shadow over American neutrality. While almost any newspaper
editor or large contributor to the Democratic Party might influence
the president, Wilson was unusually independent and the group of
real influentials was quite small. Secretary of State William Jennings
Bryan was in fact impartial, but State Department counselor Robert
Lansing (to be Secretary after Bryan's resignation in June, 1915)
wished Britain to win, as did Ambassador Walter Hines Page in

London, Wilson's personal secretary Joseph Tumulty, and most (in the end, all) of the Cabinet, including the potent figure William G. McAdoo, Secretary of the Treasury and Wilson's son-in-law. The president himself, although a man of mixed feelings, was pro-Ally. In addition to these officials, the president took advice from his friend colonel Edward M. House of Texas, and from his wife (after December 18, 1915) Edith Bolling Galt Wilson, both of whom were strongly pro-British. The chairmen of the Senate and House Committees on Foreign Relations and Foreign Affairs (Sen. William J. Stone and Rep. Henry D. Flood) were both impartial, but either they did not try or were not allowed to influence policy. Thus the people with whom the president discussed policy, and from whom he regularly received news and advice, with the one exception of Bryan, saw to it, some consciously and some unconsciously, that his patience was encouraged in one direction and his inflexibility and suspicion in another. This did not mean there must be war with Germany. It simply meant that American policy would be shaped by men who were partial to the Allies.

But more important than pro-Ally sympathies in the nation at large and in the president's circle of advisers, American neutrality was menaced by the geographic, military, and economic facts of life. When the war was not won by land armies in a few weeks, the sources of supply became all-important. The United States, industrially advanced and organized at all levels for profit, grew rather quickly into a major supplier to a Europe whose demands for steel, brass, cotton, and other materials had suddenly increased. Both belligerent blocs would try to interdict goods bound for the other, but Germany, her surface naval forces soon swept from the seas, would interdict by submarine and torpedo, while the Allies would interdict by edict, surface capture, docking, and confiscation. Death by drowning was the frequent consequence of the former; the irritations of delay and property loss, along with some very distant German nutritional problems, were the consequence of the latter. The naval and geographic facts of life arranged that the Allies purchase most of the trade, and the Central Powers deal out most of the violence. The pressure that ultimately shattered American neutrality came from these circumstances, which were little appreciated at the beginning. For two and a half years Wilson, with the help of the German Chancellor and Foreign Office, sought to alter or evade these circumstances. These were the most fateful years in the history of American diplomacy since Adams, Franklin, Madison, and Jay had navigated clear of the perils of Europe.

August 1914–December 1914

Serious problems concerning the American relation to the war arose only in 1915, and it was not until 1916 that the concentration of the president and the Congress on questions of foreign policy came to overshadow all other national business. Yet in the early months of the war, in the summer and fall of 1914, fateful decisions were made, often without extended consideration and by second-rank officials, which were to permanently narrow the range of American alternatives. The first decision had to do with the Declaration of London, a convention drawn up at British insistence in 1909 (which Commons but not the Lords had ratified) that offered reasonably clear guidelines as to rights of neutrals on the seas. The declaration left certain important American export products, such as cotton and copper, on the free list (no interference permitted), and in general provided such broad rights of neutrals as to make an ocean blockade ineffective. The British navy under an Order in Council of 20 August had set aside the contraband categories of the declaration and the rights therein guaranteed to neutrals, and on 26 September the U. S. government demanded that the British observe the Declaration of London, which the lawyers in the State Department regarded as the most definitive statement of international law. Before the British had time to reply, the United States began to yield. House, aided by the British Ambassador Sir Cecil Spring-Rice, persuaded Wilson to send a telegram softening the 26 September note, and Page in London took the rest of the sternness out of the note in his amicable discussions with Foreign Secretary Sir Edward Grey. A tone of conciliation was established, and for four weeks the two governments disagreed, the Americans urging observation of at least the "free list" portions of the Declaration, the British adamant that the present war could not be conducted by the old rules, especially if they were found in unratified treaties. On October 22, State Department Counselor Lansing gave up the struggle and abandoned the Declaration, and nothing was heard from Wilson. The American government would flounder for more than two years in an effort to establish some other clear definition of a line between those British harassments that were permissible and those that were intolerable infringements of neutral rights.

In the same autumn three other important decisions were made at various levels in the government, none of them engaging the full attention of the president, whose wife had died in August. The British Admiralty announced a mine blockade of the North Sea, and the United States acquiesced.[1] When the Americans later protested the German declaration of a war zone around the British Isles, the comparison with our acquiescence in the North Sea blockade suggested unneutrality to men from central Europe who did not appreciate the subtleties of international law. A second decision had to do with armed merchantmen. It was the duty of a neutral to prevent its ports from serving as naval bases for belligerents, but "defensive" armament against pirates remained an archaic provision of the international legal system, such as it was. When British merchantmen began to arrive in New York with mounted guns, the German government protested that they were warships intended for aggressive use and should be impounded by the United States. Counselor Lansing secured the permission of Bryan and Wilson to issue a ruling on September 19 differentiating between defensive and offensive armament, a ruling that generally permitted merchantmen to mount guns of less than six-inch caliber aft. It was a fateful decision. Six months later such defensively armed merchantmen were under Admiralty orders to open fire on submarines at sight, but they used American ports as privileged vessels of innocent commerce. Technically, Lansing had a case. Under traditional law the British merchant fleet had the right to arm itself against lurking pirates. The Germans were apparently not very good lawyers. They thought the ruling unneutral. Whatever they thought, the Armed Ship circular of September 19 was to cause endless trouble later in the war.

A third decision concerned war financing. In October, both Wilson and Bryan, under extreme pressure from bankers, allowed it to be known that the government's disapproval of private loans to belligerents, expressed on August 15, did not extend to credits, of which the government promised to take no notice. The difference between loans and credits seemed a major one to the principled men in the

[1] A weak protest was finally dispatched on December 28, and nothing was heard of it again.

executive branch, but a minor one to bankers with good European clients, and the financing of American trade with belligerents—which in effect meant the Allies—went forward at once.

By the end of 1914 the American government had made several fateful decisions, most of them by secondary officials. It had been decided that neutral rights, whatever they did include, did not include the rights specified in the Declaration of London, and that neutrality was not compromised by expanding trade on a deficit basis with the maritime belligerents. In each case the government was acquiescing in developments that had tremendous pressure behind them, and opposing ideas and interests were neither intellectually nor politically mobilized. If one expects of government that it respond to the existing pressures, it may be admitted that the course taken in these cases was not surprising. But in the anguished days of spring, 1917, Wilson would surely have given much for the chance to live the autumn of 1914 over again.

January 1915–September 1915

As 1915 opened, few Americans doubted that their country should, and would, wait out the war in official neutrality. In five months we were at the edge of war, with a new respect for the mighty, impersonal currents of events and interests that pulled a peace-loving people toward what still appeared to most of them a pointless war. In view of the inability of the German army to win a quick victory on land, the German Admiralty convinced their emperor, sometimes called "The All-Highest" (he was really a middle-aged man named William Hohenzollern) to inaugurate submarine warfare against allied shipping. The announcement was made to neutrals on February 4, and the twenty-eight German submarines were to commence what the admirals hoped would be their deadly work on February 18. The Germans not only did not know precisely what to expect from the U-boats, but were also unsure of the attitudes of neutrals carrying on commerce with the Atlantic ports. They were surprised at the general vehemence of neutral comment, but especially by the stern tone of Woodrow Wilson, who declared that Germany would be held to "strict accountability" for any infringement of neutral rights. Wilson's warning hardly clarified the situation. Neutral rights, uncertain in the face of the unprecedented de facto (but never, by anyone's claim, "legal") blockade such as Britain was gradually tightening around Germany, were even less clear in the event of a submarine campaign. At first thought it might seem that neutrals would not be affected by U-boat warfare against Allied shipping, but both Wilson and the German leadership had a vision of what was coming. U-boats crept along under the sea, their periscopes washed by brine and fog, their crews tense and cramped. If they surfaced to identify, board, inspect, and order passenger removal, all before attack, they were vulnerable to gunfire and ramming; if they did not, the job of identification, especially if Allied ships ran neutral flags, could not be accomplished without mistakes. Hence the danger to neutrals, and, if there was such a thing, neutral rights.

America's problems with England were real enough, with ships stopped and towed to port for delays and confiscation, mails interrupted, and endless arguments about what constituted contraband. But there were no deaths, and the incidents were spaced, tedious, and clouded in legal complexity. A U-boat campaign, in lurid contrast, would bring large numbers of men to their deaths, trapped screaming in iron hulls breached by the icy Atlantic. The strain of any such atrocities, which were sure to be displayed in all their horror on the front page of newspapers, might prove too much for sentiments of neutrality.

Wilson and his advisers saw this and hoped a way might be found to lift both the blockade and the submarine campaign before either became fixed. The days of February and March, 1915, were full of diplomatic activity, as befitted men who knew themselves to be at a turning point. Communications were sent to determine if the belligerent governments might retrace their steps. The German government seemed willing to call off its submarines if Britain would allow food into Germany. Secretary Bryan, sensing deliverance, persuaded Wilson to appeal to both sides for a modus vivendi—no submarine attacks without warning, in return for no misuse of neutral flags, no arming of merchantmen, and the entry of noncontraband into Germany. Germany agreed in a note of February 20, but seemed to wish the category contraband shrunk back to something like the Declaration of London limits. This meant the British would be allowed to intercept only the obvious implements of war, effectively eliminating their blockade. The British, never for a moment considering trading their stranglehold for the recall of twenty-eight submarines of doubtful effectiveness, ignored the Wilson-Bryan offer and declared a total blockade on March 11 in "retaliation" for the submarine campaign inaugurated three weeks earlier.

The Bryan modus vivendi failed, but it appears in retrospect to have been one of those moments when events might have been altered. Strong American pressure at this time might have forced both sides to strictly limit their naval war—although admittedly it was Britain, the nation we wished least to antagonize, who was required to yield the most. There were political materials inside each bloc that American diplomacy might have catalyzed against unyielding governments. The British government actually felt their position vulnerable even after the decision of March 11, and as late as June was not willing to refuse discussions of Bryan's idea. The Germans, understandably, were even closer to some arrangement whereby the submarines might be traded for supplies. Such an arrangement, or even long talks about such an arrangement, would have avoided the sinkings of April and the resultant tie-up in German-American relations, which prevented Wilson's mediation efforts from getting underway until the fall. But admittedly any mutually acceptable limits on the naval war faced great odds, and American diplomacy was far from being sufficiently resolute to capitalize on the scurrying opportunities of that spring. Soon the sinkings started, preoccupying Wilson's government through murderous months with their hardening effects on the spirit of compromise.

The mistakes that had been feared were not long in coming. On March 28 the *Falaba* went down with one American death; the *Cushing* on April 29; the *Gulflight* on May 1. Then on 7 May, 1915, the Cunard liner *Lusitania,* fast and modern, came carelessly close to Ireland, and Lt. Schweiger was able to gain a great victory for Germany and for all those fine things for which she selflessly fought, killing with one torpedo 1,198 men, women, and children (among them 128 Americans).

The American press inflamed itself in a ritual of patriotism and Christian indignation, helping to force Wilson, who turned out to be very cautious where actions were concerned, to make it clear what he had meant by "strict accountability." Had he meant a strict postwar financial accounting, as he apparently had in mind in the case of British violations of neutral rights, or would he press for satisfaction now? And would he settle with the Germans separately, or link the sides together in their crimes, not holding the one to proper behavior if he could not hold them both? Bryan advised the safest course in both instances—no showdown with Germany now, and a joint demand upon both belligerents. Wilson chose to insist that Germany repudiate her tactics at once (Britain would be given more time), and chose to deal with the belligerents one at a time, Germany first. Over these issues Bryan resigned and took up opposition on the peace wing of American opinion.

Despite Wilson's hard line, the negotiations with the Germans over the *Lusitania* dragged out. The Germans decided secretly to insure the safety of passenger liners but were unwilling to apologize. Wilson, while insisting on a curb on U-boats, gradually retreated from his early insistence that submarine warfare be discontinued altogether. Then on August 19 a submarine sank the *Arabic* with two American deaths, an act that generated more American pressure and led the German government to issue the *"Arabic* Pledge" of September 1. Germany would not attack liners, whatever their flag, without warning. The status of merchantmen was unclear; they were not included in the pledge to observe cruiser rules. But Wilson had at least forced the Central Powers to modify their tactics and leash the Admirals. There would be no more *Lusitanias*.

The War Hawks—Theodore Roosevelt, Henry Watterson of the Louisville *Courier-Journal,* and others—were unhappy with Wilson's patient diplomatic style. But most of the country could hardly have failed to reflect with some sobering effect upon how close the country had come to a break with Germany, and therefore possibly even to war, over the right of American citizens to sail into the war zone on ships of any flag carrying any form of contraband. Many were aware that the *Arabic* Pledge had settled little and that there would be more trouble with the submarine if the administration adhered to its broad definition of American rights. Wilson would find in the next round of crisis diplomacy that the dissenters were prepared to take the reins of diplomacy from his hands if he ran risks that they thought unjustified.

September 1915–December 1915

Just as the year 1915 brought no decision in the war in Europe, so it brought no resolution of the problems of the United States as she attempted to profit from the war without being inconvenienced by it. During the fall both sides continued in one form or another to injure American feelings in undramatic but irritating ways; but Wilson produced no ultimatums and passed the weeks in a kind of smouldering disagreement with both European blocs. A note of October 21 finally informed the British that we completely denied their right to institute the sort of blockade they had declared in March, but said nothing about retaliation. The principal problems were still with Germany, but here also there were nagging doubts and disagreements without any resolution. Wilson had won a respite from German attacks on passenger liners of all flags, but the status of belligerent merchantmen was uncertain. Relations with Germany were strained in November by the revelations in the *New York World* of German efforts to foment strikes or outright sabotage efforts in munitions industries, and by the November 7 sinking of the Italian liner *Ancona* with heavy loss of life. A satisfactory disavowal and indemnity had not yet been obtained from Germany regarding the *Lusitania,* and the exchange of irritating notes on that issue strung out through the final months of 1915.

One of the most important decisions of 1915 was made almost by default. While Bryan's loan ban had been relaxed to permit interbank credits, the disapproval of outright loans set a limit upon the amount of financing that American banks could offer the Allies. Informed of a British financial crisis in August, 1915, Secretary McAdoo pled with Wilson for an explicit governmental permission to the banking community to extend loans of large size to the Entente powers, even if this meant public bond drives. Wilson was hesitant, but was under pressure from Lansing, McAdoo, and the bankers, and finally responded to Lansing's argument that to refuse loans would dry up the U. S.-British trade and produce "industrial depression, idle capital and idle labor, numerous failures, financial demoralization, and general unrest and suffering among the laboring classes." In October Wilson transmitted to Wall Street an oral acquiescence (he would not put anything in writing on the subject) in an expanded loan program. Although the first public loan did not go well, credit was no longer a problem to the Allies, and the trade with them accelerated. Business was stimulated, as all had predicted, and Wilson owed his reelection in 1916 in part to the economic health generated by the war trade. In March, 1917, American loans to the Allies would total $2,262,827,544 (as against German loans of about $27 million).

Yet the situation was not without its price. Wilson's desire to mediate between the belligerents was fatally handicapped, as far as the Germans were concerned, by the fact that the United States was supplying the Allies with the implements of war. Wilson had not planned this development, but reasoned that it would have been unneutral to interfere, through an embargo on arms trade or on loans, with a natural economic development of this sort. But one suspects he would have approached this problem differently had he foreseen how the economic ties with the Allies would destroy his potential as a mediator in the desperate days of 1916.

While at the end of 1915 the state of American foreign policy, the mind of the president, and public opinion itself were all confused and unresolved, the year had revealed some things with reasonable clarity. The American president was not treating the antagonists in similar ways, in part, but only in part, because the antagonists were not treating American commerce in similar ways. With Germany, while Wilson permitted delays, he seemed bent upon forcing a humane naval war even if the land war were totally without rules. With Britain he argued American rights less insistently and seemed willing to accept postwar adjustment of claims. "We are face to face with something they are going to do," Wilson wrote Bryan after the British announced their blockade, "and they are going to do it no matter what representations we make." When the United States protested the blockade in a note of 30 March, 1915, the British were allowed an undisturbed three months in which to reply, and the State Department answered their July note in late October. Robert Lansing explained the process in his *War Memoirs:*

> The notes that were sent [to Britain] were long and exhaustive treatises which opened up new subjects of discussion rather than closing those in controversy. Short and emphatic notes were dangerous. Everything was submerged in verbosity. It was done with deliberate purpose. It insured continuance of the controversies...

There were many reasons for this dual diplomacy, among them the difference in naval methods, the pro-ally sympathies of Wilson and his advisers, the economic involvement of the country with the Entente, the adroitness of British diplomacy, and the occasional ineptitude of the German government. But while American diplomacy came to bear with more firmness upon the Central Powers than upon the Allies, American belligerency was yet far off. The American public was still overwhelmingly against military involvement, even if the

Lusitania incident had shifted public sympathies considerably. And almost equally important among those factors tending to block or delay American belligerency was the fact that the American president was not yet committed to an Allied victory, not yet convinced that both sides were not in some respects in the wrong, not willing to forgive the Allies forever for their maritime affronts—in short, still far from possessing any consistent desire to maneuver this country toward intervention.

1916

Wilson was acutely aware of how close America was to war as 1916 opened, and he worked to enlarge and activate those alternatives that history and his own decisions had left him. He was attracted, early in the year, to a proposal made by Lansing aimed at reducing the loss of life incident to submarine warfare. Wilson's demands upon Germany came down essentially to the requirement that submarines operate on the surface by cruiser rules. This idea had little appeal for the Germans, not because they preferred to lurk out of sight to satisfy some defect in their national character, but because the Allies began arming ships—usually in concealed bays—and firing on submarines that came considerately to the surface. Craft called Q-boats, gunboats disguised as dumpy merchantmen, began to operate around the British Isles in 1915. On August 19, for example, the submarine U-27 was surprised and sunk by the tramp steamer (under an American flag) *Baralong* as she was in the act of legally searching a halted vessel. The *Baralong,* which became the British Q-boat *Baralong* seconds before opening fire, made the occasion more memorable in the German navy by firing on the submarine crew in the water after the sub itself was sunk. So long as submarine commanders could expect such incidents, they would tend to attack from below surface; so long as they attacked with only periscope identification, mistakes would occur—neutral vessels, even liners, might innocently attract an undeserved and unintended torpedo.

The president was aware of this problem and was therefore enthusiastic when on January 7 Lansing suggested a modus vivendi by which the United States would force the disarmament of commercial vessels by impounding any armed vessels putting into American ports. Germany, for her part, could then observe cruiser rules. The

American government sent the proposal to the Allied capitals on January 18 for their reaction.

It seems in retrospect to have been a promising step for a president who wished to stay out of the war. The Germans appeared to welcome the idea, and the United States could have adopted such a modus vivendi whether the Allies liked it or not. Other neutrals, such as Holland, had done so from the beginning. But Wilson abandoned the modus vivendi when the British response was a bitter negative, not because he agreed with their argument that his proposal was unneutral, but because their attitude toward the modus vivendi imperiled his other and to him more important effort of 1916—mediation. To mediate he must be regarded as a true neutral by the British, and to achieve this position he was willing to sacrifice all secondary lines of strategy.

Wilson had hoped to mediate a compromise peace since the first days of the conflict. He had tendered his services as conciliator in August, 1914, and had encouraged both Bryan's mediation inquiry of September and Colonel House's exploratory trip to Europe in the Spring of 1915. Wilson had little grasp of the details of territorial demands, the military situation, or special treaties that bounded the areas of real negotiation. But he saw with clarity what only a few Europeans kept in view, that the best outcome for everyone concerned was an end to the war without victory for either side. And he had a powerful—and a very natural—desire to be the personal agent of such a healing settlement. The *Lusitania* and *Arabic* incidents lent urgency to his thoughts of mediation, and he cast about for an effective form for his diplomatic intervention.

It appeared that he had found it in a bold proposal of House, broached to the president in October, 1915. House had for some time been worried that the country might drift into war with Germany over some technical infraction by a submarine, and would in such circumstances lack the national unity and intellectual conviction that House thought necessary to carry the nation through to a proper culmination. He therefore offered the following plan: the United States would propose a peace conference when it received an Allied signal that their arms were successful and they were confident of the results of peace negotiations; the Germans would either accept the American invitation to talks, in which case there would be peace (favorable to the Allies), or if they did not the United States would enter the war on the side of the Allies. In the latter case the American people would be united by the knowledge that Germany was irredeemably warlike and insatiable.

The president was at first stunned by the boldness of House's idea (and probably also by its blatant unneutrality), but House took his silence for acquiescence, and there followed one of the strangest and most confused episodes in the records of American diplomacy. House drafted a letter to British Foreign Secretary Sir Edward Grey, sketching his plan briefly and suggesting further discussions in Europe. Grey and the British seemed interested, if cautious, and House set sail on December 28, never suspecting how cool they were both to him and to any talk of a negotiated peace. The Colonel made the rounds of the European capitals, engaging in earnest after-dinner talks with wary heads of state and foreign ministers who trusted neither him, Wilson, nor the enemy, and who knew all along that their war-embittered publics would never agree to any settlement that brought them so little advantage that the enemy could be induced to sign it. The desire to end the war short of victory was almost nonexistent in governing circles in January and February of 1916 when House made his rounds, for each side dreamed of the massive blows their armies would deal to the foe when the weather improved. But House, who avoided precise territorial details and did not sense the gap between the demands of the rivals, pressed hard for the agreement. Grey was amiable enough over the matter. He saw to it that the memo contained no action date and could be invoked only by the British when they were ready. Grey saw no risks for Britain, and there were none; the risks were in a rebuff. A delighted House returned on March 6 to present Wilson with an agreement initialed by the British Foreign Secretary.

The House-Grey Memorandum stipulated that the president, upon hearing from Britain and France that the time had arrived (meaning the Allies were winning and would deal from strength in negotiations), would propose peace talks. When the Germans did as expected and refused to consider negotiations, the United States would *probably* (Wilson inserted the word, making British doubts about the whole arrangement virtually total; Wilson, considering congressional and public opinion, could hardly have done otherwise) enter the war on the side of the Allies. To House, the agreement meant an end to the American dilemma. To the British it meant nothing at all. Yet upon it Wilson fastened his great hopes for impartial mediation; and to it he sacrificed the Lansing modus vivendi when Britain made it clear that she thought the modus vivendi grossly unfair and destructive of Wilson's status as a true neutral. Lansing withdrew the modus vivendi on February 15, and House was able to bring home his vague and meaningless agreement. Thus as March arrived America was if anything closer to the war the president did not want than she had been in September when Germany gave the *Arabic* pledge. The submarines were active again, American trade with the Allies was increasing, and all the president had for five months' effort was a note signed by a Texan of independent means but no official position, and a skeptical British Foreign Secretary.

At this point another alternative offered itself, one in many ways more promising than the two Wilson had been trying. When the modus vivendi collapsed, leaving Wilson's strict accountability policy unaltered, and with Germany intensifying her submarine warfare, a large number of Congressmen with independent ideas about foreign policy could no longer be restrained. Since the fall of 1914 congressional hoppers had never been empty of proposals to insure American neutrality, most of them involving some form of embargo on munitions or a passenger ban or both. But foreign policy is traditionally as well as Constitutionally a presidential function, and Wilson, usually engaged in close negotiations to pressure a belligerent to alter its tactics, had successfully discouraged these bills as signs of moral infirmity that undercut his diplomatic efforts. He also shunned them as being reminiscent of the Jeffersonian embargo which was so politically disastrous a century before.

But by late February, 1916, Wilson faced a Congressional revolt. Ranking Congressional Democrats learned from the president on February 21 that he would go to any length to defend the right of American citizens to travel safely even on armed belligerent merchant ships, and the House was swept by a war panic. Sentiment for a passenger ban ran three to one by some estimates, and it threatened to mass behind the McLemore bill in the House and the Gore resolution in the Senate. It is hard not to see in these bills a line of policy that surrendered nothing that was vital to the American national interest, and yet that promised to virtually eliminate the chance of an inflammatory incident. Unfortunately, this healthy initiative came from what Wilson saw as a dangerous source—the Congress. Although he had earlier toyed with the idea of a passenger ban, the president now felt that his leadership was jeopardized, and that the passage of any important foreign policy measure at all that was not initiated by the administration would be not only an intolerable Constitutional affront but would damage his influence in European capitals. Afraid that he could never mediate if his authority were in question—it was proving difficult enough as it was—Wilson committed his full resources to crushing the Gore-McLemore proposals. Presidential conferences with leaders of both parties, intensive lobbying by McAdoo and Postmaster General Burleson, and a strong presidential letter to Senator Stone made public on Feburary 24 brought many Congressmen to see another side of the issue, and support for the passenger ban fell off.

Wilson had shown again that, when fully aroused, he had no peers at the arts of politics—or perhaps some would prefer to say the arts of demagoguery. The letter to Stone must have taught any number of petty politicians and small-bore evangelists how it was done by one of the masters. In view of the long list of humiliations Wilson had found ways to live with since 1914, the most delicate thing a historian can say about such phrases as "once accept a single abatement of right and many other humiliations would certainly follow, and the whole fine fabric of international law might crumble under our hands piece by piece" is that they are embarrassing. Wilson here appears more rigid than he actually was, but talk of this sort exacts its price. While the letter and the entire presidential counterattack were successful in preserving the president's control of foreign policy, he found it hard to retreat from such principled peaks once his passions had cooled. And of course the largest part of the price was the loss of a promising alternative on the road to 2 April, 1917.

All the proposals and explorations of the fall and winter having changed nothing, the inevitable crisis promptly developed. The French packet *Sussex,* an unarmed passenger vessel, was torpedoed in the English Channel with the loss of fifty lives. Although this might sound callous to the souls of the fifty, what made the attack regrettable were injuries suffered by four Americans, who would not have been aboard (or would have been disavowed) had earlier measures to warn American citizens off ships in the war zone been enacted. Other attacks without warning on liners were reported in the days after the *Sussex* incident, and Wilson, despite reports that the public was not yet ready for a break with Germany, felt himself obliged by his entire line of diplomacy since the winter of 1915 to accept all risks and force Germany to choose between a modification of tactics and war with the United States. His note to Germany of April 18 was an ultimatum, demanding an end to submarine attacks on neutral as well as enemy commerce. The German government went through an intense struggle, and finally replied on May 4 with the *"Sussex* Pledge," promising to visit and search all vessels prior to attack. Since some vessels were armed, this meant a drastic curtailment of submarine warfare.

The president had a diplomatic victory, and the war once again seemed far away. But Wilson knew enough of the pressures within Germany—a navy with an extravagant pride in its submarines and its strategic judgment, an army stalemated, a public opinion frustrated at the leashing of the ultimate weapon in the midst of a protracted struggle—to know how fragile was the pledge of May 4. And while he had taken no official notice of it, he had read the concluding paragraph of the German pledge, which declared that if the United States did not "demand and insist that the British government shall forthwith observe the rules of international law universally recognized before the war," that the pledge would no longer be binding. Thus the German note was a kind of time bomb. In the time remaining, American neutrality rode with three historical possibilities, all of them to varying degrees improbable: a successful American effort to raise the British blockade, a quick peace through the victory of one side or the other, or a mediated peace without victory.

Wilson knew the first to be virtually impossible, and the second to be unlikely and also undesirable, since it would lay the seeds of another conflict no matter which side won a clear victory. With time running out, he tried to find the wisdom and the resolve that he might combine with the powers of his office (which he held subject to a November election) to try to bend the wild forces of European war and American domestic politics toward a type of settlement for which he and Colonel House had found no enthusiasm in two long years of probing. To be sure that Wilson understood the need for urgent action, Imperial Chancellor Bethmann-Hollweg dictated a message to the president through Ambassador Gerard on May 11, reporting that he was under extreme pressure from the Right and the Center parties in Germany as well as from the press and that he could not long restrain the admirals.

May 1916–January 1917

From May to July Wilson pressed the Allies to implement the House-Grey agreement, gradually becoming aware that they would never ask for a mediated peace, from which little territory could be gained (or regained), so long as military victory seemed possible. Allied war aims were far beyond what could. be expected from any negotiated settlement, and their political leaders declined to suggest to their respective publics that the time had perhaps come to trade hopes of vengeance and territorial compensation for nothing more than an end to the killing. There are signs that the German government, and certainly the war-weary Austrian government, might have actually gone to a peace table and acknowledged that the war was unwinnable. Yet the war aims even of the relatively moderate coalition held together by Bethmann were sufficiently ambitious that talks with the Allies would probably have led nowhere. And groups with more annexationist goals were gaining strength within Germany. It is hard to see how Wilson, even had he arranged some sort of exploratory talks, could have brought about an actual settlement. We see now what he could not see, the irreconcilability of even the minimum war aims of the opposing blocs. The Allies would insist on their rights to Alsace-Lorraine, Russian control of the Dardanelles, and the restoration of Belgium, to mention only their leading requirements. If they submitted to talks in the summer of 1916, Germany, which held Belgium, northern France, and most of eastern Europe, would inevitably secure a settlement leaving her stronger than before the war and presumably unchastised. And even if they chose to trust Wilson to fight for more acceptable territorial arrangements—and few Allied leaders had such faith in Wilson—they could not be sure he would be president after 1916. As for the Central Powers, while they were moderately interested in talks, they had no intention of allowing Wilson to be present as mediator. In short, Wilson in the summer of 1916 sought to bring about a peace between governments that wanted peace less than they wanted some other things.

But surely the *people* of Europe were ready for an end to killing, even if it meant a compromise on war aims. Wilson finally saw that his only course was to abandon the House-Grey agreement, which forced him to wait in silence until the Allied governments were ready to negotiate, and to make a general public appeal such as he had made in August of 1914, and such as Bryan and the peace groups had urged many times in the interim. While it might embarrass certain governments (i.e., the Allies, whose military position made them hostile to a general appeal, which is why Wilson never made one), Wilson was sufficiently desperate to bring to bear upon them the pressure of their own domestic public opinion to force them to some response. If he could but get a statement of war aims in print, perhaps the terms would be bridgeable.

But to bridge the gap between belligerent war aims, given their present mood, would require his active participation; and he could not participate if either side thought him unneutral. He must prepare the ground by moving to an indisputably neutral position and then time his appeal so that neither side, faltering on the battlefield, would be able to charge that the appeal was a hostile act coming when it did. We may summarize in terms that seem accurate in retrospect but, if Wilson had summed up his chances thus, would have chilled his spirits and caused the young American males who did not yet pant for war to begin to wind up their affairs: the memories of German-American conflicts since 1914 would have to be erased by an effective attack upon the British blockade; the right wing in each country must yield to its enemies on the left sufficiently so that moderate war aims might come forward; the press in each nation must reverse themselves and begin to educate the public to accept a no-win policy; generals and admirals must lose confidence in one final land battle or undersea superweapon; and the situation on the battlefront must be so thoroughly stalemated, after a German retreat to the territorial status quo ante bellum, that neither side went to a conference with a significant geographical advantage. But Wilson did not see these obstacles as he looked ahead. He saw only, as he campaigned for reelection in the fall, that the American people did not want war, that time was running short on German forebearance, and that he must somehow bring peace or face national humiliation, division, or war, and perhaps all three.

The president therefore executed a remarkable diplomatic flanking maneuver and began to put serious pressure on friendly, democratic, heroic Britain. The British blockade, vexing even in its early stages, was by the summer of 1916 one constant interference. American ships were searched at sea or towed to harbor, mail was confiscated, American firms blacklisted, coaling facilities denied. These practices had been protested before, but by a State Department preoccupied with submarine crises. Now, in the late summer of 1916, there took place a sharp change in the volume and tone of American notes to London. And in September, going beyond protests for the first time, Wilson obtained from Congress legislation (which he never used) to deny port facilities to ships of any nation that discriminated against American commerce, and urged the Federal Reserve Board to restrain bankers who were financing the Allied war trade. The British blockade was not altered by such methods, but Wilson hoped the Germans would take his new tone as proof of an independent and neutral spirit. With the election out of the way in November he began to give thought to the drafting of a peace appeal.

He was unusually slow, but he had little reason to know that the most fortuitous moment (in an admittedly unpromising venture) had already passed. Bethmann was eager for a Wilsonian peace overture in August, when Germany faced a Rumania in revolt (not knowing she would be victorious there in December), the Reichstag had recently passed a peace resolution, and the relatively moderate Falkenhayn had not yet been replaced as Chief of Staff by the aggressive team of Hindenburg and Ludendorff. But Wilson refused to make his appeal before the election, possibly because of a scrupulous regard for political fairness, possibly because he was preoccupied, possibly because he knew the Allies were furious at the idea,[2] or out of some combination of the three. After the election he was delayed by a cold, a session of Congress, and the reorganization of the British government. On December 12, his own note nearly ready, he was surprised by the release of Germany's own peace overture to the Allies. He quickly issued his own message on December 18, asking all belligerents to state their terms, and expressing confidence that the objects of all nations were actually similar. Although he had toned down his note from his first draft, which clearly threatened American action against whichever bloc did not respond properly, Wilson's December 18 message nonetheless was, as Ernest May puts it, "the most dangerous document that Wilson approved since the House-Grey memorandum and the *Sussex* ultimatum." Preceded as it was by a German peace offer, it ran a very high risk of bringing Germany and America into

[2] Lloyd George, British Minister of War, in an interview with American newspaperman Roy Howard on September 28, denounced any talk of stopping short of a fight "to the finish—to a knock-out."

sympathetic alliance, a possibility that shocked Wilson's advisers and disquieted the president, but a possibility that he was willing to face rather than drop the idea of a peace move altogether.

But if in December there seemed the chilling possibility that Wilson's action would sour Anglo-American sympathies, there was by then no chance that it would actually bring about a compromise peace. This is not to say that American intervention was inevitable, since a few reasonable alternatives still seemed open; but bringing about a peace was not really one of them, despite the time spent on it in the closing days of 1916. This may be said today because we know more about belligerent war aims than Wilson could possibly have known, even if he had been deeply interested in the wearisome study of military and geographical details, which he was not.

It is possible to make too much of war aims. Many readers of Fritz Fischer's important book, *Germany's War Aims in the First World War,* have concluded from the sweep of Teutonic visions that Germany was totally and permanently beyond reason and her complete defeat was necessary for any sort of sensible outcome to the war. But Fischer's book is not about what the German government insisted upon at a conference called in a lull of a stalemated war; it is about the terms Germans used in arguing with each other about what the Fatherland deserved, all against the background of an optimistic military outlook (the military was always optimistic) and the efforts of various groups to demonstrate more patriotism (which meant annexing more territory) than their rivals. War aims in all countries were always in flux. They functioned in part as debating points against an enemy negotiator and were accordingly inflated to permit room for compromise.

They were also inflated because they were formulated by conservative political and military leaders in a setting of fierce political conflict between Right and Left, where it was understood that annexationist war aims strengthened the Right, and vice-versa. Instead of differing openly over the real issues between them,[3] i.e., property rights and constitutional reform, the Right and the Left in Germany (and everywhere else) fought a somewhat suppressed battle over whether to terminate the war in victory or in partial compromise, in

---

3 Chancellor Bethmann practiced a policy he called "Burgfrieden," or putting domestic quarrels on ice. He discouraged all airing of divisive issues, including war aims, to keep his majority coalition intact.

huge annexations or modest ones. The Right was annexationist and victory-minded, the Left somewhat less of both, and each was sure that if it did not win on war aims the jig was up for its postwar political power and the economic interests it represented. So long as war aims were invested with such domestic political importance the terms of any discussion of them—internally, or between governments—were sure to be irrational and diplomatically misleading. This is not to say that there were important groups in Germany, out of power but capable of organizing a government, that held *moderate* war aims. War aims of the Left were simply less immoderate than those of the conservatives. But any shift of political power towards the Left would have altered German negotiation terms so as to favor Wilson's hopes for a compromise peace; so would a deterioration of the military situation, or the weakening of a principal ally. One can conceive of events that might have transformed German war aims from an insuperable barrier to merely a formidable one. The outrageous lists of territories to be annexed and indemnities to be paid that were circulated inside the German government do not, to my mind, foreclose the possibility of a negotiated settlement.

Yet even when we discount some of the discussion of war aims, which scholars now dig out of Foreign Office memos, letters, and position papers of general staffs, one has to admit nonetheless that the two sides were very far apart when Wilson made his plea. German officialdom was talking in terms of annexations including Alsace-Lorraine and indemnities against France, various territories in the East, concessions in Belgium which would make her a ward of Germany, colonial annexations in central Africa, the Azores, Tahiti, and annexation of parts of Serbia, Rumania, and Italy. The Allies were equally generous to parts of the world they deemed in need of liberation. When the Prime Minister asked various departments of the government what British terms should be in the late summer of 1916, the Foreign Office stated terms which they admitted could only be secured through Germany's defeat. The chief of the general staff argued that England should not even agree to an armistice until Germany promised to evacuate all occupied territory and surrender a portion of her fleet, and the same gentleman said in November that peace could only be considered by "cowards, cranks, and philosophers." The Allied reply to Wilson's overture, when it came on January 10, asked for the restoration of Belgium and Serbia with indemnities, the evacuation of

France, Russia, and Rumania, with reparations, and the "liberation" of all Slavs and Czechoslovaks, i.e., the suicide of the Austro-Hungarian Empire. "The war aims formulated by the Entente in camera," writes Fritz Fischer, "were not very much more modest than those of Germany."

No statesman could find common ground here. He would need the aid of internal upheavals and a large degree of luck besides. Wilson got neither in December, 1916. While he seems to have had in mind a settlement that today we would call fair, his ideas on the subject had no allure either for the Allies, who were led by men who believed their national existence required a broken Germany, or for the Central Powers, who held territory paid for in blood, which Wilson would surely confiscate if, as expected, he urged a peace along the lines of the status quo ante bellum.

War goals, of course, were not the real barrier, but a symbol of it. What prevented peace was the preference of the dominant groups in each bloc for a gamble on victory rather than submitting to the frustrations *and political risks* of compromise. In England, Asquith's government had never demonstrated the "weakness" of a real interest in going to the table with an undefeated Germany, and the accession of the Lloyd George government in early December if anything reinforced the British hard line. In Germany, Bethmann had formulated war aims in the late summer of 1916, which of course meant not that he polled the country or went to the universities to consult geographers and philosophers, but that he asked the Kaiser, the princes of the blood, admirals, and generals for their thoughtful suggestions as to what was the Fatherland's right, considering both her inherent virtue and her existing military advantages—and considering the political consequences to the ruling class if the war came to anything but a glorious end. The list of demands on the Allies that the chancellor somewhat reluctantly compiled adds new dimensions to the storied arrogance of the Teutonic mentality. Yet in both blocs the advice of the military was always to fight on, and while in normal times civilians could discount this, the war had swollen the military influence—who else would save the homeland?—to impressive proportions.

To be sure, there were in each bloc contrary pressures, groups, and individuals who urged a negotiated peace, but they were scattered and barred from power. In Germany, Bethmann's hints of a peace move in the fall of 1916 met with wide acclaim, especially from newspapers such as *Vorwarts,* organ of the Social Democratic Party, and a peace petition circulated by the socialists got nearly a million signatures. In England, the London *Nation* and the Manchester *Guardian* exerted their influence for compromise, portions of the Labour Party had similar tendencies, and the Cabinet itself contained some, including Lord Grey and Lord Lansdowne, who were at least open to the idea of a no-win peace.[4] But these were minority tendencies, and they were also at a disadvantage in that they bespoke the less satisfying human emotions—moderation, compromise, and a tiny bit of national self-doubt. Only a military disaster could have magnified their voices, and German arms were successful in the Balkans in the fall of 1916, while the Allies, bled by the Somme but no worse off on the ground than six months before, began to anticipate the submarine campaign that would bring American intervention.

Wilson's note had gone out on the eighteenth; after Christmas the replies came in, and they brought no pleasure to a peace-loving president, nor, one supposes, to the men in the filthy trenches. The Central Powers, on December 26, replied that their offer to talk had not included Wilson as mediator, and they declined to state war aims— which was taken to be a sign that their aims were shocking. Germany has been much criticized for this rebuff of Wilson. Arthur Link, Wilson's biographer, has argued that the president was by this time truly neutral and that Germany should have thrown herself upon his justice. But Link has had access to Wilson's papers. The Germans could only consult the past, and they found there little reason for trust. It is hard to see how one can expect a nation weary from three years of war, but with an advantage on the ground, to throw itself on the mercies of a man whose policies had so worked to the benefit of the Allies as to have staved off their almost certain defeat. At the same time that the president's countrymen made and sold the implements of war to Britain and France, Wilson curtailed the U-boat war to preserve the travel rights of a few tourists and businessmen. Wilson, the Germans knew, had never been neutral (they underestimated how hard it had been for him to enforce policies benefitting

---

4 Most outspoken opponents of the war were socialists: Ramsay Macdonald in Great Britain, Karl Kautsky and Karl Liebnecht in Germany, Fritz Adler in Austria. But occasionally one not only found a socialist leader hot for war to the end, but an aristocrat of unshakable social conservatism, like Lord Lansdowne, who openly questioned whether the war should be carried on much longer.

neither side, when one side commanded the sea); America had never acted impartially. They would not have been surprised at the now-famous note Wilson endorsed in the spring of 1916, which said in part: "Colonel House expressed the opinion that, if such a Conference met, it would secure peace on terms not unfavorable to the Allies; and, if it failed to secure peace, the U. S. would probably leave the Conference as a belligerent on the side of the Allies, if Germany was unreasonable." They would not have been startled had they learned that the Secretary of State in Wilson's "neutral" government wrote privately of Germany's "sinister purpose to dominate the world."

Perhaps Germany, expansionist as she was, would never have trusted a neutral. But that she should not have trusted Woodrow Wilson after more than two years of American neutrality was a foregone conclusion, and one for which Wilson himself was partly responsible. A few outbursts against England between May and December were properly regarded as inexpensive gestures,[5] and altered nothing. It was not enough for Wilson to *be* truly neutral (as he seems to have been by December, 1916). He must provide the evidence, in policies as well as words, to reverse the deep impression he had made in all those months in which he headed a government of clearly pro-Allied sympathies. He did not do this—probably could not—but as a result Germany's suspicions remained and were both understandable and tragic. "I will not go to any Conference!" exploded the Kaiser when he read Wilson's December message. "Certainly not under his Chairmanship!" This in the same month that Wilson, speaking to House, said: "If Germany really wants peace she can get it, and get it soon, if she will but confide in me and let me have a chance."

To this line of argument some will answer that Wilson did what he could in the time he had between the *Sussex* Pledge and December—a time in which he also faced an election—and that the Germans, had they possessed any real desire for peace, could have apprized themselves of his real mood. But while the Germans were admittedly stubborn, vain, brutal, and all of those German things that made them somewhat maladroit in diplomacy, they never possessed those conduits into official American circles that made British diplomatic judgment so flexible and successful from the beginning. A note from

5 Which is exactly what they were. The American Secretary of State wrote in the summer of 1916: "We must keep on exchanging notes [with England], because if we do not we will have to take radical measures."

Wilson came to the German government through Ambassador William Gerard, in whom Wilson (justifiably) placed little confidence, and it was for the German leaders to piece together what they could of this strange Presbyterian from cold print and their own skimpy intelligence reports. In Britain, Walter Hines Page carried notes to Whitehall to explain away their irritants and help compose an answer. In Washington, Colonel House, Lansing, and virtually the entire opinion-making establishment helped Wilson find the patience and insight to understand the plight of gallant England. With such friends, the Allied governments were not subject to the full extremes of mistrust as were the Central Powers, did not feel so out of communication and defensive.

A prime example—there are many—was Lansing's unauthorized activities following the president's note of December 18. The American appeal had come so close upon the German note that the Allies suspected collusion and were furious. But no less a figure than the Secretary of State relieved their minds. He called in the French ambassador Jusserand on December 20 to transmit assurances that the U. S. was firmly pro-Ally, and suggested that the Allies announce sweeping war aims (he sketched in a few, including a reformed and democratized Germany). He said the same things to British Ambassador Spring-Rice on December 22, urging London in effect to stiffen against Wilson's plans, scuttle peace talks, and await with confidence the inevitable German submarine campaign that would bring American intervention. Fortified with this news, which the ambassador at once telegraphed from Washington, the British government was not tempted to issue a peremptory refusal, which might have driven Wilson toward Germany, but at the same time was emboldened to make stiff demands, which fended off any peace talks. In a relaxed and leisurely way they prepared their January 10 reply, which conveyed terms so sweeping that a conference was out of the question, yet in language very friendly toward the U. S. The episode was one of many such occasions when the existence of special lines of communication between officials in Washington and London made Allied diplomacy proof against damaging extremes of ignorance and distrust. The severed German cable lines were symbolic of the lack of such lines of communication between Washington and the Central Powers, and this in part explains why Germany did not summon up the wisdom and the patience to entrust all her hopes to Woodrow Wilson in the winter of 1916–17, overruling the entreaties of her eager admirals, whose submarine fleet had now reached 103.

More was behind the failure of Wilson's last mediation attempt, of course, than poor communications or bad timing. War fed on sacrifices already made, blood already spilled, promises to allies of postwar spoils; peace meant sacrificing certain high and noble aims—glory, righteous vengeance, national security. Both hope and fear counseled another year of war. Hope transcended the glum facts of military stalemate, and hinted that one great springtime offensive would bring the victory that justified every sacrifice. But fear was at least as important, for it set the powerful elites of blood, land, and industry against talk of peace. The established classes sensed in their bones that a compromise peace was a strategem of the Left and would bring in its wake unsettlement, reform, revolution, the confiscation of property. They felt Bolshevism coming on. Count Westarp explained why the Conservative Party in Germany had shifted to annexationism and no-compromise after first seeing the war as defensive:

> The monarchist had to fear that the growth of radicalism, which is to be expected as a result of any war, would reach alarming proportions if the homecoming soldiers were to find as the reward for their heroism only an increased tax bill and were to become convinced that the government of the Kaiserreich had not understood how to profit from success in military operations.

In all countries, people of substance, whose governments had paid for the war by borrowing, counted upon the indemnities of victory to obviate a crushing postwar taxation, which would either bear heavily upon them, or radicalize the masses, or both. It should then be no surprise that the answer to Wilson's overture, both in diplomatic notes and in the language of the press and in windy speeches in the Reichstag and Parliament, was the language you expected from men who were not yet finished with war—talk of the righteousness of our cause, or the moral callousness of the American president who saw some justice on both sides, talk of the final and smashing victories over the enemies of humanity, hard, rigid, inflammatory talk, talk to stiffen the backs of the young men out in the mud and to underline the cowardice, the feminity, the treason of compromisers.

So the German reply of December 26 rebuffed Wilson's mediation and refused to state terms, and the Allied reply of January 10 stated terms Wilson found unreasonable. He pressed both sides to state their terms in private, where they might return to sanity. While he waited he composed and delivered before the Congress on January 22 the "Peace Without Victory" speech, in which he summarized the terms of a just and lasting peace. He thought it an important state paper, and indeed men in all countries saw in his address and his ideas a new opening out of the horror. But the interlude in which American mediation was even faintly possible ended on January 9, when, at Pless, the German government reached its decision for unrestricted submarine warfare. That door had closed. Europeans would continue to kill each other, and we were invited by both sides to leave our cash registers and pulpits and join them in the divine game.

1 February 1917 –2 April 1917

A different man might have asked for war at once, but Wilson hesitated even in breaking diplomatic relations. He was, of course, no pacifist; in two months he would ask for war. A different man might have waited forever. Even in the last weeks of American neutrality when all the big decisions had been made and there was little room, perhaps no room, to turn or reverse, a single man made a difference. Wilson was not entirely the plaything of fortune, unable to make the slightest personal contribution to history.

But granting the indeterminacy of those last days, one may say that any American president had at best one or two decisions he could make. Most courses were ruled out. Wilson's brief, vain effort of February to detach Austria from the war only underlined the absence of real, untried, promising alternatives. In this period we may see Wilson as waiting for public opinion to shift from indecision and mass behind belligerency. He waited while forces he could not see and certainly could not control—the track of torpedoes and darkened ships, the piling up of goods on American wharves, a sense of frustration among merchants and industrialists, the gradual dissipation of restraint under conditions of high tension—began to move America toward the trenches in France. But even if Wilson the politician waited for a clarification of public opinion, Wilson the intellectual grappled desperately with the issue, a pacifist intellectual with death at his back: "I am overwhelmed," he wrote a friend on 2 February, 1917; "my thought is under seas."

To say that he waited is not to say that he was idle. As February wore on it was apparent that American ships would not sail without protection, and pressure built up for some form of armed neutrality. This would mean convoying, or at the very least the arming of merchantmen with navy guns and perhaps navy crews. Wilson responded to this pressure on February 26, asking Congress to grant him authority to arm merchantmen. His resolve had presumably been stiffened by the receipt only two days before of the intercepted Zimmerman Note, in which Germany clarified the global nature of the European war by inviting Mexico to join her in the event of American belligerency. A small group of antiwar Senators filibustered until Congress adjourned on March 4, and Wilson, judging by their numbers that the public basically approved of the step, armed the ships by Executive Order on March 9.

Wilson had now played out his hand; he had no more plans. It was still his to decide whether the waiting would go on or whether he would take the only other remaining step—a declaration of war. And if he chose the latter, it was for him to decide on the timing of it and the words with which he would justify it. Sinkings, negligible in February, mounted in March: *Algonquin,* March 14; *City of Memphis, Illinois, Vigilencia,* March 18; *Healdton,* March 22; *Aztec,* April 1. Many scholars detect after the midlle of March a shift in public opinion that the president could not resist. It is certainly true that a wave of emotion swept through portions of the society, and feeling about the war intensified. Many newspapers editorialized about honor and patriotism. Uncommitted national figures, ranging from Governor Arthur Capper of Kansas to philosopher John Dewey, changed their positions in March and now asked for war. Six hundred Republicans met at the Union League Club in New York to demand intervention, and 12,000 people jammed into Madison Square Garden for a war rally on the twenty-second. Mass meetings were held in Philadelphia, Chicago, Boston, Denver, and other places. This and other evidence—sermons, speeches, diary entries, letters—suggest that many influential Americans either intensified their commitment to belligerency in these late March days, or became converted to it. Their patience had ebbed away; the waiting, the absence of national purpose when all the world seemed galvanized to heroism, began to take their toll of the hesitant and the uncommitted.

But we are not sure whether the desire to stay out of the war was not equally strong in this period. Pacifists also held mass meetings, and ran advertisements in national newspapers as late as March 29. And there were reports by contemporaries that the pressure for some sort of release from indecision was far from intolerable to average Americans out in the small towns and rural areas of Colorado, Wisconsin, or Georgia. There is no proof that the public demanded war. Most of it seems to have been satisfied to go on as it had.

But one really need not know how the people would have polled out on the question of war or peace in the last days of March, 1917. The pressure for action may not have been intolerable out in the Midwest or the Rockies. But it was felt to be intolerable in Washington, among men whose role it was to lead. Waiting, for public officials in the White House, the Congress, the State and War Departments, meant waiting for *themselves* to do something. And as they waited it must have seemed that the country had become ungovernable.[6] Among them, especially, opinion shifted in March. At the cabinet meeting on the nineteenth Wilson learned that the formerly divided cabinet was now united for war. On the twenty-first he called the Congress back into special session. When it met on the evening of April 2, he drove down in the rain with a cavalry escort and asked for a declaration of war upon Germany.

The galleries were jammed, and the atmosphere was electric. The president soberly reviewed the background to the crisis. The Chief Justice of the United States, much too old to go and fight, began to bang his hands in the middle of the long-awaited decisive sentence.

---

6 There is evidence that much earlier Wilson had become deeply concerned about the divisiveness in the nation's political and emotional life, especially "hyphenate" disunity. He directed that the theme of the Democratic Convention at St. Louis in June, 1916, be "Americanism," and saw to it that the "Star-Spangled Banner" was frequently sung by the delegates. On his instructions William McCombs opened the convention with an address in which he tried to rouse the delegates' patriotism with sentences like "the chief tenet of faith [of the Democratic Party] is Americanism, and Americans are American." But the delegates stunned observers and brought tears to Bryan's eyes by demonstrating so wildly when Keynoter Martin H. Glynn stressed Wilson's peaceful intentions that Glynn was forced to depart from his text and extemporize for the delighted crowd upon the theme, "He kept us out of war." The incident has been taken to show the pacific mood of the country at that time; but Wilson's preparations for the convention demonstrate something equally important, that he was so concerned over the division and emotional tension in the country that he resorted to a bit of very uncharacteristic right-wing demagoguery about rallying 'round the flag in order to · impose some control upon his party.

At the end of it, the chamber—excepting Senator LaFollette, we are told, and perhaps a few others—was on its feet, even on the chairs, yelling its appreciation. As Colonel House said later, "the tension was over and the die was cast"—and the feeling of relief was widespread. Wilson's secretary later remembered the president as saying: "My message today was a message of death for our young men. How strange it seemed to applaud that." They were not applauding that. They did not think of the deaths of young men when they thought of war, these representatives of the people. They thought of excitement, change, and travel, of an end to tension and ambiguity and humiliation, and of a great national coming-together after the bitter, partisan divisions that had almost paralyzed American political life.

Thoughts on the War Message

This desire to end the emotional and political division of the country was prominent among the factors leading Wilson to ask for war. Now, with the step taken, the war required unity for its prosecution. The wave of relief and enthusiasm that greeted his war message could not be expected to last beyond a few days. The articulate people who had never believed that the issues between Europeans were worth one American life would surely not be silenced by the Declaration of War by Congress. And their arguments might have a certain effect: we were not under attack, no official person had declared that our national security was in jeopardy, we would have to travel thousands of miles even to become involved in the war, and the war was sure to have its unpleasant costs, particularly in lives and money. To preserve a workable majority against such divisive thoughts would require that the war have a powerful, simple, emotionally appealing, and durable justification. Wilson may have asked for war, as a leading historian has said, because he had no other choice, but it would not do to attempt to prepare the nation for its exertions with such flimsy stuff. In April, 1917, and for the months ahead, the entry of the nation into the European war must have an explanation to enlist the energies and loyalties of a democratic people—simple, emotional, a tiny bit skeptical, deeply romantic. For this task it is impossible to imagine a more appropriate citizen than Woodrow Wilson. At calling men to sacrifice, at simplifying the complex, at extracting principle from secular confusion, no man of that generation was his equal. He understood from the start the need for public education of the most dramatic effective-

ness (although he had some doubts of its side effects), and made his
April 2 address the most impressive justification for American belligerency ever offered.

Wilson's war message, reprinted in this volume, repays close reading.
His first and presumably chief reason for calling America to arms
was to defend the rights of all mankind, now imperiled by German
submarine warfare. The human rights under attack were broader than
the right to travel safely on the seas even during a world war; they
were the rights to peace and justice, of which the present German
government had shown itself to be an implacable foe. The United
States fought also for ends that were closely related to American self-
interest and security, although Wilson did not state the matter quite
in those terms—to defend the American form of government against
authoritarianism (the Russian Revolution of March made this construction possible), to avoid those naval humiliations that would have
eliminated the nation's status as a great power, and to construct a
postwar "concert of free peoples as shall bring peace and safety to all
nations."

When Wilson left the joint session to a deafening applause, when
his old enemy Senator Lodge gripped his hand and thanked him for
expressing the "'loftiest...sentiments of the American people," he
must have known that the message was a superb success. He had
provided the vocabulary for, and started in motion, that avalanche
of "moist and numerous language," to borrow Mr. Dooley's phrase,
which informed the American people why they must now become
involved in a war that three years, and in some cases even days earlier,
they had regarded with disgust. Editorial writers, preachers, stump
speakers, teachers, and professors would see to it in the days ahead
that the reasons we fought—simple, noble, overwhelming—were com-
municated throughout the country. The average draftee who was not
a close reader of the *New York Times* or the *Congressional Record*
now could be expected to understand why we were in the World
War, and not to bother himself very much about it. But Wilson's
success at framing convincing and communicable goals did as much
as anything else to defeat those goals for which he had contended
since foreign affairs began to claim so much of his attention in 1914.

It is hard in retrospect to approve either Wilson's timing or his
reasoning in the fateful, difficult foreign policy decisions forced on

him by the Great War in Europe.[7] He argued that the United States could no longer tolerate nonbelligerency because to submit to humiliations would be to permit the destruction of human rights and national prestige. If the national prestige was involved at all it was because he willed it so; neither law, economic necessity, nor tradition required a guarantee of rights of travel on armed belligerent vessels. As for the notion that human rights were somehow in jeopardy if Americans died on the high seas, the less said about that mystical idea the better for Wilson's reputation as an incisive thinker. Yet intelligent men have found reason to defend Wilson's decision to ask for intervention, not as the best of poor alternatives, but as a wise and proper step. In the view of the Realists, armed intervention was justified by a rational calculation of the national interest. America could not tolerate the domination of Europe by an undemocratic, expansionist Germany, and her vital interests now required armed intervention in a European war to secure the balance of power and construct an unprecedented union of nations for collective security. This view of international affairs was held as early as 1914 by men like Lewis Einstein and Walter Lippmann and has been adopted by most scholars since the 1940s. Some feel that Wilson stumbled accidentally onto the right course, others that despite his abstract language about principles, he

---

[7] It is *much* harder to defend the decisions of the German government throughout this period, and I hope it is clear that my inattention to this matter represents a deliberate decision to concentrate upon American policy and in no way suggests that in any discussion of human errors from 1914 on the government of Woodrow Wilson would require more space than others. The chief German blunder, aside from their share of responsibility for the outbreak of war in 1914, was probably in not taking a slightly more moderate course in January, 1917. While I have already argued that they could hardly have trusted Wilson, they might have resumed submarine warfare only on belligerent merchantmen and not upon American vessels and passenger liners. Wilson was ready to accept this despite his *Sussex* ultimatum, as the Germans learned when he made no reply to their January 10 announcement that belligerent merchantmen would now be sunk without warning. But they chose to go the whole way, miscalculating completely the impact of American intervention. A more limited submarine campaign would have delayed American intervention, and, their Eastern divisions freed by the Russian collapse in late 1917, the Germans would probably have forced the Allies to sue for peace. But they preferred to strike for total victory, trusting to American lethargy and their own submarine fleet to prevent effective American military intervention. At the end of the war they had sunk one American transport; two million men had come over to Europe safely.

intuitively understood that a German victory constituted a threat to
American security and so conducted American foreign policy as to
refuse to permit it. If he did not use phrases like "balance of power"
and "American vital interests," it was because he faced a public of
implacable naïveté and uninformed idealism, one which could only
be motivated to the necessary sacrifices through the thrilling language
of Protestant evangelism. But his drive to put himself and his country
in a commanding position to mediate was strong from the beginning;
it was one of the reasons he finally decided to intervene, and the sort
of peace he wished to mediate did bear a close resemblance to the
balance-of-power compromise the Realists approve.

Respected scholars have repeatedly made this argument for Wilson's
intuitive realism, even though it requires some redefinition of his
terminology and some careful scrutiny of the spaces between the lines.
But if the president saw that our security was involved in the contest
going on in Europe, as a few of his private remarks suggest, he made
no effort to explain the matter to the American public. This may be
credited to his own uncertainty rather than to political timidity. Wilson
proved in the Brandeis appointment and later in the League fight that
he was not afraid of political risks. But whether he was a slightly confused half-realist or a secret realist with exaggerated fears of the
political risks involved in candor, Wilson spent the years from 1914 to
1917 talking about ideals, rights, and proper naval behavior. When he
wrote state papers with his unrivaled eloquence, they were usually for
the purpose of educating the Germans in their human and Christian
responsibilities, not in educating his countrymen in the hard realities
of modern geopolitics. When he asked for military preparedness, a
logical step for one who wished his country to be in a position to
influence events, he shaped a program of naval rearmament and left
the army still puny—exactly what one would do who was in fact
concerned with maritime rights rather than with European power
dispositions. When he finally asked for intervention, he came across
as a pure idealist on a mission of rescue for high, unassailable, but
somehow precious ideals.

Guided by their president's words, which were repeated many times
by pulpit and press, the boys went to beat the hell out of Germany
for sinking our ships and for not being peace loving and democratic.
Apparently the thrashing would be educational for the Germans,
would produce great moral improvement among them, and would

not only restore threatened human rights to their rightful place but would vindicate them forever. The attractiveness of this high enterprise, along with a general boredom, a habit of obedience, and perhaps above all an unrealistic expectation of what war would be like (Wilson himself thought the war would be over in six months and that our part in it would be primarily naval, and he was not alone)[8] was enough to call the nation to arms.

Of course, it is almost certain that he could not have persuaded the country to enter the war for realistic reasons. He could never have convinced an isolationist and parochial society to participate in history's most horrible war for such uninspiring goals as the restoration of the balance of power and the defense of England's security on the novel grounds that both had a close relation to our own *vital* interests. The number of Americans who thought in such terms was so small that the entire group could easily be locked into a White House bathroom. Many wished to declare war, but merely wishing a declaration of war on Germany did not make one a Realist. Even those around the president who favored war did not know until after April that the Allies were in grave danger of losing. They, too, in the days before April 2, had talked of principles and human rights. Wilson himself might have tried over the months from August, 1914, to create a realistic public understanding of the American stake in the war, but no sensible person argues that this would have been enough. Twenty years later another persuasive president tried, and never convinced a majority of his countrymen. But if an effort to achieve limited but attainable goals was ruled out by American tradition and the state of popular education, by what logic does one take the nation into war for goals that are unattainable and in fact hardly coherent, and whose only virtue has not to do with their connection to reality but their ability to move public opinion behind belligerency? Wilson got the country to act, but for the wrong reasons at the wrong time.

There were men, like Theodore Roosevelt, who thought that war

---

8 The *American Banker* editorialized on 24 March, 1917 that our armed forces would "be entirely confined to the chasing of U-boats....Of course there can be no transportation of American troops to the scene of war across the sea." And *The Economist* on February 10 predicted that "it will be difficult to find points of contact." More realistic judgments were not nonexistent. The military had made plans for an expeditionary force, and Secretary Lansing in a diary entry of April 7 wrote: "Now to make ready our millions and send them overseas to bring victory to the cause of Liberty."

had no costs of any consequence, that fighting was in some way a beneficial experience for men and nations.[9] But Wilson was wiser than that. There is an apocryphal story, told by the journalist Frank Cobb, in which Wilson on the eve of the war message predicted that going into the war would cost the country most of the New Freedom gains and much of its internal tolerance and sanity. Although Cobb's story has recently been challenged, we know that Wilson reckoned the costs of war much more realistically than most contemporaries, especially the domestic costs. In addition, he knew that the language and ideas he must employ to create a large, enthusiastic majority out of the refractory isolationists and temporary pacifists who surrounded him would create a type of fervor that would probably make his goals unattainable. For Wilson, whatever his talk of moral absolutes and "force without stint or limit," went to Europe basically to effect a compromise. He remained more interested in diplomacy than in victory, and while he led the nation against the forces of darkness he was sure the guilt in Europe was not all on one side and insisted that the United States be designated an "associated power," not an ally. Three times in his war message he spoke of restraint, of the necessity to fight without passion or vindictiveness. But Americans listened to the Wilson they preferred: the moralist, not the conciliator. To get the nation into the war he had proclaimed war aims that made restrained action and limited involvement impossible and made reaction inevitable among a people who had not been dealt with candidly.

The disappointments he feared—but did not fear enough—came in full measure. Germany was beaten, but she did not learn the moral lessons Wilson intended. If human rights were better off for American entry, no man has yet found a way to measure the improvement. Nor did the American influence at Versailles create a lasting peace. Because we were there, the settlement was a bastard compromise, "fairer" than the one the Germans would have dictated if the United States had not entered, but by no means more conducive to the stability of Europe and the avoidance of the horrors of 1939–45. The democracies won the war, but their victory did not stem the slide of Western civilization into dictatorship and philosophic malaise.

These disappointments came to Wilson's international aspirations,

---

[9] Theodore Roosevelt loved war and is better described as an adolescent than as a realist. Marshall Joffre once said: "It costs from ten to fifteen thousand lives to train a major general." T.R. was eager to learn.

and there is no evidence that he foresaw the possibility of such defeats, although a number of hardened cynics were predicting them. Domestically, the costs of American involvement were far, far beyond even Wilson's relatively astute premonitions: 130,000 American lives lost in combat, 35,000 permanently disabled, approximately 500,000 influenza deaths in the U. S. in the winter of 1918–19 from a virus imported from the battlefields; an expenditure of $33.5 billion by 1919, to which may be added at least the $13 billion spent as of 1931 (according to economist John M. Clark) on veterans' pensions and interest on the war debt; 20 million person-years of labor diverted to war, or six months' work by every American; the 25 race riots of 1919; the stimulus to private indulgence and social irresponsibility; the decimation of the liberal center and the hobbling of the Left.

Such a brief sketch of the high costs and low yields of American participation in the war suggest an error in judgment. While Wilson had nothing like the influence over events that either he or his critics assumed, many doors of history hinged on his decisions. If it is too much to ask of any mortal political leader that, given the circumstances of spring, 1917, he choose division and national humiliation over unity and pride, it is not too much to ask for a different line of diplomacy reaching back to 1914, one that would not allow such restricted and self-defeating alternatives to hem him in.

It might be objected that a concentration on Wilson's decisions from 1914 forward ignores the historic trend toward a more active world role for the United States that commenced in the 1890s, and that this short-sighted perspective exaggerates his freedom. True, the United States in the twenty years before Wilson's Presidency had acquired an empire, intervened militarily in four countries where affairs had not gone to our liking and exerted diplomatic pressure in countless others, had built a modern navy, and had steadily expanded her international commercial contacts. But while this trend meant the inexorable approach of world power and involvement, it did not imply intervention in World War I. Our early military interventions had been limited in scope, had occurred in Latin America and the Far East, and had not been wildly popular.

Another argument with which I am not sympathetic holds that progressivism had an affinity for war. Progressives were activists, moralists, and had a strong sense of mission. They were therefore especially prone to foreign crusades, so the indictment runs. Those advancing this argument point to the fact that wars followed hard upon the reform eras of the 1890s, the Wilson years, the New Deal, the Fair Deal, the New Frontier. Further, they point to progressive Theodore Roosevelt's activist role in Panama and elsewhere, to Wilson's bellicose Mexican policy and his strong internationalism after World War I was over. A progressive President, a progressive country in 1914–1917—war was inevitable! But as plausible as these associations may appear, the case fails to convince. Close studies of progressive attitudes toward foreign policy consistently fail to detect a "progressive" position, whether activist, isolationist, or any other. Progressive T.R. wanted to intervene early, progressive Wilson tried for three years to stay out, and progressives LaFollette and Bryan fought intervention before 1917 and disapproved of it later. Reformers were of diverse minds on American foreign policy, and while some were quite jingoistic, the most opposition to the war came from the Left, liberal as well as radical.

Nonetheless, there is a tendency among modern students of Wilson to be so impressed with the long-term trend toward international involvement, and the supposed predisposition of the reform mind to crusades, not to mention the President's political and diplomatic difficulties, that Wilson's policies are presented as virtually inevitable. Sympathetic scholars point out that Wilson presided over often uncontrollable tides of passion and group interest and that he was forced many times to drift and wait, passive before forces he knew to be beyond his Constitutional and personal powers to shape. But he also acted decisively many times, channeling events within a reasonably wide belt of possibility. Where he had no alternatives or no reasonable ones, we cannot be revisionists. Where he had them we must make judgments, so long as they are tempered with a respect for historic forces which always dwarf men, and with sympathy for this brilliant, patriotic Christian who inherited such baffling dilemmas.

Perhaps no other president would have seen the importance of the early decisions regarding the British blockade and the Declaration of London. The way was politically clear for the administration to insist on the declaration, but most men would have weakened and let it go. No one expected a long war. But many of the decisions of the spring of 1915 bore Wilson's personal stamp. Demands on the belligerents could have been linked, and Germany could have been held to the same postwar accounting reserved for the Allies. Bryan requested a passenger ban at that time, and Wilson was not on principle opposed. Yet he declined to suggest one, insuring that the idea would come from Congress and require his opposition.

The loan decision is an interesting case. Charles Beard showed some years ago that Bryan himself flinched before the bankers' arguments. The country was in an economic recession in 1914, a recession that produced "the largest number of business failures in our country's history," according to *Bradstreet's Journal,* and that brought Andrew Carnegie to write Wilson on 23 November, 1914: "The present financial and industrial situations are very distressing. I have never known such conditions, such pressing calls upon debtors to pay. . . . " No one, from the Harvard Economics Department through the entire range of federal agencies, had any idea how to cope with it beyond maintaining a happy investment climate for the men who hired other men. We now know that recovery could have been achieved by having the government borrow funds from New York banks and reemploy people by a program of spending—on ships and tanks if it wished, but preferably on schools, hospitals, and housing. But this was advocated only by a few unbelievable socialists. The bankers showed Wilson a golden opportunity to put idle funds to work by simply *allowing* Europeans to borrow in New York and spend the money in this country. The pressure was enormous, and there were no real counterpressures and no constructive countersuggestions. Here was an apparently painless cure for America's economic troubles, and the enthusiasm for Allied loans and trade would certainly have broken Wilson politically had he blocked it only with arguments drawn from moral repugnance. *The New York Times* editorialized in early 1915:

> We have oversupplied ourselves with forces of production and they are idle in unusual proportion. . . . The Promise of the new year is that we shall accomplish a peaceful penetration of the world's markets to an extent we have never dreamed of. What others have shed blood to obtain through politics and force we shall obtain while bestowing our benevolence. . . . It is a new translation of the old beatitude, revised: blessed are the keepers of the peace for prosperity shall be within their homes and palaces.

Well might British ambassador Spring-Rice write to Grey in October: "When it became apparent that a loan was necessary, many secret forces began to act in its favour." It may now seem incredible that to achieve recovery the United States must ship to Europe both money

and goods and call it a sharp bargain. But it made sense in a capitalistic order with only a rudimentary economic science, and there was
literally no other plausible way in 1915 to get idle funds to work. The
loan decision, while not inevitable, must be seen sympathetically in
this light. Keynes' *General Theory* was twenty-one years away.

But if Wilson could hardly have been expected to maintain the ban
against loans to good customers abroad, he might have eliminated
munitions from the resulting trade. The Hitchcock bill of December,
1914, would have accomplished that, and there was ample precedent
and political support for it. Embargoes on munitions were imposed
by Denmark, Sweden, Italy, the Netherlands, Spain, and Norway.
The United States itself had embargoed munitions to Mexico in 1913.
A passenger ban might have easily been added in the spring of 1916, if
not earlier. When the liner *Persia* was sunk on January 3, the principal
Congressional reaction was anger that *American citizens had been
aboard*. That month Wilson left for a speaking tour to gain support
for preparedness and learned that the Congress accurately reflected
the country's mood. A passenger ban was his for the asking; and
while this would not have diminished the Allied trade, there would
be no loss of American life to inflame the issue if Germany eventually
resorted to unrestricted submarine warfare despite a ban on munitions,
as she well might.

These two changes in policy taken together would have vastly
altered the equation of forces. There were no other good alternatives
of comparable importance, although Wilson passed up some minor
opportunities for a more neutral course. The Lansing modus vivendi
on armed ships could have been put into effect, but probably would
not have made cruiser warfare the rule. Britain had been sending few
armed ships to America anyway, and with Q-ships operating in
British waters the submarines were still in danger on the surface. Yet
the move would have been helpful. As for Wilson's mediation efforts,
it is hard to fault his intentions or his persistence, except to wish that
his general appeal had been issued earlier, and from a position of
greater neutrality. But there was never much interest in a negotiated
peace. Some small things he might have done. He might have fired
Page and secured an ambassador to London who would not weaken
protests against the blockade. He might, as some progressives urged,
have dampened some enthusiasm in important quarters by declaring
that, in the event of war, he would draft capital as well as men.

But the passenger ban and the munitions embargo were probably enough, and they were politically possible. Naval troubles with Germany would have arisen, but would have been manageable. With Wilson's rhetorical power and discipline of mind, the road to neutrality was diplomatically and politically passable.

Had Wilson acted along these lines the result would almost certainly have been a German victory, either in the form of a negotiated or a dictated peace. Hohenzollern Germany would dominate the continent —a nation adept in the industrial arts, astonishingly vigorous, nominally Christian, capitalistic, racially arrogant, militaristic, deep in its own internal struggle between the socialists and the entrenched and unimaginative conservatives of land and industry. At least the last years of the war and perhaps more, with their relentless butchery and crippling moral and political consequences, would have been averted. One is permitted to doubt the November, 1917 success of Lenin. Speculation could go on. It should also be noted that the education the American people supposedly received in their new international responsibilities would not have taken place, or at least not in the same way. In view of American foreign policy attitudes from 1919 through 1941, one contemplates the loss of this schooling with relative calm.

The allure of a different American diplomacy springs not from a blind aversion to warfare but from a reasoned conception of the nature of American security. Wilson was sure that our security lay in a respect for law, in the spread of parliamentary governments, in the prestige that comes to nations that do not tolerate the infringement of their rights, in a defeated Germany, in a just peace, and in a postwar league of nations. Much of this is silly, but some of it represents the deepest insight into modern international relations. His mistake lay not in his instincts, a compound of the profound and the harmless, so much as in his judgment of the circumstances. Given the circumstances —the uncontrollable passions of Europe and the ignorance that gripped his own great democracy—there was only one *sure* way to pursue American security, a familiar way, without staggering risks, and without death. It was by an intensification of that surge of internal reform to which he had already become committed: the purification of our own democracy, the diversion of more resources to the education and physical well-being of our people, the broadening of the sway of equality, the conservation of our resources, the humanizing of our hours and conditions of work, the enhancement of the efficiency of our industry, the beautification and ordering of our cities, the narrowing of the gap between the classes. But a decision was reached to interrupt this work for a different approach to national unity, a different approach to economic prosperity, a different approach to the respect of nations.

Ernest May has guessed that Wilson would have chosen differently if he had foreseen the casualties of the Argonne and Chateau-Thierry. In the last speech before his stroke, delivered at Pueblo, Colorado, on 25 September 1919, Wilson said, his face streaked with tears, "What of our pledges to the men that lie dead in France...? There seems to me to stand between us and the rejection or qualification of this treaty the serried ranks of those boys in khaki, not only those boys who came home, but those dear ghosts that still deploy upon the fields of France." We have seen much more of the twentieth century than Woodrow Wilson, and the doubts grow stronger.

part three

REFORM: 1917-1928

I.

Once the war intervened, conservatives were happy to predict that reform would be shelved. But their expectations were only half realized. Proving once and for all how different were the impulses making up progressivism, the war encouraged some reformers and withered the spirits of others.

To many progressives the goal of reform had been to generate a great secular revival, lifting men's thoughts above self to what was shared. Such reformers had occasionally appeared as radicals, dedicated to *removing* the inequalities that divided society. The war proved that they were glad to settle for an easier solution—getting men to *forget* those inequalities in a time of common danger. Unity was their end; justice had been a means to that end, but war served admirably. Wilson's Assistant Secretary of Agriculture Carl Vrooman, for example, a reformer of varied credentials, regarded the war bond drives of 1917–18 as the high point of progressivism. Progressives like Vrooman had been critics of capitalism because it fostered a spirit of competition and rivalry and division. The war provided a shortcut to the cooperative spirit they had sought through social reform, and they took it with enthusiasm. An editorial in the General Federation of Women's Clubs *Magazine* in June, 1917, expressed this sense that the war was the fulfillment of reform:

> We shall exchange our material thinking for something quite different, and we shall all be kin. We shall all be enfranchised, prohibition will prevail, many wrongs will be righted, vampires and grafters and slackers will be relegated to a class by themselves, stiff necks will limber up, hearts of stone will be changed to hearts of flesh, and little by little we shall begin to understand each other.

For others who did not so easily forget the substantive goals they pursued, the new federal responsibilities of the mobilization period brought unexpected opportunities. Multiplying federal agencies offered positions for those who had longed to offer their skills in the service of the public. For those in the Croly-Van Hise tradition of national planning, the war was a time when American industry could be directed by experts in search of productive efficiency, not entrepreneurs avid for profits. The War Industries Board was only the most prominent of the wartime agencies where such experts found fulfilling work. The few reformers who were interested in housing welcomed the first experience in public housing when the Department of Labor's U. S. Housing Corporation built dwellings to house six thousand families and seven thousand single men. It was a small but useful precedent.[1]

The war was also a brief but unforgettable experience for social workers, ministers, and other reformers who had long wished to direct

[1] Another federal agency mandated to oversee war workers' housing, the U.S. Shipping Board, preferred to lend money to corporations, and this produced about 16,000 more dwelling units. The total, obviously, is quite small, and the hopes that it might serve as a useful precedent to initiate postwar federal housing programs were shattered by the Congress in 1919 when it required that all federal housing and federally funded housing be sold (at bargain prices) and the entire experiment terminated. See Roy Lubove, "Homes and 'A Few Well-Placed Fruit Trees': An Object Lesson in Federal Housing," *Social Research,* 27 (Winter, 1960), 469–85.

Americans toward a more upright life. They found their chance in the establishment and management of training camps and recreation facilities for the army and the Red Cross. Progressives like Raymond B. Fosdick and the Boston social worker Robert Woods were able now with government backing to provide the sort of health and sanitation facilities, wholesome recreation, creative use of leisure time, and freedom from alcohol and loose women that they had yearned to bring to the urban working classes. As Woods put it:

> In no previous decade, certainly in no previous generation, would it have been possible that every nook and corner of our cities would have been under the close, responsible, friendly surveillance of men and women representing much that is best in our national life.... It (the mobilization) has been the occasion of a new and better order of things affecting the restraint of the liquor trade and of prostitution, and the promotion of ...old and new forms of health-giving community recreation.

Another prominent social worker, Edward T. Devine, described their new opportunities in more specific terms:

> Enthusiasm for social service is epidemic.... A luxuriant crop of new agencies is springing up. We scurry back and forth to the national capital; we stock offices with typewriters and new letter-heads; we telephone feverishly, regardless of expense, and resort to all the devices of efficient "publicity work".... It is all very exhilarating, stimulating, intoxicating.

If there is a bit of surprise at learning that a mature, urban American could become so stirred over such trifles, this reflects our ignorance. In view of the prewar resources of America's social welfare movement, Devine's excitement is entirely understandable. And whatever the initial reaction of the social workers at finding themselves so affluent, they adjusted their expectations quickly enough. After enumerating the new opportunities open to reformers in the wartime period of "true national collectivism," the busiest year of his life, Woods added: "Why should it not always be so? Why not continue in the years of peace this close, vast, wholesome organism of service, of fellowship, of constructive creative power?"

As the planners and social workers found employment for their talents, so the war created a climate that advanced other progressive goals that had seemed so distant. The Americanization movement had aimed at assimilating the immigrants who were coming in such indigestible numbers since about the turn of the century. Americanization bore all the marks of progressivism. It expressed a benevolent purpose, it took on the urgency of a crusade, it shared with the rest of progressivism the conviction that the powerful social forces that were reshaping America ought to be brought under control and that legislation was the way. Frances Kellor, a leading figure in the Americanization movement and appropriately enough a New Nationalism progressive, put it succinctly: "Nation building is to be in the future a deliberate formative process, not an accidental...arrangement." Accordingly, Miss Kellor's New York branch of the North American Civic League for Immigrants, allied in the effort with patriotic societies like the Daughters of the American Revolution, many of the settlements, the Young Men's Christian Association, and other groups, busied themselves with the staggering job of "educating" the immigrant in American behavior and principles. But all their efforts before 1917 had produced only uncoordinated city and state efforts at night classes in English or an occasional official "investigation" of conditions among the immigrant population. Americanization had not caught on with the public or their elected representatives, and private efforts were inadequate to the task.

The war brought the chance to involve the federal government in the Americanization struggle, and Miss Kellor, now head of the New York Committee for Immigrants, tirelessly pressed for the recognition of Americanization as a vital part of the war effort. Under her prodding, somnolent federal bureaus like the Bureau of Education and the Bureau of Naturalization took a new interest in the immigrant and his skills as worker and citizen. Social worker Josephine Roche joined the Committee on Public Information and guided a large amount of their propaganda toward immigrants. Interest in Americanization sprang up everywhere. Cities, patriotic groups, and industrialists like Henry Ford suddenly exerted themselves to accelerate and direct the melting-pot process—something they had been content to leave to chance in the past. The war in a few short months did what Frances Kellor's patient organizing efforts had failed to do in the years since T.R. first heard her reformer's plea in 1906. It brought to this sector of progressivism an undreamed-of public support.

Opportunities for other types of reform arose out of the mobilization, and they were not all lost. White women gained some forty thousand new jobs as they replaced men or moved into war industries,

and the government formed the Committee on Women's Defense
Work under Anna Howard Shaw to coordinate the woman's preparedness movement. The war provided the right climate for passage of
the Constitutional amendment granting women federal suffrage, and
the Nineteenth Amendment was ratified in 1920. Just earlier the Congress had finally yielded to the prohibitionists by passing the Eighteenth
Amendment against the sale of alcoholic beverages, and in this case
also the wartime need to conserve grain and preserve health offered
reformers a decisive argument.

The war also produced among progressives a heightened determination to attack inequalities of wealth. One of the leading failures
of the entire progressive movement had been its inability to appreciate
and use the taxing power. This was especially true at the federal level,
where the potentialities of taxation as a weapon of social policy were
greatest. The federal revenue structure in 1914, after the reformers had
done about all they seemed interested in doing in the area of taxation
at the time of the Underwood Tariff battle, raised only $71 million of
a total revenue of $734 million out of a graduated income tax. The
rest, $663 million, was raised from customs duties, excises on liquor
and tobacco, land sales, and the like, which meant that American
federal tax burdens were carried by the consuming public. "The
wealthy, obviously," writes Arthur S. Link, "enjoyed relative immunity
from taxation."

It took the preparedness controversy of 1916 and its demands for
new revenue to stimulate progressives to a heightened interest in one of
their most promising and little-used weapons, taxation. In the spring of
1916, progressives in the Congress, led by North Carolina's Claude
Kitchin and Wisconsin's Robert LaFollette, beat down an administration proposal to pay the cost of armament by a tax bearing predominantly upon lower and middle classes. Then these Congressional
radicals, assisted by reform pressures outside the Congress such as
the Association for an Equitable Federal Income Tax formed by
John Dewey, Fred Howe, and others, pushed through a tax law
in September that raised the surtax from 6 percent to 13 percent,
doubled the tiny corporate tax, and added a small inheritance tax.
In 1917 progressives again raised individual and corporate rates
(to a maximum of 67 percent), increased estate taxes, and passed an
excess profits tax. These efforts to insure that no one became a mil-
lionaire while young men died in France fell short of success. Huge

profits were made from the war, but they would not have been taxed at all had no progressives made the effort, and each dollar taken from profits meant a dollar that would not have to be borrowed from the wealthy to finance the war and be repaid, plus interest, in the 1920s. Secretary of the Treasury William McAdoo finally raised about one dollar in three by taxation, which represented a failure to progressives like Amos Pinchot whose American Committee on War Finance had demanded pay-as-you-go (paying for the war entirely out of taxes, which meant virtually confiscating all higher incomes). But due to progressive efforts a tax program was enacted that was too radical for J. P. Morgan, Jr. and men of his class, who had preferred a rate of one to five. When the Bristol (Tennessee) *News Bureau* editorialized in 1918 that "war is a hothouse of income taxation," it spoke the truth only with reference to the ineffective tax efforts of prewar reformers.

II.

Yet while the war years brought new opportunities, which some progressives seized, we know that in the total story the war was fatal to the humanitarian, liberal component of reform. No historian has described this process in full detail, for it involves matters of mood and spirit as well as the traditional pull and haul of politics. The effect of war was, of course, uncomplicated in one area: to the peace movement it represented defeat and brought immediate dejection. A number of other reforms were simply shouldered aside by the preoccupations of wartime. The Federal Trade Commission, institutional embodiment of the anti-trust drive, had scarcely organized when the need for maximum wartime production forced it into a passive role. There were stirrings of the old New Freedom fervor after the war, but these were effectively scotched by the Court and by the 1925 appointment of that former lobbyist and genial friend of the corporation, William E. Humphrey, to the chairmanship. In another area, Wilson added one more defeat to the progressive conservation movement when, pressed by wartime concerns, he simply forgot to appoint the Waterways Commission, which conservationists had finally established by the Newlands Act of 1917 (the authority for the Commission was withdrawn in the Water Power Act of 1920). In still another, the war aborted the establishment of a government-owned armor plant proposed by Secretary of the Navy Josephus Daniels and mandated by Congress in the Naval Bill of August, 1916. Without American entry the government would have taken at least this step toward supplying a "yardstick" portion of its own defense tools, a small but interesting step away from the military-industrial complex of recent lament.

But the chief damage done by war to the progressive movement came not from the interruption of various prewar reform projects, for while war diverted energies from some causes it seemed to provide at least as many new outlets for the urge to social service as it directly or indirectly stifled. What hurt progressivism most were two products of the war: the perversion of the idea of a regulatory state as business groups came to dominate governmental policy, and the war-induced alteration of the reform mentality in the direction of ideas and impulses at once less confident and less generous.

Wilson himself, a man with as highly developed a sense of the dynamics of national opinion and political power as any of his generation, had anticipated that reactionary pressures would rise along with patriotism. Even if he did not speak prophetically along this line to Frank Cobb prior to the Declaration of War, others remembered similar predictions. "Every reform we have won," Secretary Daniels recalled Wilson saying before he made the decision for war, "will be lost if we go into this war. . . . War means autocracy. The people we have unhorsed will inevitably come into the control of the country, for we shall be dependent upon the steel, oil, and financial magnates. They will run the nation." And in they came: Wall Street's Bernard Baruch, B&O Railroad's Daniel Willard, International Harvester's Alexander Legge, Union Pacific's Robert Lovett, Cleveland industrialist Frank A. Scott, energetic, successful, patriotic capitalists who would man the new federal agencies such as the War Industries Board, the Food and Fuels Administration, the War Finance Corporation, the Railroad Administration, and who for two hectic years shared with the Congress the power to decide how the rewards and burdens of the wartime economy would be distributed. The well-being of any given American in 1919 was shaped by decisions made in Washington to a degree unprecedented in American history. The Congress determined who would be taxed and how; the financing activities of the Treasury and the Federal Reserve allocated the burdens of the second tax system, inflation, and the third tax system, interest rates on the federal debt; myriad agencies, led by the War Industries Board, wrote the cost-plus contracts, agreed upon prices (i.e., profits), allocated scarce resources among competing industries, and extended credit to stimulate expansion in uneconomic areas. The results, as Wilson and others had dimly foreseen, were reactionary. Despite efforts to tax away war profits, despite an unparalleled attention to the legitimate claims of labor (through the War Labor Board and labor representation on the War Industries Board), and despite some well-meaning attempts by Baruch and others to prevent profiteering, the wealthy seem generally to have managed to have the war paid for by somebody else. While the evidence is somewhat spotty, it appears that real wages went up imperceptibly if at all during the wartime boom, and working people put in longer hours and endured crowded living conditions to hold their own against inflation and taxation. For the great mass of salaried employees, the fiscal system worked out in Washington brought them, in George Soule's words, "unmitigated disaster:" the purchasing power of their pay dropped 22 percent between 1916 and 1919. Presumably it was just such people who, in a blind desire to punish those responsible for this injustice, supplied most of the energy for the postwar campaigns to eliminate aliens, radicals, and uppity blacks.

While these groups were permitted the morally bracing experience of sacrificing for their country, other groups were finding war nothing like the hell that Sherman had described. Farmers experienced a 25 percent gain in real income between 1915 and 1918, although it was a prosperity with only one or two more years to run. But the largest and most lasting benefits came to the larger capitalists. Corporate profits jumped to three times their prewar level in 1917, and even after the higher wartime taxes took effect it was estimated by John M. Clark that business profits were up 30 percent from 1913. A Federal Trade Commission inquiry into profiteering showed that in some sectors of the economy the war was literally golden. The profits of U. S. Steel went from a prewar average of $76 million to $478 million in 1917. In 1918 the profits of the largest ten steel mills ranged from 30 percent to 319 percent of invested capital, and a grateful management of Bethlehem Steel voted its top four officers a shared bonus of $2.1 million. After taxes in 1917, forty-eight lumber companies netted 17 percent of invested capital, oil companies averaged 21 percent, and twenty-four copper companies averaged 24 percent. The net earnings of national banks increased more in the 1914–19 period than in the preceding forty years. The number of taxpayers in the thirty to forty thousand dollars-a-year income bracket roughly tripled between 1914 and 1918, and at the war's end it was estimated that steep taxes had not prevented some forty-two thousand Americans from accumulating a million dollars or more.

Such figures reflect a secure grip upon government by the larger capitalists. The governmental machinery put together to organize war production was manned, with few exceptions, by men drawn from industry. There had been no alternative to this. When Bernard Baruch and the War Industries Board accepted the job of centralized control of the wartime economy they found themselves obliged to intervene in countless decisions about prices, wages, transportation and materiel priorities, and the only real source of talent in these complicated questions was the affected industries themselves. The universities of that day, the foundations, and the older governmental agencies could contribute only a handful of trained, experienced men. Newly appointed government officials with an industry background and point of view were naturally something less than implacable when bargaining with industry for terms that protected the interests of the public treasury and the labor force, especially since there was a war on and the army must be supplied. One result was high profits, but more important than this was the lesson absorbed by all those involved in the wartime cooperation between business and government. The uncertainties and tight profit margins of the competitive market could be replaced by the steady output and predictable, high profits of a system of government-sponsored planning. Nothing was lost save the worn-out doctrine of laissez-faire. The government proved sympathetic to industry's problems; it extracted no painful sacrifices in return for its gift of asylum from the hazards of competition and inadequate demand. The "entente" between big business and government that some scholars think they perceive in the administration of T.R. had indeed become a reality by 1918.

There are those—the younger Woodrow Wilson was among them—who have argued that such an outcome was inevitable, war or no war. A regulatory state in a capitalistic setting must wind up regulating in the interests of the largest and most powerful corporations. Thus progressivism, to the extent that it meant a regulatory state, has been seen as deeply conservative and involving no real reform at all. The relations of government and business during and after the war offer much support for such a view, but I think it mistaken. The enlarged powers of government in the prewar period were always potentially and sometimes actually out of the control of the large capitalistic interests. Even during the war, when government policy was most benign toward capital, the "entente" was uneasy and government officials could prove unreasonably stubborn in the defense of the public interest. Melvin Urofsky, in his very useful book, *Big Steel and the Wilson Administration* (1969), argues that the steel industry had its way on every important decision affecting its interests. But much that we know, and in fact much of Urofsky's evidence itself, points another way. At various times during the war the government threatened to take over plants, adopted revenue schedules designed to recapture up to 70 percent of excess profits, refused to drop the anti-trust suit against U. S. Steel instituted in 1911, and forced on the steel industry both an eight-hour day and promises to hold free shop elections and bargain with the resultant unions. No plants were actually commandeered, the revenue schedules were evaded by ingenious accounting procedures, the anti-trust suit was lost, and preoccupation with the League struggle undercut the administration's support of labor just at the crucial moment in the fall of 1919. But the President and stubborn New Freedom Democrats such as Josephus Daniels of the Navy Department, William McAdoo of the Treasury and Railroad Administration, Newton Baker in the War Department, and Felix Frankfurter, Secretary of the War Labor Policies Board, proved ideologically ill-adapted to an entente with big business. They were so unpredictable that leading businessmen wavered in their attachment to the idea of a post-war continuation of government planning and began to talk again of cutting government back to a minimal role and managing their economic problems through trade associations.

In the end the spirit of wartime cooperation did dominate the future. The dream of several government officials and dollar-a-year businessmen of an Industrial Board to continue government-industry cooperation into peacetime was shelved, but the regulatory powers of the progressive-era state—the ICC, FTC, Federal Reserve Board, Food and Drug Administration, Tariff Commission—were retained and did in fact prove friendly to capital in the 1920s. But it had not always been so. Wilson may have claimed too much when he said that the New Freedom had "unhorsed" the wealthy, but national progressivism had since 1902 managed to direct a significant proportion of the powers of the state toward the needs of groups other than the eastern corporate elite. Is it answered that the capitalists benefitted most from regulation? True enough, the benefits to large corporate interests seem to have outweighed the benefits to labor, small business, agriculture, and consumer, as of 1916. But the situation was fluid right up to the war (and even to some extent during the war, as government relations with the steel industry show), and the regulatory apparatus was capable of being used for predominantly public rather than predominantly private ends. There are many reasons why this was so, the chief among them being that the idea of the public interest as a distinct entity, overriding claims of property *and requiring frequent conflict with property,* was widely implanted in the heads of men —politicians, intellectuals, lawyers, even businessmen—who would shape public policy in the future.

But the decision to mobilize for war did turn out to be a decision to alter both the idea and the· practice of federal economic regulation. Progressivism may have laid the egg of the regulatory state, and hatched it, but the formative wartime years were spent with foster parents from Wall Street. American industry did in fact work a miracle of production, and the natural result was a deep admiration and respect for Big Business and for the government-industry cooperation through which the miracle was arranged. The experience made a deep impression not only on the general public, but on the national elite of men who, as federal bureaucrats or as people flowing back and forth between private life and public service, would determine the nature of federal regulation in the future. To attain maximum wartime production, the federal bureaucracy, infused with industry-based personnel, put harmonious relations and uninterrupted production above stable and reasonable prices. It was a pivotal experience; the economy had never worked so well, and the cost was easily forgotten. The way of the future was the way of business-government cooperation. The 1920s, with their cozy government-industry relations, commenced when the dollar-a-year men entrained for Washington in the spring of 1917 to shoulder their patriotic duties.[2]

2 It took years for the reform mind to work its way free of the WIB experience. Even in the early days of the New Deal it was still thought that regulation and economic planning could best be accomplished through a cooperative, friendly process in which business helped to man the controls. Only in the late 1930s did men in government in significant numbers return to a more austere conception of federal regulation and make another start at realizing the promise of independent regulation in the public interest. Then war intervened again, production became paramount, and the regulatory tradition was warped a second time by military exigencies. Because of the Cold War we have never emerged from these conditions. In this century, war has aborted the regulatory experiment.

In addition to the advantages that it conferred on some of the traditional antagonists of reformers, the war undermined central progressive assumptions. A faith in the inherent goodness of The People underlay all the political alterations of the Direct Democracy component of progressivism, and a faith in man's rationality underlay the work of reformers who wished to substitute expertise and social control for drift. For those with the Jeffersonian confidence in the many, the sight of masses of men docilely and even in some cases with relish killing one another, and then throwing away the military victory by refusing to insist upon a just peace, suggested that the Jeffersonian view of man might be insufficiently pessimistic. And one could not help but be further discouraged by the news (revealed in *Army Mental Tests,* edited by C. S. Yoakum and R. S. Yerkes [1920]) that army mental tests showed some 30 percent of recruits to be illiterate, with forty-six thousand men in the first nine months of 1918 showing up for induction with a mental age of ten years or less. Such discoveries immobilized the pressures for Direct Democracy and worked havoc in any number of minds.

Those reformers in the Hamiltonian tradition who had all along been somewhat elitist could draw no more solace from the war period than the Jeffersonians. The pessimistic anthropology taught by the war stunned even the elitists, for a thorough skepticism about human nature undermined their faith even in the rationality of the experts. They were if anything more elitist after the war than before, but less sure where the elite was to be found and now reasonably certain that it would not be heeded.

And if loss of confidence in human rationality were not enough, the experiences of 1917–20 dealt a blow to progressive confidence in the state. Reformers had supposed that the state was benevolent, but Attorney General A. Mitchell Palmer, with the president's support, turned the power of government to the persecution of immigrants with European political views as well as native American radicals. Against a background of banned publications, arrests, and deportations under the Espionage Act of 1917, the Trading with the Enemy Act of 1917, the Sedition Act of 1918, and the Alien Act of 1918, veteran reformer Frederic C. Howe wrote in his autobiography: "I hated the new state that had arisen, hated its brutalities, its ignorance, its unpatriotic patriotism, that made profit from our sacrifices and used its power to suppress criticism of its acts." But if a liberal government could not be trusted, where were reformers to turn? Many became disoriented and entered a period of intellectual armistice, adopting the sort of cynicism which H. L. Mencken (whose cynicism, unlike that of most intellectuals, was not recent) expressed when he said: "If I am convinced of anything, it is that Doing Good is in bad taste."

The war thus revealed how much progressivism had rested upon certain vulnerable assumptions. It also demonstrated how the thrust and shape of the movement depended upon a very fragile mood. Progressive reform represented an intervention to project the values of the genial and neighborly nineteenth century into the twentieth, but the nineteenth century unfortunately offered a number of contradictory values to complicate the job of its defenders. It was little understood during the progressive era how vitally important was the mood of the time in determining which values would be uppermost, both as social goals and as guides to acceptable tactics. Some of these values were the generous values of Jefferson, Lincoln, and Theodore Parker, and in the sunny atmosphere of the prewar years these humane and liberal values were strong in the movement. But some of the values of the class from which progressivism was drawn were moralities of a different sort—the norms of the Anglo-Saxon Protestant New Englanders, ranging from sobriety and continence through an identification of "American" with white skins, northern European extraction, and small-town capitalism. The balance, as we see it in retrospect, was always a close one between the generous and the coercive impulses. In the tense, anxious war years with their bewildering changes, progressivism changed its mood and turned increasingly into a cultural counterattack against deviance from the traditional New England norms. The experiences of two progressive organizations document the ascendancy of the reactionary spirit that coincided with and was evidently caused by the war experience.

Nowhere do we see this line of struggle more clearly than in the Americanization movement. When Frances Kellor founded the New York branch of the North American Civic League for Immigrants in 1909, the league was financed by industrialists who were glad to contribute to an organization that would teach English, hygiene, and the rudiments of a patriotism that amounted largely to orderly behavior. Not scorning these goals, Miss Kellor from the first tried also to direct Americanization into areas such as factory safety legislation.

Thus the movement had a dual nature: one wing of the Americanization impulse sent industrial spies into the ranks of foreign-born workers or drilled law-and-order civics into them at night, and the other wing tolerated their language, religion, and habits and worked to improve their living and working conditions. The war ended the ambiguity. The conformist tendency became paramount and the permissive, humanitarian side almost vanished. Frances Kellor herself, in her book *Straight America* published in 1916, called for loyalty, discipline, and universal military service. The national crisis had tipped the delicate balance of this reform effort toward its hard, repressive aspect. To be Americanized after 1917 meant to be watched, to be forced to stop attending the local socialist club or workers' meetings designed to organize the shop. Americanization in wartime carried the early signs of the approaching red scare.

The same process may be seen at work inside the Southern Sociological Congress, a civic organization established in 1912 to improve social conditions in the South. At first the Congress had a strong social welfare and social gospel orientation, and its chief interests were in child welfare, public health and housing, adult dependency, recreation, temperance, and racial relations. Efforts along some of these lines—public health, for instance—benefitted the entire community, and while laborious they were not socially disturbing. But the Congress also took an advanced position on the treatment of the disadvantaged and on the question of race. It always had a strong evangelistic tone, but at first this sort of fervor was *social* gospel fervor, with the emphasis upon justice at least as much as upon morality.

The war caused a change of emphasis in the work of the Congress. In the convention of 1918 in Birmingham the new note was discernible. Clergy began to outnumber welfare workers, and the effort to improve the South was now seen by Congress speakers as less a matter of scientific study and social reform as a matter of spiritual inspiration. The Congress began to lose interest in changing conditions and take an interest in changing hearts. In the 1919 convention at Knoxville, the organization's historian tells us, "several speakers expressed concern over radical movements. Bolshevism was a product of atheism, they argued, and should be countered by 'genuine American patriotism.'" Women were advised to stay out of politics, to "give us happy homes and happy firesides and bolshevism cannot come in." In 1920 the nationalistic note was dominant, with Bishop Theodore D. Bratton telling the convention in Washington that the task of the Congress was to keep America American. The Congress had shifted entirely to the defensive. Five years later, with bolshevism put down in the United States, the Congress, its reform spirit thoroughly played out and domesticated, became the Home Betterment League.

III.

Transformations of this sort occurred across the range of progressive activities as the postwar atmosphere turned defensive and sour. Reactionary tendencies ultimately won out over desires to change the system so as to make it more democratic and more receptive to new impulses, and because they did, we see this rightward turn in American politics and social thought as the significant development in domestic affairs in the period 1918–20. But in these years just at the end of the war there was also a strong Left in the United States, ranging from the familiar progressive elements through a briefly invigorated Socialist Party and including, after 1919, two small communist parties. These "parties of movement," as Arno J. Mayer calls them, were in ferment and apparent growth both in Europe and America. Many contemporaries, observing the wave of strikes of 1918–19, thought the Left might be within months of a seizure of power. New York clothing workers went out in late 1918, followed by longshoremen; a general strike paralyzed Seattle in February; New England was swept by walkouts among telephone workers, railway labor, and even Boston policemen; and in September the great strike against U. S. Steel began. The Socialist Party itself experienced dramatic growth in 1917–18, polling 27 percent in the New York mayoralty election (a 500-percent increase over their showing in 1913), 34 percent in Chicago, and 44 percent in Dayton. In North Dakota, a number of ex-Socialists had organized the Non-Partisan League around the grievances of Dakota farmers, elected their own Governor, and were establishing state-owned enterprises from banks to grain elevators and flour mills. At least parts of the American public seemed to have been radicalized by the war,[3] and this included some intel-

---

[3] And by wartime inflation. With 1913 as a base year (index of 100), the cost of living was 104 in 1915, 131 in 1917, in 1918 was 159, in 1919 was 183, and in 1920 was 208 (calculated by A. Hansen, in Bureau of Labor Statistics, *Historical Statistics of the United States, 1789–1945* (1949), p. 235.

lectuals. Woodrow Wilson himself spoke of the need for a third party, and mused to a friend in 1918 that the world would probably be moving to the Left and that he would be going with it.

Thus both the Left and the Right were active, ambitious, and growing in strength just after the war, and there were abundant predictions of the success of each. In those months there was an air of expectancy, anxiety, chiliasm; opinion began to polarize, with both radicalism and reaction feeding on the reported successes of the other. We now know that the Right was much stronger and that the ferment of 1918–1919 would be rather decisively stifled. The triumph of the reactionary spirit was not engineered by some manipulative business elite, but was a national phenomenon expressing the ultimate decision of the great bulk of the American people that they would not tolerate any further disturbance or uncertainty, and were in no mood for idealism. The role of the Wilson administration in the postwar reaction, however, was far too cooperative. Different national leadership might have moderated, even if it could not entirely blunt, the swing to the Right. Wilson, preoccupied with the Versailles meetings and the fight to gain treaty ratification, allowed himself to make an almost complete default in the area of domestic leadership in 1919. He was in the country only ten days between December, 1918 and July, 1919, and in all of 1919 sent only three messages to Congress, none of them mentioning any specific reforms. Progressives needed and appealed for his leadership, but long before his stroke in September it was clear that Wilson would neither lead the Left nor actively combat the Right—except in the matter of the League of Nations. Despite progressive protest he terminated federal housing efforts and returned the railroads to private ownership; declined to help labor in its difficulties with steel management and secured injunctions against striking coal miners; and signed laws in the areas of water power, railroads, and merchant marine in 1920 that were more than generous to capital. In the area of civil liberties the administration could not even claim to have been the nonresisting accomplice of a conservative Congress. Attorney General A. Mitchell Palmer and Postmaster General Albert S. Burleson had enforced the wartime Espionage and Alien and Sedition Acts with excessive zeal, and Palmer ultimately put the Justice Department at the head of the Red Scare of 1919, with Wilson's consent.

It was a poor record for a progressive administration. Harding might as well have been in the White House from 1918 forward. Indeed, this might have been an improvement, since Harding freed Debs. But it is doubtful that the postwar triumph of reaction could have been entirely averted even had Wilson tried to chart a clear course to the Left. Liberals were shocked by the treaty when its unexpectedly harsh terms were revealed in June, 1919, and many were beginning to pull away not only from Wilson, who had talked them into the war and then failed to redeem their decision by bringing home a statesmanlike peace, but from idealistic exertions under any leadership. The broader public showed signs of moral fatigue as early as November, 1918, when the Republicans captured control of both houses of Congress. And although Attorney General Palmer's activities helped encourage the postwar politics of rigidity and fear, they were not only matched and exceeded, but also preceded, by grassroots repression and vigilantism directed against any ideas tainted with a critical edge. Beginning in the early days of 1919, the local groups who had been so vigilant against antiwar sentiment began to shift their attention to subversive political and economic ideas. From January, 1919, to May, 1920, the Republic was saved not just by a few FBI raids on immigrant political groups, but by local harassment of intellectually unconventional teachers, beatings administered to Socialists and Wobblies, and a few well-placed gunshots and hangings to emphasize the sincerity of popular feeling. It is not pleasant or particularly enlightening to repeat the details of the Red Scare of 1919–1920, especially the stimulus it gave to America's racial antagonisms. There were 25 large race riots in American cities in the summer of 1919, and more than 70 *reported* lynchings (whites lynching blacks; none of the other kind were reported, and one may be sure they would have been). The Red Scare was really a red-and-black-scare, aimed (if the word does not imply too much rationality) not only at political radicals but also at any Negroes, particularly the young males just back from France, who might have come into contact with the idea that their postwar existence would be any different from their existence before they put on a uniform or moved into war work in Detroit and Chicago. Any observer could have stated the principal reasons for such a constipated social climate: the Russian Revolution and the "threat" of international Marxism, the bombings and labor problems of 1919. But there would undoubtedly have been a red scare even without Leninism. Stanley Coben, in a perceptive article published in

1964, argues that the red scare was not so much aimed at Bolshevism as at the disturbing changes in values and behavior that everywhere undercut familiar things in postwar America. Undoubtedly the term "Bolshevism" denoted a number of sins. The bourgeois public broadened the term to include all forms of social criticism, and counterattacked to prevent the imminent onset of riot, expropriation, and free love. Bourgeois society, under the goad of the unrest of 1919, closed ranks against subversive ideas of all kinds, proscribing not only the really revolutionary sentiments of a few anarchists and Marxists but virtually all forms of social criticism.

So the atmosphere closed in by 1919, and the dreams of the socialists, the railroad nationalizers, the stray radicals hoping to convene a third party, all were shown to be the dreams of a small minority. The red scare, of course, was "over" by mid 1920; it required a degree of emotional excitation not far from that required for reform, and it was just such exertions the public was seeking to avoid. But the underlying doctrine of the anti-red crusade, that dissent in all its forms was revolutionary and intolerable, persisted in the 1920s in the stifling form of a credulous complacency. When the Right won the brief struggle of 1918–19, it won not just a year but a decade of dominance. The presidential politics of 1920 would mark the beginning of an extended reign of those forces committed against social criticism, against all forms of social change but the technological and commercial innovations of the private sector. The public, or most of it, continued until 1929 to find the economic order nearly perfect, and lived easily under the benevolent rule of the well-paid decision-makers in the worlds of industry, commerce, advertising, education, and religion. Such outbreaks of indignation and dissent as occurred were repeatedly put down by the political leadership of the established order. It was not a flourishing climate for social criticism, broad vision, or sustained attention to the public interest.

IV.

There was a time when historians left the story of progressivism here, fading Wilson and LaFollette out as Harding and all his hosts of conservatives reclaimed the country. While the stereotype of the conservative, complacent 1920s contains its truth, it needs to be emphasized that the eclipse of reform was never total. Ideas and projects distasteful to entrenched commercial groups continued to emanate from angry people, and if these efforts are forgotten simply because they were beaten back, we then exaggerate the placidity and consensus of the 1920s, and in addition are unprepared to understand 1929. Note the signs of insurgent activity with which the custodians of the ongoing social enterprise had to cope. In late 1919 Amos Pinchot, J. A. H. Hopkins, and other progressives organized the Committee of Forty-Eight to keep alive the prospects of political action, and the committee was the nucleus of a progressive coalition that met in Chicago in 1922. The majority of those at the Chicago meetings were representatives of the farmer-labor parties that had been springing up in states such as Minnesota, Iowa, Nebraska, and as far west as Washington, in angry response to the high unemployment and low farm prices of 1920–22. Out of two conferences in Chicago grew the Conference for Progressive Political Action, an assortment of old reformers, trade unionists, moderate socialists, and Non-Partisan Leaguers. What brought them together and held them together was a distaste for the conservatism of major party politics, and they had no difficulty persuading Bob LaFollette to run for president in 1924 on a Progressive Party ticket. LaFollette polled five million votes, a poor third, but his campaign was plagued by mistakes and difficulties, and that five million votes becomes an imposing sign of dissent when we understand it to be the hard core of a progressive vote that was in potential much larger. Had LaFollette not antagonized the Klan, had he not opposed America's participation in the war, had the progressive organization been more efficient, more states might have returned totals like those of California, where LaFollette received four times as many votes as the Democratic candidate, John W. Davis. Coolidge was easily elected, and the vote showed that most of the country was not only conservative but apathetic; only about 50 percent of registered voters bothered to vote. But under the apathy and conservatism of the majority ran an unmistakable current of protest.

This pressure for reform was felt in more places than presidential politics. The farm bloc in Congress secured passage of the Packers and Stockyards Act of 1921, the Grain Futures Act of 1922, several complicated farm credit arrangements enacted in 1921 and 1923, and the Cooperative Marketing Act of 1922. These legislative exertions did nothing to stem the slide of farm prices, but they were the only display of creative legislative power that spokesmen for what might be called underprivileged social groups were able to muster in the years of Republican dominance. Yet if insurgents did not have the strength to pursue their positive goals in the congressional atmosphere of the 1920s, they had considerable obstructive strength. In the Senate, George Norris was at the head of a list of reform-minded men full of irreverent language, dislike of large fortunes, distrust of large corporations, and sympathy for the underdog. Later generations have forgotten Frazier and Lemke from North Dakota, Shipstead and Johnson of Minnesota, Hiram Johnson of California, Brookhart of Iowa—have almost forgotten Norris and LaFollette. And with the exception of the latter two, the "Sons of the Wild Jackass" in the Senate *were* cranky, contentious, uninterested in sustained action, and effective in a negative way only on selected occasions. But they held the line against a few of the schemes of conservatives, such as the selling of government rights at Muscle Shoals, the appointment of John J. Parker to the Supreme Court, or a few of the more outrageous features of Andrew Mellon's tax plans. As Cedric Cowing reminds us in his *Populists, Plungers and Progressives,* these senatorial mavericks sustained a vigorous criticism throughout the 1920s and especially from January to October, 1929, of speculative excesses on the market and the timidity of the Federal Reserve Board in curbing the call loan market. They stand as a reminder that there were rebellious constituencies all over the country in the years of Harding, Coolidge, and Hoover.

Outside the government, voluntary associations in the social welfare and social service movements remained in existence and continued their struggles on behalf of labor legislation, social insurance, public housing, and adequate relief. Organizations like the National Consumers League, the Women's Trade Union League, and the group associated with *Survey* magazine refused to allow reduced budgets and public apathy to put an end to their efforts. The National Child Labor Committee helped push its Constitutional amendment through the Congress in 1924, and then lobbied it in the states. New organizations actually arose to join the old, such as the American Association for Old Age Security, founded in 1927 by Abraham Epstein. Fruition along these lines was delayed until the 1930s (and in some cases, such as those of adequate relief or national health insurance, did not come even then), but the 1920s were a time of at least theoretical advance toward some of the unattained goals of the progressive social welfare wing. A more successful reform campaign of the 1920s, in which some of the social service group also participated, was the effort to outlaw war. The peace forces of the progressive years regrouped after the war, and gained their pact against war in the Kellogg-Briand Treaty of 1928. In this battle at least the reformers had not only agitated and educated, but had won exactly what they wanted.

A review of the surviving reform activities thus produces no mean list. It is well to remember these pockets of resistance to the "let business alone" ethos lest we stereotype the 1920s, and, more important, lest we lose sight of the alternatives actually offered to the American public.

V.

Arthur Link wrote an article in 1959 in which he reviewed some of this evidence of dissent in the 1920s, and he nonetheless entitled the article "What Happened to Progressivism in the 1920s?" Economic reform in that period was almost totally frustrated, the scattered forces of reform in crippling disarray. A fairly widespread prosperity, a memory of the radical frights of 1919, a cycle of weariness and complacency, these constitute the chief causes of the weakness of progressivism in the 1920s, according to the classic external explanation. There is much to recommend such a line of argument; indeed, it is indispensable. But we know how much economic discontent there was, and no purely external explanation can account for the poor results attained by groups in revolt. Throughout the 1920s the forces of economic reform were frustrated by their inability—which went all the way back to the split of 1912—to concentrate sufficiently to capture one of the two major parties. This organizational problem was to a large extent a result of that factionalism and unruliness that had always characterized and hampered the reform forces. Their leadership problems in the 1920s were serious, with Wilson ill, Roosevelt gone, and LaFollette aging, but here again the problem was not new—they had never been able to unite behind one leader or one program. It was in the area of the reform program that the 1920s revealed inadequacies few had suspected. The progressives had largely run out of relevant ideas, Link argues, citing the stale formulas of the LaFollette platform and the helplessness of reformers in dealing with Secretary Mellon's tax cut proposals without benefit of a modern understanding of what public-sector spending could accomplish. Link and others have exaggerated the intellectual inadequacies of the reform universe (as distinct from individuals within it, who had plenty of inadequacies); while it would require a book to argue this conclusively, it is my impression that reform intellectuals and political leaders were in possession during the 1920s of a rather thorough understanding of the nature of poverty, the activities of antisocial groups in American economic life, and the principal steps necessary to seek humane adjustment. Undoubtedly they had an insufficient (almost nonexistent) understanding of the social uses of fiscal policy, but the New Dealers' conservatism in this area indicates that the concept was difficult to assimilate. Even given this undoubted intellectual inadequacy, the apparent obsolescence of the progressive mentality in the 1920s was as much a matter of will as of intellect.

This is not to directly disagree with critics like Randolph Bourne, Harold Stearns, or the historians David Noble and Eric Goldman who show that the pragmatic reform mind was so much more interested in action and technique than in goals and ultimate values that it did not function well in adversity. In the days when the entire nation was aroused, social evils seemed many but simple, their solution a matter of public enlightenment and applied intelligence, and the volunteer army of reform was large and enthusiastic. But once the bosses and slums did not vanish, public apathy began to silence the muckraking journals; the war crusade brought the hard knowledge that The People were ill-informed and irrational and the state preferred intellectual conformity to social service. Then the liberal mind was forced to rethink its task. This should not have been such a morale-shattering bit of work. The principal ideas of progressivism were sound enough: it was still true that private economic forces had made the cities close to intolerable, plundered the natural environment, and virtually eliminated (or perpetuated the lack of) real freedom from the lives of the great mass of Americans who had no capital and little education and therefore no real chances of spiritual and physical emancipation. And it was still true that intelligent, humane people who confronted such a social system knew what they must do: expose social maladjustments; denounce social drift; awaken a vision of a society made more just and more free through intelligent and democratic social control; amass and analyse social data; write; organize politically on all levels; revitalize public education; and above all, learn to use the state on a sustained basis.

All this had been known for years and had not lost its validity. Individual reformers certainly expected too much from simple exposure or the Australian ballot, and their resolve and ingenuity perhaps flagged when the world proved hard to remake. But despite its association with much that was fatuous, peripheral, and sometimes repressive, progressivism had identified America's social problems rather accurately, and had formulated and even experimented with many quite promising remedies. Reform faced political problems, since man was not what the reformers had thought. But in the universe of reform ideas there were priceless insights, which, had they been more widely adopted and implemented, would have made the way ahead much easier for the American nation. Such intellectual problems as remained were problems of technique that a normal amount of intelligence, flexibility, and inventiveness could solve. The malady of the reform mentality after the war was not so much bewilderment as discouragement. While the reformers' loss of effectiveness was naturally enough related to external circumstances, to the extent that it was internal it owed less to a poverty of suitable ideas than to the structure of the reform coalition and the nature of the reform calling.

To examine the surviving reformers in the 1920s is to gain a better sense of that mix of internal and external difficulties that so depleted reform ranks. Progressivism failed to hold the recruits it had attracted before the war, and it could ill afford to lose any reform-oriented person, least of all its chief intellectuals and politicians. The scores of reformers who dropped out of the movement after the war remind us not to overestimate the joys of their campaigns. Reform was tedious, hard, disappointing work. A few men established political careers through reform, but for most progressives there was little more in the game than sacrifice of time and energy for impalpable and transitory feelings of guilts eased and duties shouldered. Sacrifices such as they made were trifles when they were young and the movement so new that it was possible to believe that one or two elections would bring them home. But sacrifices and deferred personal lives seemed more burdensome as the 1920s wore on, with prospects for uplift and improvement now so dark. Whether or not a reformer any longer believed the thing could be done, he was usually ready for someone else to do it.

Accordingly, many reformers became ex-reformers and turned their hands to long-deferred private concerns. Those who had come from the professions into public service simply took up again the practice of law or medicine. Various business interests occupied those who had interrupted commercial careers. The reform journalists continued to write, but the shift away from public crusades was plainly outlined in their new themes. Muckrakers who had written of social evils now wrote innocuous romances, short stories for the *Saturday Evening Post,* or novels of the old West. History had a strong appeal for men who were disoriented and disappointed with the present. Samuel Hopkins Adams, for example, who had exposed the patent medicine industry in a series of articles for *Collier's,* wrote of the Erie Canal country of his youth, and Burton J. Hendrick began a history of the Confederacy. Some, like Ida Tarbell when she wrote a life of U. S. Steel's Judge Gary, eulogized men whom twenty years earlier they had stigmatized as Robber Barons. Of the muckrakers, historian Louis Filler found only two—Upton Sinclair and Ray Stannard Baker—who continued in the 1920s to write on contemporary social problems.

Lucrative law practices and pleasant little novels were not the only allurements that stripped the progressive movement of much of its intellectual talent. Brand Whitlock went to live abroad; Fred Howe to live in Nantucket; Carl Vrooman retired to his Illinois farm and the solace of religion; Charles R. Crane grew dates in Palm Springs or travelled in Europe; Raymond Robins became a grower and a banker in central Florida; Hutchins Hapgood grimly pursued the bohemian life in and around New York. But the effect of such new interests was the same—these reformers had laid down their burdens of duty and conscience and sought entirely private ends in the years that remained to them.

These defections thinned progressive ranks and exposed the environmental and internal difficulties that must have hampered even those who kept up what reformers called "the fight." In themselves, of course, defections do not explain the failure of reform in the 1920s since they are to be expected in some degree and would naturally have been replaced if the status quo continued to be abrasive among certain social groups. Since the status quo was well supplied with flaws and injustices in the 1920s, there were indeed recruits for the army of reform, even some for the idea of revolution. We wonder that there were not more, that the unemployed and the urban lower class and the blacks and the landless farmers did not join with those who *were* somewhat radicalized in the 1920s, the railway brotherhoods, Dakota farmers, middle-sized landowning farmers in the grain belts. Yet even when one counts out the old progressives who had resigned and the disadvantaged classes who were so strangely and pathetically docile, *still* we have the impression that the amount of discontent was considerable. What saved the day for the conservatives was not the success of the economy nor the happy loyalty of the citizenry but the fragmentation and disunity among the disinherited, the indignant, the apprehensive, the bored, and the morally sensitive. It was this disunity that allowed the decade to take on its misleading air of self-satisfaction.

Disunity among progressives derived from many factors, some not peculiar either to progressivism or to the 1920s. Any campaign to change institutions and practices is more prone to internal disagreements than the effort to defend them. Conservatives have always had that advantage. Woodrow Wilson had explained this to the young Franklin Roosevelt by likening the conservatives to a fist and the reformers to the extended, unjoined fingers of a hand. Another problem the reformers had faced since the beginning in the 1890s was the obtrusive individualism of Americans, which made coalition, organization, persistence and patience so difficult. The highest virtue among progressives—this was to some extent a generational trait—was "being true to my own ideals" or "a lonely fight against all the odds," the assumption that a man was never so right as when he stood alone and refused to compromise. This trait reared splendid individuals; it crippled political action. Progressives had always been plagued by it. And to make prospects for unity worse, there was the intense partisanship of American political life, which meant that reformers of essentially the same mind and purposes but of different parties would only under the rarest circumstances agree to ignore the party label of some otherwise useful person.

All of these potentially divisive factors were present when progressivism arose in the 1890s, and they hampered reformers over the years, although of course they were occasionally overcome. But the

1920s, fortunately for defenders of a status quo so flawed that it bred a mass of enemies, was a decade when the divisions among reformers were exaggerated into a chasm. The issue that divided them—the issue that dominated the decade—was the cultural antagonism between the urban and the rural ways of life.

That antagonism predated the 1920s, of course. Indeed, a large part of progressive reform had been an effort to insure that the standards of small-town, rural America would not be replaced by undesirable new habits imported from Europe, or spawned in the permissive, crowded, impersonal city. There was fervor in this, but in the hopeful atmosphere of the prewar period the attitudes of middle-class, white, farm, or small-town raised Americans (this included almost all the progressives) had not hardened into an obsession with the city's evils. Reformers, like everyone else, flocked to the city and took up residence there without hesitation, attracted by its opportunities and certain that its blemishes and bad habits could be corrected. Once there, reformers worried about the moral conditions of life, but they also worried about the physical conditions, about wealth, poverty, economic advantages, power. Agrarian and small-town reformers were rarely warm toward urban labor, but they took seriously their duty to "uplift" the laborer in both his physical and his moral life. As a result, coalitions could occasionally be effected between the urban working class and the rest of the progressive movement with its predominantly rural or small-town outlook. Their various goals might coincide on any number of material (as contrasted with moral) issues—locally, an improvement in city sanitation, or a shift in the tax burden from households to industry, or the humbling of a utility company; nationally, an antitrust law, a lowering of the tariff, a progressive income tax.

In the 1920s the chances of such coalitions plummeted. This was certainly not because material grievances had been removed. The urban and small-town middle class, true enough, had become less responsive to economic reform because of the increased flow of con-sumer goods that the non-agricultural middle classes enjoyed. But economic complaints were still widely felt by the urban labor force and a major part of rural America, especially the large staple crop areas. Persistent agricultural depression put rural people in the mood for insurgency, and the urban working class had not escaped its unsteady employment, its low wages, its exposure to industrial accident, its squalid housing. Inevitably and naturally, efforts to create a farmer-labor coalition were made many times in the 1920s because the logic of common interests and common enemies was so obvious. The most notable effort was the campaign of 1924, preceded by the farmer-labor parties formed in the upper Midwest.

Such efforts failed despite what appear in retrospect to have been promising circumstances. For just at this time when cultural differences between urban laborers and agrarians needed most to be ignored, they became the leading concern of the agrarians. As a result, most of the political energies of economically disadvantaged people were directed against other economically disadvantaged people.

It is not entirely clear why cultural antagonisms became strong enough in the 1920s to kill all chance of a coalition of rural and urban insurgents when roughly similar moral reforms before the war had not polarized the progressive movement. We know that urban areas continued to grow at the expense of the countryside, so that the census of 1920 showed more Americans lived in cities than on farms or in towns of less than 2,500. Young people drifting into the cities in 1900 seem to have had a sense that the old ways could be restored in these new cities, and that the dominance of the old New England culture was basically secure. Twenty years later they had a number of reasons to feel that the initiative had shifted to the vulgarization of morality, that time was running out and the utmost urgency was called for to halt the decline of a once proud, clean, white, Bible-reading, homogeneous society. Economic reform would have to wait until the more important matters of morals and behavior and ideas were dealt with.

The main outlines of the politics of cultural counterattack are well enough known. Defense of the Protestant-rural way of life required that alcoholic drinks be outlawed, that the flow of swarthy, Jewish immigrants be stopped, that the teaching of any biological theories that might undermine Scripture be terminated, that the public in general be alerted to the city-based moral deterioration that had resisted prewar progressive cleanups and now threatened to mongrelize the race, socialize the economy, and introduce in one intolerable package the practice of free love and the tyranny of the Pope. Given these priorities, the highlights of the public life of the 1920s may be reviewed without surprise: the quarantine from alien ideas and peoples accomplished by the red scare; the defeat of the League of Nations and the World Court; the Immigration Restriction Acts of 1921 and 1924; prohibition and its comic enforcement; the string of antievolution laws in southern and border states leading up to the trial at Dayton, Tennessee, which was a victory for the fundamentalists whatever the eastern press may have said; that most publicized and politicized of murder trials, the Sacco-Vanzetti case, which inflamed feelings for seven years (1920–27) and turned less on criminal evidence than on the anarchistic ideas and European identity of the accused; and the Ku Klux Klan. Above all one remembers in this connection yesterday's Mafia, the "Invisible Empire" of the Klan—reborn in Georgia in 1915, moribund until the fear-ridden atmosphere of 1920, mushrooming into a political force of some 2–4 million members, which made and broke politicians in Texas, Oregon, Oklahoma, Georgia, Alabama, Indiana, and Washington, D.C., tearing apart the Democratic Party in 1924 before subsiding toward the end of the 1920s in scandals, a returning prosperity, and disenchantment at its lack of constructive results.

The important effect of such crusades lay not in whether drink was really outlawed, Catholics-Jews-blacks permanently barred as political and sexual threats, or the Bible secured against all heresy, since in these, as all other reforms, legislation and aroused opinion proved inadequate to the task. What was significant about such political efforts was that they set potential allies at odds—ruralists and portions of the urban middle class whose cultural identification was rural, against the non-English ethnic component of the working class and urban intellectuals emancipated from Victorian standards. While one cannot be sure, it is at least possible that in the absence of such cultural agitations, with their drain on energy and their claim on analytical powers and political attention, a broad class alliance might have been formed, in portions of the country, if not nationally. Some rural people talked of industrial prices and profits, the tariff, the cost of credit, the existence of virtually untaxed fortunes—complaints that could have formed the core of an alliance with labor and stray progressives from the professions. But so long as most ruralists worried as much or more about the birth rate, drinking habits, and general unworthiness of the Dago, the Wop, and the Jew, the relative economic situation of the classes was sure to remain the same.

The spectacle of people on pinched incomes exerting their political talents against differently dressed people on pinched incomes must have given considerable pleasure to the masters of capital and their retainers, those who were not themselves, like Henry Ford, so unsophisticated as to be seriously involved in the holy war against city ways. Ford, of course, was deadly serious about the peril of the city, but had he been a political genius, which no one has ever suggested, he could not have devised a campaign better designed to shelter his wealth and prerogatives from his restless employees. Ethnocentric politics are conservative politics, as the southern ruling classes learned long ago. The summary of political life in the 1920s is brief enough: cultural conflict made it impossible for economic radicalism to mass.

Ironically, the illiberal crusades of the 1920s against urban lifestyles and heresies bear strong resemblances to the crusades of the prewar period. The 1920s were not so totally different from the decade before the world war, when citizens were aroused by Tom Johnson and T. R., leaders now departed. In both periods one has popular movements to restore the lost community, to cleanse, to uplift, to do good. We lack the solid evidence on the social composition of prewar and postwar social movements that would be necessary to announce that progressivism was carried on in the 1920s by the same social groups and classes, soured by the war experience and now putting the old methods to reactionary purposes. But in the absence of such evidence the similarities between the popular movements of 1912 and 1922 are striking enough to suggest to some historians that the 1920s ought to be thought of also as a progressive decade—but a progressivism with its illiberal side now having the upper hand.

Too much stress may be placed on continuities. Prewar reform may not be studied in the 1920s. Too much had changed, the ranks of the aroused had been depleted and refilled, the juxtaposition of issues was fundamentally altered. But the suspicion of a substantial continuity between prewar and postwar crusades has much to recommend it when one thinks particularly of rural and small-town rather than urban progressivism. Notice how the veterans of a certain type of reform often made the decision that the defense of the village way of life required a cultural rather than an economic emphasis: after the war we find old Tom Watson railing at Negroes and Jews, William Jennings Bryan putting down the Darwinian heresy, A. Mitchell Palmer straining every nerve to round up and export dangerous political ideas and their carriers. The case of Bryan is most instructive, for it shows how slight an alteration in stress and mood was required to adjust at least one variety of the progressive impulse for its postwar career. We remember Bryan's last years as a time of church services and revivals, and especially for the inept defense of the Fundamentalist reading of scripture at Dayton, Tennessee. This period has been pictured as an apostasy, but Lawrence Levine, in his fine book on Bryan, *Defender of the Faith,* makes two points about these last years that underline the consistency of Bryan's life. Bryan never forgot about, and certainly never changed his mind about, the economic injustices that he had been working against since the early 1890s. He labored to make the Democratic Platform of 1924 a progressive document and predicted that the leading election issues would be inequitable taxation, profiteering, agricultural distress, and governmental regulation of railroads and mines. His Dayton activities represented no total reorientation of values or effort; he was still for economic justice in the 1920s. But he had always stood for certain narrow moralities, and saw himself as fighting the same battle at Dayton in 1925 as he had fought when he made his convention speech in 1896, a fight to defend the integrity of rural America. He had always been an economic radical and a cultural reactionary. Rural progressivism had this same dual character. There was less of the first kind of progressivism in the 1920s because there was so much of the second.

VI.

How may progressivism be summarized, its various forms and extended history managed in the fewest generalizations? Historians must mediate between the untidy details of the movement and the desire of their readers for generalization. Scholars, as did contemporaries, strike out for two or three categories—more would be an intolerable mental burden—into which they may fit all the complex facts of an historical era such as this one. The oldest set of categories into which progressives have been put was one established by progressives themselves. It is the New Freedom–New Nationalism distinction, arising out of the political struggles of 1912. For all its flaws this is a useful division. A considerable number of reformers may be described as citizens who were primarily or even solely worried about large industrial and financial combinations, who wished them broken into competitive units, and who were uneasy with a powerful state whatever its motives.

And there were men of quite a different reform mind, who saw the combination movement as a natural feature of modern industrial life and were eager to control it through a vigorous government with both regulatory and welfare responsibilities. It is of no great importance that the labels do not entirely fit either Woodrow Wilson or Theodore Roosevelt, or that the parties they led under those labels were even more than the candidates' minds a mixture of creeds. Many progressives held views of the New Freedom or the New Nationalism variety with considerable tenacity, and whatever party they favored, the categories mark off and help us to speak about large areas of consistent attitudes and behavior. The New Freedom had reactionary tendencies, which became evident later on (T.R. and others perceived this at the time, calling it "rural toryism"), but it kept alive a healthy distrust of private economic power. The New Nationalism had affinities for a government that knew what was best and would put an end to the squabbling of groups, a government preferring unity to justice. In this respect it bore a few slight resemblances to the theories and practice later to be strutted about by Mussolini. But it understood industrial civilization better than the New Freedom, and it tried to teach the American mind to accept the necessity for constant management in the public interest by public officials.

These categories, as useful as they are, do not contain all the important styles among reformers. Another pair of typologies might be designated the moralists and the scientists. The moralists were those men and women who thought the answer to the "social problem" lay in a return to the values that had served the nineteenth century— honesty, abstinence, continence, individual effort, fiduciary integrity. They filled the prohibition ranks, tried to abolish prostitution, hounded men from office if they were stained with a bit of graft. Because they did all of these things with an air of righteousness (and because they did some of them at all) we do not remember the progressive moralists with nostalgia. Today we like neither their moral code nor the aggressive way in which they held it.

Quite in contrast were men who had rejected the Victorian code in their personal lives and had no thought of applying it to America's social problems. They preferred to apply science, or at the very least, rationality, rather than the Bible or tradition. Lincoln Steffens is perhaps best remembered (because of his *Autobiography*) for such attitudes, although he had little knowledge of science. He was uncomfortable with the upright reformers he encountered in his observation of American cities, dubious of the efficacy of mere honesty in office, and irresistibly drawn to the flexible, affable, wordly bosses who had a sense of humor he missed in the Goo Goos. To Steffens and men like him neither the moralistic reformer nor the political boss could bring America out of her crisis; the answer lay in science, in technically trained people, in "trained intelligence." If Steffens was the popularizer of a reform type uncomfortable with moral certitudes and full of confidence in the critical intelligence, John Dewey was its preeminent philosopher. This preference for science over received moral absolutes appealed to engineers, public health officials, economists, statisticians, architects, physicians, and even some businessmen, social types who had learned orderly and critical processes of thought and who were eager to bring their expertise to bear upon an unruly society in need of reorganization.

It is clear to us now that the reformers who were pragmatic and had a respect for science understood better the America of their time and the America in the making than did the moralists. They seemed to perceive the need for mental flexibility in a society so caught up in change, and they understood that progress would come only to the nation that trained and utilized its scientists and social scientists. They sensed that modern society required social control guided by a constant flow of data and that it could not proceed on the rigid truths of dated sermons. The saloon was not the prime menace to the well-being of Americans, nor was the political boss. An unregulated economy holds that honor, crashing on toward profits and blind to the social consequences. But while the scientific progressives were best equipped temperamentally and occasionally also intellectually to cope with modern problems, in retrospect we have been unable to commend them wholeheartedly.

In the first place, talk as they might about critical intelligence, technique, and urbane sophistication, most of them had not traveled very far from the fervid style that marked their entire generation. A scientist like Harvey Wiley might ground his crusade in figures and experimental data, but in ways he was as moralistic as the heavyset ladies of the WCTU. This was simply not a cool generation, and those in it who spoke admiringly of trained intelligence never managed to spring their own intelligences loose from service to some unexamined values. This inconsistency, however, is not what we chiefly regret in the scientific school. A consequence of their thought and activity seems to have been the impersonal, bureaucratic world that envelops us, crushing out spontaneity, disrupting community, and in general robbing us of some of the finer by-products of a premodern social order.

Every student may be allowed a third category, those reformers who had just the right vision and balance, who took from the moralists their passion for risky, worthy causes, and from the scientists their mental flexibility and their respect for technical expertise in the service of the public. But for anyone this is a small list, since so few men and women then or now avoided the excesses of dogmatism or manipulative urges. My own list includes Jane Addams and Lillian Wald, Benjamin Marsh, John B. Andrews, George Norris, Paul U. Kellogg, Judge Ben Lindsey, Mary White Ovington, and that "unwearied hoper," Florence Kelley.

VII.

One could go on noting these efforts at a taxonomy of progressive reform, but we are perhaps in a position to see the main outlines of what we wish to summarize. The progressive era was a compound of these elements: (1) attempts to impose order and modern procedures upon an archaic nineteenth-century society; (2) attempts to come to the aid of the casualties of industrialism—the ghetto dweller, the female factory laborer, the working child; and (3) attempts to impose nineteenth-century moral codes on a twentieth-century world. Each of these major objectives enlisted different social types, drew strength from different social classes, and more often than complementing each other, contradicted each other. Some overlap in leadership, and the usual confusion of legislative struggles and their inevitable blend of impulses and interest groups, have naturally blurred the outlines of these three types of reform effort. So also has the fog of self-justifying and generally sincere rhetoric. The common use of phrases such as *The People, Justice, restoration of American ideals,* helped obscure what was distinct about the components of progressivism. Yet even if these categories reflect the reality of what contemporaries saw as one undifferentiated movement for greater democracy, important and difficult tasks remain. How may these various objectives be ranked so that we understand with reasonable accuracy how that generation was apportioning its corrective energies? And what results were achieved in each area?

On the question of which objective predominated at the time, we have only impressions, uncorrected by any methodology capable of measuring the intensity of commitment of reformers in prewar America. The urge to submit social processes and governmental institutions to the discipline of technology and industrialism seems in retrospect to have been the most significant motivation of the period and one that met with the most far-reaching results. America at the beginning of this century was a modernizing society, shifting from agriculture to industry, from crude and small-scale industry to larger units, becoming daily more urbanized, technological, rationally and specially organized for specialized tasks. Efficiency, the hope of efficiency, and the sheer desire to expand meant that broad commercial interests would impinge upon narrow, local ones with mounting success. Ambitious entrepreneurs followed a vision of nationwide and predictable operations, and it was shared by experts who longed to manage large projects. Expanding enterprise confronted localized jurisdictions and habits, irresistibly pressing them toward subordination or obliteration. The bureaucratic habits of orderliness and regularity were prized, eccentricity and lack of planning discouraged. The initiative rested with the forces of centralization, integration of systems, rationalization, coordination, and efficiency, even though these were slowed by tradition and other impediments.

What has all this to do with reform? The rationalization of systems meant the internal reform of those large business enterprises that meant to participate in the future, and this required men with a respect for the methods of science, a passion for order, an expansionist psychology, and a sense of mission. Such men, and women, arose in business and the professions, and they may be called reformers as readily as we have used the word for public servants like Roosevelt, LaFollette, Pinchot. Samuel Haber's book *Efficiency and Uplift,* tells of the Taylor movement to bring efficiency to industry with stopwatches and efficiency studies, and the moral fervor and guiding principles of Taylorism mark it as a cousin to the well-known political aspects of progressivism. In the medical profession, the Flexner Report of 1910 should be equally recognizable as an event in reform history. The report exposed the chaotic manner of preparing and certifying physicians in the United States, and led to the rationalization of medical education through common standards and effective examination of aspirants. Another example from the private sector would be Seaman A. Knapp's pioneering efforts to establish demonstration farms and to educate adults in rural areas in the practices of scientific farming.

It was inevitable that this aggressive, modern spirit moving in the larger capitalist institutions and the professions would discover that it also had a calling to the reformation of public life. Indeed, the challenge here was even greater, since the world of business had forged ahead with modern methods and left public institutions stagnant and backward by contrast. Modern corporations were increasingly in command of their environments—gathering data, anticipating the future, eliminating uncertainty and waste. But the cities were fragmented, ignorant, leaderless, directionless. Roy Lubove's *Twentieth Century Pittsburgh* (1969) provides a good example of the shocking contrast between growing private order and public disorder. The steel industry was planned and poised for the future, while the city in which it sat was framented by class, ethnic, and residential divisions, unable to respond to its desperate problems. Not unnaturally, the coalition that emerged to attack the problems of Pittsburgh and other cities not only borrowed the methods of modern business, but enlisted the businessmen themselves. Those whose operations were citywide (or greater) wished a city government that answered to the data generated by experts rather than the haphazard appetites of a welter of wards with their local and parochial preoccupations and their tendency toward drift. For them, reform meant a strong, routinized government they could control or influence, with well-staffed regulatory agencies at all levels—public health, finance, police, public utilities, city planning, and the like. The ranks of urban reform were filled with people of lesser economic stake but a similar determination to have a modern, orderly city. They were often individuals of small-town background, lawyers, and other educated citizens ready for new professions, people who brought to the city the evangelical style of the Protestant countryside, which disguised urban progressivism with the rhetoric of moralism when its inner dynamic was really rationalization.

Men with similar outlook but with broader investments or professional horizons came to see the need for reform at the federal level—and reform meant new and enlarged functions performed by trained and properly oriented men. The regulatory measures at the federal level that form the best-known part of the progressive record—regulatory commissions in railroading, banking, special industries from meat-packing to pharmaceuticals, and a commission for all large industry[4]—were largely created by a special type of businessman and a special type of young professional. We have earlier reviewed the sources of regulatory statutes: disgruntled shippers demanded railroad regulation and enlightened owners and managers concurred; a coalition of noneastern bankers and small businessmen demanded banking reform and were joined in the idea if not all the details by the Wall Street financial leaders; meat-packers wanted a meat-packing inspection act; food processors and retail druggists pressed for a food and drug administration. And in all these struggles to reform business practices the pressure came not only from business interests but also from professional men, many already in the federal service, who had caught a glimpse of the public and personal advantages of bureaucratic control over the existing chaos.

This type of progressivism might occasionally talk of democracy, but it was elitist rather than democratic, efficiency-minded rather than justice-minded. Where it was successful, power was not diffused among The People but was concentrated in a knowledge-elite without whom no modern mayor or industrialist would dream of proceeding. While the opposition was fierce and often lumped this sort of reformer with the do-gooders who worried about the urban poor, poverty was no prime concern of theirs. They were out to end the diffusion of power and the randomness of social processes; they wished to vest social control in safe hands, and fewer hands.

Because of this conservative potential, and because they were in tune with the logic of industrialism, the exponents of efficiency and orderly procedures lost little momentum after the war. The effort to bring the advantages of centralized, bureaucratized government to the cities continued in the 1920s, with 303 cities turning to the commission-manager plan (only 31 cities had adopted the plan from 1905 to 1915). This was an innovation that centralized responsibility, with a few men elected on a citywide vote in place of the old unwieldy

---

[4] And the less well-known agencies established by the same pressures, whose functions were promotional rather than regulatory, such as the National Bureau of Standards (1901), the Bureau of the Census (1902), or the Bureau of Mines (1910).

council elected on a ward basis. Reformers promised that the result would be lower taxes even as services were strengthened and expanded. These changes had the strong support of most businessmen, who thought the old mayor and council system cumbersome and wasteful and deplored the strength (or at least, autonomy) it gave to working-class wards that would be underrepresented under a system of citywide elections.

The bulk of the postwar activity of this sort came at the state level, where a series of reform administrations wrote a reform history that has received insufficient attention. New York under Al Smith (1920–28), Pennsylvania under Gifford Pinchot (1924–28), California under Clement Young (1926–30), North Carolina under Cameron Morrison (1921–25), Alabama under Bibb Graves (1926–30), Louisiana under John W. Parker (1920–24), these and other states were the scenes of legislative activity and administrative reorganization that George Tindall has described as "business progressivism." Businessmen may have supported the new policies of the 1920s, since part of what was involved was a series of subsidies in the form of increased expenditure on transportation improvements and state agencies for promotion and research. But the central idea was not subsidies, but efficiency. By 1931 at least forty-one states had followed the lead of Indiana, which had in 1909 established an agency to coordinate other state agencies (in Indiana, the Department of Inspection and Supervision of Public Offices). In 1912 no state operated with a budget; by 1930, all but one had adopted that prerequisite to financial planning. No state in 1910 had a central purchasing agency; by 1930, thirty-five had centralized their purchasing. The 1920s in state government was a time of the integration and rationalization, as well as the expansion, of modern governmental bureaucracies.

After the war there were also continued efforts at the federal level to bring order to the economy through a scientific and technical bureaucracy. Federal government spending in 1930 was 350 percent greater than in 1915, and while much of this was war-related, the functions of government expanded yearly through the 1920s as bureaucrats and constituencies agreed to let fewer things alone in America. Spending on health and welfare did not keep pace with population increase, but the government became very active in the promotion and regulation of commerce and agriculture. The largest increases came in expenditures on transportation, the postal system, aid to shipping, the data-gathering functions of Bureau of Foreign and Domestic Commerce and the Bureau of Agricultural Economics. The Commerce Department under Herbert Hoover, an engineer who was impressed with the success of the War Industries Board at bringing rationality to sectors of industry (the WIB, for example, had standardized the shape of auto tires and bricks), became an agency with a mission—to foster efficiency and coordination in American business. Under Hoover's guidance (1920–28) the department gathered information on trade conditions, prices, and markets, and distributed it (free) to competing firms to allow them to eliminate wasteful competition. Agricultural economists like Mordekai Ezekiel and Louis Bean were doing the same things for farmers from their offices in the Department of Agriculture. The goal was predictability and control, the reduction of the bad guesses and wasteful duplications—in a word, the inefficiency—of American producing and selling. There were similar opportunities in the agencies involved in resource management for those bureaucrats who were ambitious to bring their expertise to bear upon decisions affecting irreplaceable natural resources. "Pinchot-type conservation did not deteriorate in the 1920s," historian Donald Swain tells us, "but expanded and matured" as agencies such as the Forest Service enlarged their operations.

The same thrust toward rationalization was apparent in the streamlined public administration at the federal level. The Budget and Accounting Act of 1921 carried out many of the recommendations of the Taft Commission on Economy and Efficiency (1911–13), most importantly establishing a Bureau of the Budget to coordinate not only federal spending plans but its bureaucratic procedures. Outside government one finds the same tendencies. City comptrollers, police and fire chiefs, state auditors, even mayors and governors organized in the 1920s, if they had not done so just before the war, and began to share information and standardize procedures. *World Convention Dates* for 1920 shows forty-five annual conventions of national organizations of public officials, and by 1930 the figure was ninety. President Hoover's Commission on Recent Social Trends reported that the 1920s had been a time of great change in American public administration, and the words the commission used over and over again were *centralization, simplification, supervision, research, efficiency.* There were no dramatic victories— this sort of reform rarely provided them. But the gains for social control progressivism were measurable and permanent.

Progressive speechmakers, our fathers who read the older textbooks, and our children now frowning their way through the social studies curriculum in junior high schools would all fail to reccognize the foregoing account as a description of the real core of the progressive movement. We see social control where older histories described liberation, we attribute reform measures to professional and commercial elites rather than the indignant rhetoricians of Congress, pulpit, and magazines, and we describe the goal as the rationalization and centralization, not the democratization, of American society. What jars most in all the new writing on progressivism, if one had been reared on more traditional accounts, is the discovery of businessmen swarming throughout the domain of reform, originating, shaping, modifying, and in general lobbying—unassimilable notion—for regulation. One may wonder what took us so long to discover them, and the answer seems to be a compound of the beguiling rhetoric of the reformers themselves, the advent of better sampling procedures, the intensification of monographic studies, and the congeniality of the discovery to the radicalized intellectuals of the 1960s. There is some reason to wonder if, under the latter influence, the younger historians are discovering too many of them. The most important task now is to try to learn the precise extent of the influence of commercial groups in the various sectors of that wave of deliberate social change we call progressivism. It is sufficiently clear that many of those working to impose rational processes upon the mass of individual liberties that made up the pretwentieth-century American economy and social order were in fact businessmen, and that the old Beard and Parrington theory that reform meant the common man was thrashing the predatory interests was no good at all in explaining progressivism—or what appeared to be the main or most significant part of progressivism. Two new theories have recently been offered to explain the emergence of a broad drive, at many levels across an entire nation, to achieve greater social control. Gabriel Kolko, in *The Triumph of Conservatism* (1965), and James Weinstein, in *The Corporate Ideal in the Liberal State, 1900–1918* (1968), see progressivism, at least at the federal level, as a businessman's drive to use the state to stabilize the large-scale capitalist system, which was threatened both by the uncertainties of vigorous competition and by a rising tide of political radicalism. These are brilliant, challenging books, but they are not entirely persuasive. Data formerly ignored are now being overemphasized.

Businessmen were reforming, but they were also being reformed. The scene is not at all tidy. A more convincing and conceptually much broader interpretive framework has been offered by Samuel P. Hays and by Robert Wiebe. In this view the nineteenth-century social structure, characterized by a local focus, small-scale operations, and personal, face-to-face relations (in Frederick Tonnies's encompassing term, *community*, or *Gemeinschaft*), was giving way at the turn of the century to a social order based on a cosmopolitan and national focus, large-scale operations, and impersonal, bureaucratic procedures (*society*, or *Gesellschaft*). Social groups who had a stake in hastening this transition—this would-be large businessmen and their professional allies in law, engineering, city planning, and the like—turned to the state to build a bureaucratic environment conducive of stability and congenial to greater social control. Their rhetoric obscured their real purposes, but this was not because they dissimulated but because in an exciting time when the young and enlightened were reordering society they turned to the only moving rhetoric they knew, the language of the Protestant Reformation, the Old Testament prophets, the Declaration of Independence, the great national vision of Lincoln. In any event they hardly understood the historic function they were performing. They were reformers, but in this view what was being reformed in the progressive years was not only or even primarily graft or poverty, but disorderly, inefficient, and unsystematic ways of doing things.

The conceptual scheme of Hays and Wiebe is an invaluable contribution to our understanding of the progressive era, preferable to the view of Kolko and Weinstein in that it accounts for the extensive role of business groups in various reform areas without ignoring the professionals, and without overemphasizing elements of conspiracy and naked self-interest. Wiebe's *The Search for Order* is the only systematic effort to place the diverse facts of the progressive era into this conceptual framework. The book clarifies so many things that one must make a decided effort to remember that in Wiebe's hands the community-society framework has not yet comfortably been made to contain all the data. Wiebe, intent on demonstrating the transcendent importance of the reformers who represented industrial and governmental rationalization, did not devote sufficient attention to the continuing counterattack of another set of reformers, the spokesmen of community.5 But if this is a flaw, it is a flaw of proportion, not a flaw of his framework, which accommodates nicely the prohibitionists along with the apostles of scientific management. A more serious problem is the tendency of this framework to squeeze out the element of conscience in progressivism, i.e., the social welfare volunteers, the ladies of the settlements, the Social Gospel ministers and novelists, and every other contemporary whose Christian or Emersonian principles brought him, however briefly, into the orbit of progressive activism. Hence, in this study I have tried to devise categories that allow us to utilize the community-society concept, but that also provide a framework for understanding contradictory evidence. But that reform was to a great extent a drive to stabilize large-scale industrial society by centralization of decision-making and rationalization of social processes can no longer be seriously doubted.

Because the principal beneficiaries of this side of progressivism were the owners and managers of corporations and the experts who staffed the powerful new governmental and educational bureaucracies, progressivism is on its way, especially among younger scholars, to becoming a much resented social movement. It accelerated the demise of small, neighborly communities, about which we are nostalgic, and brought the domination of a bureaucratic, scientized, depersonalizing world, which feeds our bellies so well and our souls so badly. It talked of coercion and the imposition of restraints more effectively than it talked of freedom. It educated leading capitalists in how to use the state to prevent real change, and the mental lock-step and high profits of wartime America further revealed to them the conservative possibilities of large government.

But there were both liberating and radical possibilities in the urge to coordinate and plan for greater efficiency. In the minds of Croly and Veblen and T.R. himself efficiency led away from a profit standard toward standards of social usefulness, with efficiency only a way station. Engineers who harkened to Veblen, intellectuals who read Croly, were likely to find their minds permanently occupied by the

---

5 Wiebe, of course, knew that they were operating contemporaneously with his apostles of order and modernity, but he discussed them at length only in his section on the 1890s. A brief treatment of the forces of community in the years between the wars may be found on pp. 172, and 179–80 of his book, a sensible and perceptive discussion but all too brief.

subversive idea that profit was not the point. Admittedly, neither the coordination and cooperative practices of the war nor the 1920s much resembled the radicals' social vision or followed their priorities. But the social control strain of progressive thought need not have been put to reactionary and repressive uses. Its leading thinkers sought freedom through order, not order for its own sake. They did not intend for the liberating possibilities of social discipline to be lost sight of. Croly sought to restrict certain economic liberties, but only because he knew there was no real freedom in a disorderly and uncontrolled economy. Margaret Sanger and the progressives of the eugenics movement proposed to submit the "right" to procreate to certain social controls; and while Adolf Hitler succeeded in putting such proposals under suspicion, Margaret Sanger was unquestionably right that real freedom in the future depended upon greater control over the production of human beings. The path that history actually took should not obscure the fact that the social control movement was at least in the beginning a liberal movement. Its leading theorists, people like Thorstein Veblen, Herbert Croly and John Dewey, assumed a basic conflict with the profit motive and saw in more cooperative forms of social organization a great step toward freedom. This legacy of progressive thought was reactivated in the 1930s as men like Adolf Berle and Rexford Tugwell took from that tradition their dream of an integrated economy run by social engineers responsible to the public. Ingrained individualism and jealous interest groups swept them aside as it had their progressive forerunners, but as the planet fills up with humanity the management of freedom will bring men back to the philosophers of social control.

VIII.

Another distinctive type of reformer was the social justice progressive. *Justice* was a word frequently used in progressive circles. Some defined justice as equal economic opportunity (equal access to resources and markets, not to jobs or housing), others as the right to exercise meaningful political power. But by *social* justice the progressives understood all those efforts to give assistance, usually but not always through an agency of the state, to groups that had for any reason fallen into an intolerable arrears in the "natural" social arrangements of modernizing America. Conservatives argued that what social justice progressives sought was neither just nor socially desirable; but whether it was justice or generosity, it was impossible to ignore. Had pressure for humanitarian legislation come only from directly affected groups it would have made little headway, for such groups were unorganized and apolitical. But support came from middle and upper classes—the professional altruists of the social work–social settlement movement, and their allies in law, journalism, and even politics. When these progressives were added to the groups who would be the beneficiaries and who happened to be organized or at least aroused—railway labor, retail clerks, seamen, certain groups of farmers—it became a coalition to be reckoned with. While a coalition of altruists[6] and beneficiaries was still not wealthy or numerically very strong, under fortunate circumstances it proved able to manipulate the political machinery with tangible effect.

Writers have been attracted to the social justice progressives, and for good reasons. On the whole these were attractive, humane people. But such writers have often implied that social justice was the central concern of the era, which it was not. Recently it has been implied by young scholars that the social justice component was either nonexistent or unimportant; but it was not that either. Compile a brief list of the men and women, the organizations, and the accomplishments of this effort, and the list has a familiar ring and a not inconsiderable bulk: Jane Addams, John B. Andrews, Roger Baldwin, Louis Brandeis, Paul Kellogg, Florence Kelley, Benjamin Marsh, Owen Lovejoy, Margaret Dreier Robins, Mary Simkhovitch, Graham Taylor, John A. Ryan, Stephen S. Wise, Lillian Wald; organizations so well known that their initials are enough, such as the NCL, WTUL, AALL, NCLC, NAACP, ACLU; institutions like Hull House, Greenwich House, University Settlement, Denison House, Chicago Commons, and all the Charities Organizations in the major cities; The Pittsburgh Survey of 1906; the Industrial Relations Commission Report of 1915; the New York Tenement Law of 1901; the child labor laws in the various states, and the long national campaign; thirty-nine maximum-hour laws for women by 1917, and fifteen

6 Their motivation was, of course, not quite this simple. Altruism was bred into these sons and daughters of the better families as a part of the code of their class; but it was abetted by a strong presentiment of doom to the middle classes if the proletariat should become so numerous and miserable as to turn to violence.

minimum wage laws for women by 1923; factory safety laws in most industrial states; workmen's compensation in forty-two states by 1920 —the list could easily be extended, but the outlines are clear.

Does such a list not sketch the outline of a kind of revolution, a shift from the heartless, devil-take-the-hindmost industrialism of the nineteenth century to a humanized, early version of the welfare state? Unfortunately, a close, skeptical look at the record does not sustain such optimism. Paper victories, though hard enough to win, had a way of melting away in the mazes of administration and judicial interpretation. Despite the child labor laws passed by the states after the founding of the National Child Labor Committee in 1904 (southern anti-child-labor groups had operated earlier) the census of 1910 showed more children at work than in 1900. State laws were notoriously weak, levying minimum penalties or none at all, providing for elaborate court review, excluding many industries, and—in nineteen of the thirty-one states passing child labor laws, providing no funds at all for even one inspector to enforce the law. Among other reasons for such inadequacies, state legislators complained that strict laws drove industry to relocate in friendlier states and argued that child labor regulation was properly a federal matter. When the NCLC overcame its Constitutional scruples and resorted to a federal law (the Keating-Owen law was passed in 1916 after Woodrow Wilson overcame *his* Constitutional scruples), it was declared unconstitutional in *Hammer* v. *Dagenhart* (1918). A differently phrased law of 1919 met the same fate, and the despairing reformers turned to a Constitutional amendment (passed finally by Congress in 1924) only to see it smothered in the tangle of state legislatures. A national ban on child labor came only in 1938 with the passage of the Fair Labor Standards Act, and it came then not so much because of four decades of agitation by reformers as because the most radical force of all, the dynamic American economy, had undermined the institution. State child labor and compulsory education laws had cut the proportion of working children from 18 percent in 1890 to 15 percent in 1910. The decline of the family farm and the farm labor force in general, along with the automation of the more repetitious jobs, brought a rapid postwar drop to a figure of 4 percent by 1930.

But victory over child labor, whatever the share of credit between reformers and impersonal economic forces, actually produced additional evidence of the superficiality of so many progressive remedies.

Even had the child labor reformers taken the children out of the mills, their home environments would have remained in many cases as brutalizing as the work environment. Industrial labor was hard on children, but the home lives of most such children were unrelieved by adequate recreational or educational opportunities. The child-labor reformers, like most progressives inclined toward simple, negative solutions, gave little thought to the total environment of the child. At the passage of the Fair Labor Standards Act, NCLC leader George Alger, ignoring the problem of school dropouts, delinquency, and the like, closed the books on their crusade with the remark that he "knew of no further legislation to suggest." The historian of child labor in New York State was forced to conclude that "child labor reform was purely surface in nature and failed to reach the basic problems of New York's youth," leaving them after the victory of 1938 worse off than when the reformers started thirty-five or forty years before.

The failure of child-labor reform was widely admitted and broke the hearts of many social justice progressives, as well it might. But it was not an atypical case. State labor legislation proved equally porous when it was enacted. Fifteen states passed minimum wage laws for women, but when the Supreme Court ruled the law for the District of Columbia unconstitutional in the *Adkins* case (1923), six of the state laws were nullified along with it. Yet while the *Adkins* case "killed all enforcement," as Elizabeth Brandeis wrote, the laws had never amounted to much in the first place. Of the fifteen laws only five were enforceable at all, the others being so badly drafted that they either failed to set up a minimum wage or established one beneath the prevailing minimum. Of the fifteen states willing to take even these shaky steps toward the protection of women workers, only two, Massachusetts and Wisconsin, were important industrial states. The others found the laws palatable because they had little industrial labor to regulate.

In the area of housing, it must be remembered that the legislative reforms that enhanced the record of progressives in cities like New York and Chicago built no new housing units but only purported to regulate the existing ones, or some of them. Leading housing reformer Lawrence Veiller was typical in his concentration on restrictive legislation to make existing tenements more livable; he explicitly rejected the idea of public housing. So long as such attitudes characterized progressive housing reformers, even had funds for tenement inspection and enforcement of restrictive laws been sufficient (which they never were), there would still have been no new units as the result of reformers' efforts, and no racial integration in the old ones.

The progressives' experience with housing reform well illustrates not only the intractability of modern social problems but also the occasional intellectual deficiencies that restricted the progressives from making much headway against the social evils they bravely attacked. Sweep away the slums with one clean legislative stroke, progressives like Veiller believed, and the cities will bustle with happy people. Their analysis in this instance was shallow and their remedy simplistic. Of course they were too optimistic and the law would be evaded; but even had the hallways been cleaned and lighted, the increased costs to tenement owners raised the whole question of who would build more urban housing, where would they build it, and how would it be designed? This was left to take care of itself. When the profit motive did not produce the right sort of housing for urban human beings, the New Dealers, feeling somewhat superior, took the next necessary step into public housing. They then learned how little both they and the progressives before them had known about what the "right" sort of housing was. People lived in neighborhoods, in a total environment; it was not enough to pile clean, well-lit apartments on top of one another in towers. We gave the slum-dwellers new buildings with modern elevators and kitchens, one New Dealer complained, "and they're still the same bunch of bastards they always were." The urban environment was not corrected to insure human happiness by the progressives—or by the New Dealers—not only because the scale of the job went far beyond both their awareness and their resources but also because they had no positive conception of what that environment ought to be. Yet it must be said for them that they at least launched the scientific study of housing and city planning, the ultimate source of better ideas than their own.

Social justice progressives are credited with bringing to America the idea and inaugurating in a modest way the practice of social insurance —the public assumption of responsibility to compensate victims of industrial accident, illness, old age, and unemployment. The unbearable private cost of industrial accidents generated a drive for workmen's compensation laws, pressed initially by "altruistic" organizations like the AALL and the NCL, which provided skilled lobbyists and careful studies based on the available data. Forty-three states had enacted workmen's compensation legislation by 1920. But we know from recent studies by Roy Lubove and James Weinstein that the workmen's compensation movement drew its main support from the employers, who preferred the predictable costs of such systems to the uncertainties of legal proceedings. The National Association of Manufacturers proved more important in the workmen's compensation drive than the tiny AALL. Businessmen adopted the workmen's compensation movement and saw to it that the system covered only about one-fourth of actual medical costs, and that (in most states) private insurance companies held and administered the funds rather than the government.

Whatever its defects, workmen's compensation was the only compulsory social insurance program operating in the United States before the 1930s. Conservatives often frightened themselves with the theory that any concession to reform would open the floodgates to socialism, but in practice the reverse was often the case. Roy Lubove writes: "Social insurance experts mistakenly assumed that the rapid spread of compensation legislation after 1911 would lead to other compulsory programs... (but) far from providing an entering wedge, it solidified the opposition of private interests to any further extension of social insurance." A small group of progressives began to agitate for health, old age, and unemployment insurance in 1915, calling health insurance "the next step." The step was likely to be a small one in any case, but the war killed whatever chance health insurance had, as opponents were able to condemn the idea as "Germanic." Absolutely nothing was accomplished along any of these lines at any level until the 1930s.

Thus, progressive social justice legislation brought very meager gains to the intended beneficiaries. The central statistical indicator that illuminates the social justice record is income distribution. Progressives were quite conscious that income redistribution was crucial to social reform, both as a matter of equity and to preserve the society from dangerous social extremes. Herbert Croly in his *The Promise of American Life* (1909), for example, argued that the decision to pursue "constructive national purpose" meant that "the American state will in effect be making itself responsible for a morally and socially desirable distribution of wealth." Many other reformers gave redistribution high priority. While the data on income and wealth leave much to be desired for the years before the 1930s, it appears that the distribution of income became, if anything, slightly *more* unequal over the period from 1896 to 1929, the period when reformers thought themselves to be diminishing such inequalities both through taxation and through regulatory laws that shifted more of the costs of production onto the employer. Walter Spahr estimated in 1896 that 2 percent of the people owned 50 to 60 percent of the wealth, but Willford I. King in 1917 judged that the intervening years had seen "a marked concentration of income in the hands of the very rich." King's studies of income distribution showed the top 5 percent of families receiving 28 percent of the national income in 1910, a slight increase (so far as he could tell) over 1896; ten years later, in 1920, the war had apparently caused some leveling, with the top 5 percent of families claiming 22 percent of the national income (according to Simon Kuznets); by the mid 1930s, the share of the top 5 percent had risen to 29 percent. Of course, income is much less concentrated than "static" wealth. King found that in 1910 the top 1 percent of families claimed 15 percent of the national income but 47 percent of the national wealth, a figure roughly comparable to that for socially reactionary Prussia. All such estimates are rough, and unquestionably underestimate the maldistribution, as they do not cover capital gains, gifts, and other forms of untaxed compensation, which are substantial in the higher and negligible in the lower income brackets. The main outlines of income distribution are clear: the first thirty years of this century saw a gradually increasing concentration of income in the hands of the top income tenth, generally at the expense of the middle- rather than the lower-income receivers. "Reform" made no impact on this trend; only the war interrupted it, and after the war the concentration commenced again. Despite the lowering of the tariff in 1913, the pathbreaking little income tax of the same year, and the other measures that the wealthy claimed were tantamount to socialism, income distribution at the very best remained about where it was when the fiddles of reform tuned up in the 1890s.

While the actual results deriving from a few legislative victories were often discouraging to social justice progressives, in some areas of glaring inequality they achieved no victories at all, symbolic or otherwise, because they never made the effort. Solicitous toward white women and children, the social justice progressive was typically uninterested in the plight of two groups in the most serious economic difficulties in those years (as now), the Negro and the rural poor.

To some extent these were overlapping categories, but most farm laborers and tenants were white, and they had a strong claim on the middle-class conscience if the degree of poverty established such a claim. But while progressives were often shocked by the state of life among the urban lower classes and addressed themselves to their improvement, they gave little time to the hidden agricultural lower class. There was a modest awakening to the problems of country life before the war, but the attention of men like the educational reformer Liberty Hyde Bailey or the founder of agricultural demonstration work, Seaman A. Knapp, was directed toward modernizing the middle-class, commercial farmer. Theodore Roosevelt's Country Life Commission studied the problems of rural life, but its report of 1909 neglected the landless farmer almost entirely. Considering the state of public and Congressional opinion, the flaws in their vision made little difference. Congress ignored even the slim recommendations of the Commission—better conservation, investigation of middleman profits, the banishment of the saloon, and similar measures of middle-class appeal. Progressivism came and went, leaving rural poverty untouched. Tenancy, the condition of 36 percent of American farmers in 1880, was up to 49 percent in 1920 and rising. Progressives, with very rare exceptions, were too busy to notice.

Also largely unnoticed was the Afro-American. The facts show that blacks were in a condition of sustained emergency. They were confined to the menial trades and the more brutal levels of agriculture, poorly paid, intellectually isolated, socially ostracized, and physically intimidated. The black illiteracy rate in the South approached 50 percent, as against a rate of 12 percent for whites. The life expectancy for blacks at birth was 32 years in 1900, while for whites it was 47. Blacks were harder hit by most diseases because their environment was harsher; yet they were also less likely to find or afford medical care. But, incredible enough, worse was yet to come. As the progressive era opened, the condition of blacks was in important respects deteriorating.

The last years of the nineteenth century produced a powerful tide of racism, more virulent and dangerous than had ever before marked American race relations. There had been earlier cycles of xenophobia that excited native Americans to abandon their uneasy tolerance and find ways to persecute alien peoples. But the nativism of the 1890s and after was not only more intense, but it now bore upon the blacks, who before had been somewhat protected by their status as chattel property. As the 1880s gave way to the 1890s one could notice the changing signs: rumors of the inundation of native Americans by hordes of unassimilable immigrants (these, in northern cities, included blacks), a torrent of speeches and books elaborating on the theme of white supremacy, talk of racial world conflict just ahead. To the Catholic and the Jew this spelled intolerance, suspicion, political and social discrimination. To the black it meant all these things, and also a degree of physical danger, which brought him in these years to the point Rayford Logan calls "the nadir of the Negro's status in American society."

C. Vann Woodward in *The Strange Career of Jim Crow* has described the legal expression of the new racism. A system of enforced segregation, unevenly developed before the 1890s, was perfected in the early progressive era, with the black everywhere confined to inferior civil rights and public facilities, or denied them altogether. The Negro had suffered economically perhaps more than any other group from the depression of the 1890s, but when prosperity returned the hurricane of racial intolerance made sure that the blacks would not fully participate in the recovery that other groups would experience. The agricultural black may have shared slightly in the rising farm prices after 1898, but the small black middle class was deliberately decimated. The rigid caste system of separate railroad cars and toilets was extended to jobs as well. The black began to disappear from trades he had formerly monopolized—tailoring, painting, smithing, carpentering. The depression initiated this downward pressure, and the intense nativist emotions after the turn of the century caused further displacement from reasonably attractive jobs. There were occasional pockets where blacks held out, such as coal mining, but for the most part they were the losers in a bitter struggle with whites for jobs that permitted an urban existence and something better than a marginal standard of life.

More dramatic than his economic difficulties was the increase in racial violence. Lynching in America had always had a strong class incidence—the rate was high among the poor and the transient—but it had been relatively color-blind before the 1890s. From 1882 to 1888 some 595 whites were lynched, and 440 blacks (this, of course, is a higher rate for blacks); by 1892 lynching was becoming racialized, with 169 blacks and 69 whites lynched that year. At the peak of the progressive period, 1906 to 1915, ten times as many blacks (620) as whites (61) were burned, beaten, or hanged to death. Inevitably the racial feelings behind these acts against individuals found occasion to shift to entire communities. Savage race riots broke out in New York and New Orleans in 1900, in Atlanta in 1906, in Springfield, Illinois in 1908. Between the reports of such incidents in the history of American race relations one could observe in the press and even in the best journals such as *Harpers, Scribner's,* and *Century,* the white mind at work reinforcing its racial stereotypes: the black man was subhuman, childlike, docile, comic, lazy, criminal, superstitious, oversexed, lying, and stupid, a nigger, a spade, a pickaninny, a coon. This view of the black, we now suspect, was more damaging to the black and his aspirations for the future than the economic deprivation and physical danger that burdened his body.

Surely this exploitation and suffering would not go unnoticed in the progressive era, when sentiment for the underdog ran high and the ideals of the Declaration of Independence were being revived. And in fact the conscience of the white community began to stir. A few journals, such as *The Independent, The Arena,* and *Charities,* spoke out editorially against lynching. *McClure's* displeased its southern readers by printing a mild denunciation of race relations by Carl Schurz in 1904, and a splendid series of articles in *The American Magazine* by Ray Stannard Baker gained further circulation when bound into the book *Following the Color Line* (1908). Baker's book was widely noticed, and, along with more detailed investigations such as Mary White Ovington's *Half a Man: The Status of the Negro in New York* (1911), Louis D. Bowen's *The Colored People of Chicago* (1913), and John Daniel's *In Freedom's Birthplace: A History of the Boston Negro* (1914), took at least the first, fact-gathering step toward intervention. Several Negro settlement houses were established, and one or two settlements mixed the black and white poor. The philanthropic urge was quickened in the progressive era generally, and some attention was paid to the educational needs of blacks in the establishment of the General Education Board by the Rockefeller Foundation in 1902, the Anna T. Jeanes Fund in 1905, the Julius Rosenwald Fund in 1913. And it was a group of white progressives and socialists, among them Miss Ovington, William English Walling, Charles Edward Russell,

Henry Moskowitz, and Oswald Garrison Villard, who took the organizational steps that led to the founding of the National Association for the Advancement of Colored People in 1909.

But these efforts do not add up to serious attention to the condition of blacks. The progressives had more pressing business than the welfare of the Negro, and the handful of reformers who concerned themselves with racial issues was unrepresentative and essentially ineffective. Progressivism at the local level discovered graft, captive political systems, inadequate public services; it never discovered the almost total lack of educational, medical, and eleemosynary institutions available to blacks. There were praiseworthy efforts in the South to abolish the infamous convict-lease system (six southern states had done so by 1917), but the southern jails and prison farms remained, as Frank Tannenbaum's *The Darker Phases of the South* reported in 1924, inhumanly brutal.[7] Race relations being what they were, the penal institutions of the South were the places where blacks had their most sustained, damaging contact with white power and where reform was both most urgent and least likely.

At the national level, progressivism disappointed the few articulate blacks and whites who heard the language of humanitarianism from presidential campaigners and misjudged the limits that would be set by the pervasive racism of the American public. Theodore Roosevelt showed an initial independence in the matter of black civil service appointees and dared to invite Booker T. Washington to dinner at the White House. But when there was criticism of his appointment and dining policies he not only abandoned them but further reassured his white critics by his handling of the Brownsville affair. The white citizens of Brownsville, Texas, had worked themselves into an ugly mood over the presence of black troops stationed at the edge of town, and a controverted shooting incident on the night of August 13, 1906, was at least partially and perhaps entirely their fault. But T.R. accepted the questionable evidence of black culpability and dishonorably discharged three companies of black infantry, thereby holding black soldiers to standards of docility, discipline, and collective guilt that

---

[7] The rest of the country also had a long way to go toward rational and humane penal institutions by the end of the progressive era. Social worker Homer Folks told the National Conference of Charities and Corrections in 1911 that while America might lead the world in the treatment of juvenile delinquents, "as to jails, the world leads us."

would have been unthinkable in the case of whites. After Brownsville, T.R. neither harmed nor helped the American black, and the Republican Party through 1912 continued to collect black votes and ignore the platform remnants of its Lincolnian heritage.

Despite the racial conservatism of the Democratic Party, Woodrow Wilson hinted strongly that blacks would be included among those aggrieved groups the New Freedom would help. But the humanitarian strain in Democratic progressivism was no match for its deep-seated racial attitudes. The Treasury and Post Office Departments segregated lunchrooms and bathrooms shortly after Wilson's cabinet took over, and, with Wilson refusing to intervene, black-held jobs dropped from 6 percent in 1913 to 5 percent in 1918. Despite repeated entreaties the president would not denounce lynching, never visited a black picnic or school. Booker T. Washington admitted in 1913 that he had "never seen the colored people so discouraged and bitter as they are at the present time." Wilson was personally no bigot, mixed with blacks when the occasion demanded it, and in fact had Washington to dinner at Princeton. But as President he would take absolutely no risks on the issue of race relations. Oswald Garrison Villard finally gained an interview with Wilson in October, 1913, and presented him with a plan for a national race commission to study the question. Wilson admitted that he would not endanger his program or administration by even that degree of involvement with the delicate racial issue: "I say it with shame and humiliation," he told Villard," but I have thought about this thing for twenty years and I see no way out. It will take a very big man to solve this thing."

Why had progressivism made such an infinitesimal difference in the racial attitudes and customs of Americans? The failure to place this issue higher on the agenda ought to be seen in historical perspective, or it will appear merely as a monumental and inexplicable display of callousness. At that time *all* white Americans were raised in an atmosphere of sustained racism. They were convinced of Negro inferiority and armed against reality by separate institutions and racial stereotypes. White Americans learned how to see (and not to see) the black from casual comments of parents and peers, from "Uncle Remus" stories, from novels such as the trilogy of Thomas Dixon, *The Leopard's Spots* (1902), *The Clansman* (1905), *The Traitor* (1907). A United States Senator (Benjamin Tillman, Dem., South Carolina) condemned Roosevelt's dinner with Booker T. Washington with the comment that "entertaining that nigger will necessitate our killing a thousand niggers in the South before they learn their place." To some that remark seemed proper; to the rest, understandable. Roosevelt himself thought blacks inferior and admitted the dinner was a mistake.

In such a climate, whites did not "think" about the black. Their notions were fixed; their armor against aberrant thoughts was impenetrable. Progressives were white Americans and their culture equipped them with these attitudes. And in those rare instances when an individual, through some combination of perhaps an abolitionist heritage and an unusual personal encounter with black refugees in the northern cities, broke free of the old attitudes and began to sympathize and seek reform, the state of public opinion made the race issue the most unpromising subject a reformer could raise.

But to credit their ineffectiveness on this issue to the racist climate of opinion is to miss an insight into the progressive mentality. The black was overlooked because the entire culture overlooked him, but he was overlooked by a reform movement that made a specialty of uncovering neglected social evils because that reform movement had built-in blinders when it came to the desperate troubles of society's lowest classes. Progressivism was a middle-class movement, and only in a few instances, such as the social welfare movement in New York City or the state movement in Oklahoma, did progressivism take up the grievances of really submerged people. Its faith in political democracy was in conflict with, and often overruled by, the instinctive elitism of the confident, educated people who were the backbone of reform. In the end progressivism was better at directing than at listening.

Progressivism was also associated with the rising group self-assertiveness and solidarity of the native white American. Reform was not only contemporaneous with nativism but seemed to have a symbiotic relationship with it. While there were reformers who were free of the fever of a Nordic mission, there was a tendency for people who became excited about progressive causes also to be excited about the duty of "the race" to preserve and extend its dominion. Recall the careers of Roosevelt, Albert Beveridge, William E. Borah, Hiram Johnson, or Woodrow Wilson, with their happy union of Nordic nationalism and progressivism. Reform required a bold, crusading, self-assertive temper and aggressive moral certainty. As subversive as it may have sounded to smug conservatives, reform did not encourage doubt or tolerance. Such qualities were dysfunctional in a war, which is the analogy the reformers most often drew upon in describing what they were doing. Reform drew its strength from the unquestioned moralities of the white Protestant American. From such an impulse the descendants of slaves could expect at best occasional paternalistic advice and charity, at worst the disfranchisement associated with southern progressivism and the harassments against Orientals common in Hiram Johnson's California.

These qualities of the reform mind help to explain its insensitivity to a social problem more serious, both in terms of fundamental human morality and of social efficiency, than the trusts, or political corruption, or child labor, or alcohol. White progressivism offered little aid to blacks. Yet the expectation that a time of idealism and social introspection would bring some breakthrough for the black American was not in error. Currents of thought found in white progressivism had their parallels among blacks. These were the years when Booker T. Washington's program of black self-effacement and industrial education began to lose its grip on the younger blacks, and men like W. E. B. DuBois and William Monroe Trotter revolted against white assumptions and social arrangements. Their speaking and writing expressed and encouraged a heightened group consciousness not unlike that which swept the white community. In the Niagra movement of 1905, and in the NAACP, this awakening of black professional and white-collar elites found organizational form. There were also several black organizations aimed, like their white counterparts, at rescuing the victims of urbanization—Victoria Earle Matthews's White Rose Industrial Organization founded in 1897 in New York, for example, or the Committee for Improving the Industrial Condition of Negroes in New York, founded by the black educator William Lewis Bulkley in 1906. Rejection of the status quo, the conviction that something could be done, organization, political pressure for state intervention, racial self-assertion, and the rhetoric of liberal humanitarianism—all these phenomena were found on a small scale among blacks at the same time that they appeared on a larger scale among whites.

We slight these beginnings because they were too little and too late. Yet from this distance it does in fact appear that a corner was turned in this period for this most exploited of America's oppressed groups. When real change in American race relations finally came, it would build upon the awakened conscience bequeathed by white progressivism, and the organization and self-discovery stimulated among blacks in this same era. If the social justice movement for blacks later took on a radical, even violent aspect, it was not because these early black reformers willed it so, but because the few hesitant steps of white progressives proved so ineffectual against the misery of blacks or the racial attitudes of the mass of whites.

So this problem was postponed. It was the progressive generation's most conspicuous failure, and yet, in view of the social realities in which they moved, their most understandable one. And it did not go entirely unnoticed. Walter Weyl, for example, wedged an important insight into his *The New Democracy* (1912) in one lapidary sentence: "The Negro problem is the mortal spot of the New Democracy."

IX.

Reform had a third major thrust, toward restoring the economic arrangements of small-scale capitalism and the social values of small-town America. To this cause rallied businessmen from the South and Midwest, and from small towns in all parts of the country where New England memories were strong. The most effective exponents of economic individualism were articulate young lawyers like George Record, William Borah, and Woodrow Wilson, who thought they were defending liberty rather than the interests of a dwindling entrepreneurial class. In its most intelligent forms, as in the thought of Louis D. Brandeis, this antitrust, and, at least covertly, antiurban school did have something to contribute to a dialogue about freedom and made a useful critique of the dominant tendencies toward centralization. In less intelligent hands its psychology was defensive and negative to a fault, and its social vision neither generous nor—since immigration was shut off so late—plausible.

The achievement of the economic individualists is ha·d to estimate, but the word *failure* suggests itself, despite its rough sound. The courts, the war, and a deep public ambivalence about economic concentration, all kept the progressive antitrust efforts from anything like a restoration of the conditions of nineteenth-century littleness. The worst fears of the economic individualists have come true: most Americans *have* slipped from self-employment to employee status. What is more, they seem to be adjusting to it. That was the main disaster these progressives feared, and they could not avert it. It is true that a few of their campaigns produced apparent victories. There was great vitality in the drive to break the stranglehold of eastern interests upon credit and transportation advantages, and some legislative successes were secured. But in the end small interests were usually outmaneuvered. The Federal Reserve Act set up a system of twelve decentralized districts so that New York could not dictate to Main Street or Market Street, but Wall Street actually emerged stronger than before, dominating the New York branch, which in turn dominated the system. The ICC gave southerners no satisfaction in their efforts to eliminate the long and short haul differentials in freight rates. Some have argued that the antitrust efforts of progressives at least humanized big business and taught it a sense of public responsibility, even if no real dissolution was achieved. Perhaps so. At least beginning in the 1920s, most corporations had sufficient concern for the public to hire public relations assistance.

This defensive component of progressivism had a cultural as well as an economic side. Its aim was a restoration of the nineteenth century community—classless, neighborly, hard at work, devout, morally disciplined. The threat came from the moral loosening of urban life, and from the sheer number and fecundity of the immigrant. The remedies they devised constitute a subcategory of the progressive uprising: exhortations to unity, the prohibition movement, the Americanization movement, the drive on prostitution, the eugenics movement. Return progressivism fought a reasonably successful rearguard action against the cultural challenge of urban America, but unfortunately it coerced an urban milieu that won out in the end, especially among the intellectuals. Since urbanized intellectuals write the histories, this sort of reform is treated with a conspicuous lack of sympathy. Some criticism is deserved. If the excess of progressivism identified with social control was to abandon under stress its democratic sympathies and to set an elite to dispensing national discipline, the excess of the school seeking to return to nineteenth-century values was to reduce reform to a drive for enforced conformity to a compromised moral code that was no longer held by a majority. What was valuable in that moral code has unfortunately not received its due, since the moral reformers were unable to make distinctions between lasting and outmoded virtues. Much can be said for small communities (including those found in large cities), for stable, small-family agriculture, and

for "Victorian" virtues such as sobriety, self-discipline, and honesty—
all, of course, in moderation. They were not much advanced by progressives, since they chose to identify the nineteenth-century moral
inheritance with such obviously defunct ideas as the notion that drinking beer was an evil. We are in great need of some of the virtues of
the premodern generation, but if we are to recover them we must
ignore their public crusades and turn to biography, to the lives of
splendid and untiring men and women like Louis Brandeis, Jane
Addams, or the rabbi Stephen S. Wise.

Only a few perceptive contemporaries sensed that the goal of
returning to nineteenth-century virtues was an odd bedfellow for the
impulse to aid the underprivileged of the cities, or the impulse to
enlarge the sway of trained intelligence in American life. Crusades to
keep America a place where the Yankee culture was dominant were
a part of progressivism by every test—chronology, fervor, middle class
base, pressure for legislation, interlocking personnel with other reforms—but one. They were not liberal. At the core they expressed
a reactionary spirit—hostile to change, suspicious of the cities, fearful
of the future. They preferred faith and tradition to reason and were
wedded to narrow racial, regional, and national loyalties just at the
moment in history when basic forces urged broader perspectives. Some
have been uneasy that the term *progressivism* has been arched to
spread over illiberal social movements as well as those of a generous,
tolerant, and rational cast. These irregularities should not drive
us from the term. Parts of progressivism blended nicely with what
later came to be known as liberalism, and parts did not. There
is no need to define certain activities out of the movement simply
because they contradicted other activities, reform values, or subsequent
preoccupations. Internal contradictions existed at the time, but contemporary journalists, not blessed with the analytical and taxonomical
skills of college professors, perceived the common elements in the
uproar around them, and they were right to speak of a progressive
movement. Prohibition, immigration restriction, and the antiprostitu-
tion drive were different in spirit—and usually attracted different
types of reformers—from the scientific management effort, or conservation, or housing reform, but they were all middle-class, aroused,
marching Americans, vintage 1910, and they shared a core of intellectual traits: they were activists, they had an unshakable confidence in

intervention, they were equally optimistic that social practices could be changed by exhortation, scientific study, the police power of the state, or some combination. Abraham Flexner, writing in 1914, used the sort of language they used whether they were Social Gospelers, engineers, social workers, or young lawyers running for city council:

> Civilization has stripped for a life-and-death wrestle with tuberculosis, alcohol and other plagues. It is on the verge of a similar struggle with the crasser forms of commercialized vice. Sooner or later, it must fling down the gauntlet to the whole horrible thing. This will be the real contest—a contest that will tax the courage, the self-denial, the faith, the resources of humanity to their utmost.

Rhetorical similarities among the various sectors of reform went beyond an exhortative, crusading style. The word *efficiency* was a kind of litmus of reformism. All the renovators and innovators believed in efficiency, counted on its strong appeal to a generation impressed with the promise of science, and used it to justify the most diverse activities. The municipal Goo Goos wanted to make city government more efficient, not a difficult argument to follow, but we also find social worker Crystal Eastman justifying workmen's compensation on the grounds of efficiency, Louis Brandeis justifying railroad regulation and a complete social insurance system on the grounds of efficiency, Charles Edward Russell arguing that urban poverty was an inefficient use of human resources, and Irving Fisher appealing for prohibition on the grounds that it would so increase the national efficiency as to produce a 10–20 percent addition to the GNP. If nothing else tied together these various and occasionally contradictory crusades—and much else did—their common resort to the ideal of efficiency would be enough to suggest some sort of fundamental identity. Frederick W. Taylor, the father of scientific management (a synonym for efficiency), wrote in *The Principles of Scientific Management* (1911) that his principles "applied with equal force to all our social activities; to the management of our homes; the management of our farms; the management of the business of our tradesmen, . . . of our churches, our philanthropic institutions, our universities, and our governmental departments." His generation was in agreement. Each in his own way, the member of a civic voter's group, the city planner, the settlement worker, the prohibitionist, all had caught a common vision of a society happier because social engineers had brought an end to wastefulness and irrationality in all its various activities. So to a large extent they spoke a common tongue.

But the most compelling reason for spreading the word progressivism over somewhat contradictory social objectives is that one often finds some single reform or campaign that unites quite dissimilar values beyond any effort to factor them out. The most objectionable strain in Return progressivism was its racism, but it is possible to find even this harnessed with concern for some part of exploited and suffering humanity. Aileen Kraditor tells us, in *The Ideas of the Woman Suffrage Movement 1890–1920* (1965), how often anti-immigrant and anti-Negro sentiments appeared alongside the noble ideals of the Declaration of Independence in the inspirational literature of the movement. An equally good but less well-known example of a reform born of mixed impulses is the LaFollette Seaman's Act of 1915. The act improved the pay and working conditions of an historically exploited group and strengthened their hand in contractual arrangements with shipowners; it enlisted the support of progressive altruists who responded to Andrew Furseth's pleas for justice. But the act had strong southern support in the Congress because it was openly racist. In Jerold Auerbach's words, it was frankly designed "to drive Asiatics from American vessels" by eliminating the economic advantage in hiring orientals who either depressed "white" standards or drove occidentals from the merchant marine.

Another such combination appears in the drive against prostitution. It was often pressed by people who did not like sex, and who appear to modern eyes as not only prudish and coercive, but ethically misguided and probably no real friends of the American female. At the same time prostitution did involve exploitation and a threat to the public health, and the fight against it attracted nonprudish and thoroughly admirable people like Lillian Wald and Jane Addams who urged a scientific rather than a moralistic approach to the matter and who were primarily interested in the protection of virtually helpless individuals (females) from overpowering environmental pressures against their dignity and freedom. Some reformers spoke of the evils of prostitution and thought of how much they disliked not only the sex act but Jewish immigrant girls who were probably producing ethnically undesirable bastards; others spoke of the evils of prostitution and wished to stamp out disease and economic exploitation, not non-WASP breeding and nonconjugal love. Many reforms had this same schizophrenic composition, and virtually every campaign was laced with contradiction. Hiram Johnson's progressives in California found time and motivation to work on conservation, workmen's compensation, and laws excluding Japanese from landholding and citizenship. James K. Vardaman's progressive administration in Mississippi (1903–7) raised teacher's salaries, increased expenditures on mental and tuber-culosis hospitals, attacked the convict-lease system, advocated the reduction of interest rates and higher taxes upon corporations, and at the same time cut appropriations for Negro education and set new lows in the rhetoric of bigotry. These and other progressive campaigns brought together impulses one might have thought incompatible until observing them in some dynamic blend. But the world of the progres-sive was confusing, and many emotions combined in their sense of social crisis. They sacrificed logic to action, and made reform a house of many mansions.

X.

Where in this scheme does one place the friends of political democracy? Most progressives of whatever type thought of themselves as advocat-ing changes that were widely popular and would instantly prevail if the people were awakened by the written and spoken word. When this did not happen they suspected defective political machinery rather than the accuracy of their estimate of the state of public opin-ion. Blaming the political machinery for immobilizing their latent majority, they pressed for procedural reforms widening the suffrage and extending the popular influence. But the Direct Democracy aspects of reform do not constitute a distinct category, for they were usually not ends in themselves but means to other ends. The grant of federal suffrage to women was presented as a concession to the idea of individual worth, done because it was right for men to do so if they claimed to be democrats. But Alan P. Grimes shows, in *The Puritan Ethic and Woman Suffrage,* that in the western states where woman suffrage was strongest it drew strength not so much from egalitarian sentiment—there was some of that, mostly among women—as from the expectation that enfranchised women would further the drives to enact prohibition and immigration restriction laws. There were usually similar substantive hopes behind all the campaigns for pro-cedural democratization. The Oregon reformer William S. U'Ren worked for years to democratize Oregon politics, but he was not primarily interested in Direct Democracy. "All the work we have done, for Direct Legislation," he wrote late in life, "has been done with the Single Tax in view." U'Ren was, in this respect at least, typical of reformers interested in Direct Democracy measures. Progress depended not merely on enlarging the political community, but on pursuing certain ends with the newly acquired power. There was hardly a distinct Direct Democracy component of progressivism since invigorated electoral procedures were almost invariably pressed as preliminary to and valued subsidiary to substantive changes. Jane Addams, in an article "Why Women Should Vote" published in 1909, justified their enfranchisement on the ground that they might then extend to the entire city the cleanliness they maintained in their own homes. Woman suffrage was a reform, but it was also a means to reform.

It is worth noting that disappointments in this area were the rule rather than the exception. Enlarged electorates showed a stubborn tendency to continue to vote for machine politicians (Boss Boise Penrose, astonished that he was still in the Senate after the first Pennsylvania election in which Senators ran before the people, was supposed to have said, "give me the people every time"). The females enfranchised in the Rocky Mountain states did in fact help the prohibition forces, but the enfranchisement of women generally disappointed its supporters. As John Gordon Ross wrote in 1936: "After a fair trial of 16 years, it seems just to appraise women's suffrage as one of those reforms which, like the secret ballot, the corrupt-practices acts, the popular election of senators, and the direct primary, promised almost everything and accomplished almost nothing." And, much to his disappointment, U'Ren and the single taxers in Oregon wore themselves out on their procedural reforms only to find that the broader electorate had as little interest in the single tax as the smaller electorate of the late nineteenth-century.

The general ineffectiveness of Direct Democracy measures to accomplish the fine things promised by overexcited reformers has been noticed many times, almost invariably with a touch of scorn that men could believe such tripe about "the people." "A man that'd expict to thrain lobsters to fly in a year is called a loonytic," said Mr. Dooley, "but a man that thinks men can be tur-rned into angels be an iliction is called a rayformer an' remains at large." It is hard to see why observers of the progressive faith in democracy are so pleased at discovering such gullibility; if the reformers were wrong, and it appears that they were, the implications are not at all pleasant. Their simple faith in the efficacy of drawing more and more people into the voting booths reveals them—in view of the record—as hopeless innocents. But men who remark the proven invalidity of that faith are hardly realists if they do so smugly. We may know man better, after army intelligence tests, the analysis of dreams, pogroms, and a procession of regicides, but the last emotion this justifies is a sense of superiority.

XI.

Surveying this record of dreams of justice and promises of uplift in the moral and physical life of the people, and finding that it all came to so much less than the progressives had wanted, one wonders what meaning to draw from the gap. Some would say that capitalism was not substantially reformed because it cannot be, others because it need not be. Every person must decide whether such modest gains are the best a citizen can wish, or whether he prefers one of those twins who offer themselves as substitutes for reform—apathy and revolution. But a number of lesser inquiries are equally enlightening.

Notice the advantages held by the conservatives. The American character, individualistic, sanguine, and suspicious of the state, fought on the conservative side, resisting a movement that relied upon the irritations of criticism and the exertions of collective action. The holders of privileged positions were united by economic interest, by social outlook, and usually by intermarriage. The potential allies in any uprising were largely unorganized or at best poorly organized on the eve of the struggles of the progressive era. Of American workers, only 7 percent were in unions in 1904, and these were largely in the Gompers-led American Federation of Labor, emasculated politically by his doctrine that nothing could be expected from political action. Consumers were unorganized until Florence Kelley and others started the consumers' leagues in the late 1890s, but even after this their real power was negligible. The same is true of other social groups who might have joined any crusade to redistribute the good things of earth —Negroes, farmers,[8] and the more recent and less advantaged im-

---

[8] The Grange enrolled only 200,000 members in 1900, the Farmer's Union emerged in 1905 but shunned political activity, the Alliance movement was dead, and the politically powerful Farm Bureau Federation was not founded until after the war. The American Society of Equity (est. 1902) enrolled perhaps 150,000 farmers, largely in the wheat regions. Landless farmers were totally unorganized.

migrants. Of course the progressive era was the era of organization, and such gains as they made were made largely by organization, but it was slow work.

After men had been brought to see the necessity of organizing, either around their own interest or around a shared concern for the exploited and unfortunate, the job of actually redistributing advantages and burdens was staggering. It required endless patience, sustained pressure, and luck. An acceptable and talented leader had to be found, campaigns had to be pressed beyond the initial defeats and delays, public opinion had to be mobilized or at least neutralized, political and legislative machinery mastered, bureaucracies shouldered aside and new bureaucrats recruited, mistakes unraveled and the game begun again. As the months and years went by, both tedious and breathless, the Social Justice coalition tended to fragment, its components to return piece by piece to that apathetic impotence from which they had with such difficulty been aroused.

Even when some angry coalition forced its will through a legislative body, the courts could always be counted upon to defend property, and corporation counsel could always be counted upon to bring each reform enactment to judicial attention. Note the list of toppled regulatory, labor, or social insurance laws: in *E. C. Knight* (1895) it was learned that Congress had no control over manufacturing; in *Pollack* (1895), that Congress could not directly tax individuals; in *Lochner* (1905), that the legislature of New York could not set maximum hours for bakers; in *Hammer* v. *Dagenhart* (1918), that Congress could not outlaw child labor (although the Court had earlier decided that the memory of the Founders would not be outraged if Congress prohibited lotteries and the white slave trade; apparently property losses in the shady areas of capitalism were tolerable to the Constitution); in *Adkins* (1923) that Congress could not fix minimum wages for women who lived in the District of Columbia; and so on. When the Federal Trade Commission gave signs just after the war that it might construe broadly its mandate to investigate and indict practices in restraint of trade, the Court ruled the FTC findings of fact would not be accepted as prima facie evidence, but must pass through the filter of nine more reliable men than the commissioners. In all, American judges understood that their most sacred trust was to use the Constitution, with its wonderfully ambiguous language and varied precedent, to safeguard property rights. It must be said that they

shouldered their responsibilities to civilization with that combination
of determination and a passion for duty that has long marked the
American patrician class. Wrote Chief Justice William Howard Taft
as he held the conservative majority together in the 1920s: "I am older
and slower and less acute and more confused. However, as long as
things continue as they are, and I am able to answer in my place, I
must stay on the Court in order to prevent the Bolsheviki from getting
control. . . . The only hope we have of keeping a consistent declaration
of Constitutional law is for us to live as long as we can."

The People, admittedly, *could* ultimately override the judiciary
if they blocked the popular will; they *could* alter constitutions through
the prescribed, laborious processes and bring the courts to heel. A
number of progressives, among them Roosevelt in 1912, talked openly
of the need for action against constitutional barriers and even against
judges themselves. But constitutional alterations required the most
sustained political effort, and curbing individual judges was an idea
that made slow headway against the deep popular respect for the
robe and the bench.

So conservatives—those who wanted wealth, economic and political
authority, and social status to be held tomorrow and forever where
they were held today—could throw up a formidable defense against
meddling levelers. They were barricaded behind public and interest-
group apathy, unrepresentative political systems, a conservative judiciary drawn from their class, conservative and intellectually stagnant
universities, a genteel and irrelevant literature, a folklore that insisted
that complete social mobility was a reality, and mass media owned by
men who could be counted on (or if necessary forced by advertising
cancellations) to mesmerize the public with trivia and either ignore
or smear the radicals. It was a deep, complex maze through which few
redistributionist proposals could pass at all, and none without crippling
concessions. But this is to speak only of the defenses of conservatives.
The progressive years saw them take the offensive, at first haltingly,
and then with mounting success. Conservatives learned that their
greatest advantage lay not in their defenses against government, but
in their ability to manipulate it.

While the state had always been used by dominant groups to protect or extend their economic advantages, it is nonetheless true that
the American ruling classes had not had a sustained and comprehen-

sive resort to governmental power until the twentieth century. Admittedly there had always been a tariff, there had been railroad grants, and as the nation industrialized the upper classes saw to it that their government shouldered the task of repressing, through force or injunction, the restless laboring masses. Yet Barry Goldwater learned it to be a fact in 1964 that the dominant economic interests now demand a use of governmental power that is not sporadic and punitive but continuous and positive. The change did not come overnight, but we can state that if it did not exactly begin it at least accelerated sharply in the progressive era.

Prior to this century, those whom the industrial system (and the land) had made rich and comfortable used the state only infrequently, despised politics, counted upon conservative politicians to keep things quiet, and beat off the occasional inept attempts of radicals to actually use the state for other than police purposes. Basically the ruling classes were Sumnerians, or social Darwinists. They had no real vision of what the state might do for them beyond hiring policemen and judges and delivering the mail.

The progressive period was apparently a very educational period for them. Obviously, they learned that the state could be used against them, as waves of angry "little" businessmen from the South and West (shippers, commercial farmers, small bankers), as well as smaller waves of assorted do-gooders, assaulted the sleepy halls of legislatures and the Congress with coercive and confiscatory programs. The first impulse of the conservatives was to fight the very conception of the state as an active force in the economy, and because some of the less intelligent and imaginative among them still follow that impulse, it has come down to us that the business community has always been negatively oriented toward government. Actually, those few historians who have turned from the political life of intellectuals to the political life of American businessmen have found that a more positive conception of the state took hold in certain sectors of the American upper class in the years before the war. The more sophisticated members of the upper classes overcame their doctrinaire Jeffersonian suspicion of state power and moved from obstruction to a position resembling that of the reformers—demanding sustained governmental intervention in the nation's economic life. There was no reason, they saw, why the regulatory agencies of the modernized state must serve the purposes of the radicals. In the words of such an enlightened conservative, Richard Olney, at the opening of the modern era:

The Commission (ICC), as its functions have now been limited by the courts, is, or can be made of great use to the railroads. It satisfied the popular clamor for governmental supervision of railroads at the same time that the supervision is almost entirely nominal. Further, the older such a commission gets to be, the more inclined it will be found to be to take the business and railroad view of things. It thus becomes a sort of barrier between the railroad corporations and the people and a sort of protection against hasty and crude legislation hostile to railroad interests.

Olney spoke for a small minority of businessmen in 1892, but his view made headway among men of his class. There was every reason for his confidence that a government of new and useful but potentially dangerous powers could be controlled by the owners of industry rather than the dispossessed. The only disadvantage of the entrenched classes was numerical inferiority. But they had instant access not only to legal talent for persuasive testimony before congressional committees but also to the sympathetic ear of politicians of a common ethnic and social background who respected wealth and breeding, sometimes despite themselves. If the politicians on infrequent occasions were pressed so hard by angry groups that a regulatory agency was set up under a law at least potentially dangerous, the corporations on the commanding heights still held numerous advantages. The agencies were kept on miserly appropriations and were never large enough for the research, field, and legal work required to survey a national economy. The FTC, in a rare mood, investigated the meat packing industry in 1919 on suspicion of fixing prices, and in that year the advertising budget of Swift and Co. was six times the total budget of the agency. But there was more to the matter than size. Governmental bureaucracies were composed of men who were cautious, basically conservative, and—largely because of the meager salaries the public was willing to pay—likely to be men who in intellect and energy were quite inferior to their legal and technical adversaries from industry. There is a revealing passage in Secretary of the Treasury William G. McAdoo's autobiography where McAdoo, whose $12,000 yearly salary was the highest in the American government excepting only the president's, set out to hire into the federal service the presidents of the railroads he had just seized (1918) in the wartime emergency. To men with salaries ranging upward from $100,000 yearly, government employment with its rewards ranging steeply down from $12,000 was a virtual disaster and an insult. McAdoo was embarrassed, and the government hired its railroad directors at $40,000–50,000, depending upon the region. Any contest between such men with their New York lawyers against the civil servants of the Interstate Commerce Commission was likely to be, as it had been since 1887, an unequal contest.

These advantages of the dominant interests were not necessarily permanent. Time brought changes that tended to make the governmental bureaucracy more independent—slightly larger appropriations for staff and research, the enhanced attractiveness of federal service to talented people, the gradual organization of more interest groups, the gradual improvement of public understanding of the stakes involved in public policy decisions. But these trends had not developed very far by the end of the progressive era. As a result, using government to reduce the economic advantage of those who *have* the economic advantage was uphill work. As the entrenched interests accepted the inevitability of enlarged government, they found themselves in a post position in the race for its favors.

XII.

This gloomy account derives largely from contemplation of the record of social justice progressivism. Progressive attempts to rationalize habits and institutions must be accounted partially successful and in the end irresistible. Progressive efforts to restore the moral consensus of the nineteenth century were moderately successful in the short run and served their therapeutic purpose. But while social justice progressivism was demonstrably the least successful component of reform, the preceding review of the advantages of conservatives in frustrating it gives us a perspective from which to estimate social justice accomplishments as a bit higher than nothing at all. Progressives of this sort had done a substantial damage to the conservative outworks, and although beaten back, their sappers' trenches were still at the wall for another day of siege.

Think of the advantages of conservatives that, while proving enough in the defense against social justice progressives, had been eliminated or weakened. For its defense the status quo counts heavily on abstract modes of thought—a legalistic constitutionalism, a fixation upon natural law or the divine order, and in the realm of education a curriculum firmly limited to the "classic," i.e., resolutely nonrelevant studies. But progressive thinkers riveted the attention of their era upon the current and the real. Realism was the most pervasive intellectual quality of the leading thought of their day, whether political theory, law, literature, or the arts. There is an obvious kinship between muckraking and oil paintings of ashcans and alleys, between social investigations like the Pittsburgh Survey or the Industrial Relations Commission of 1911, and short stories about denizens of saloons. That kinship resides in a common preference for the real, which to the progressive generation usually meant the hard and sordid side of existence, as against what William Dean Howells called "the smiling aspects of life." As perceptive conservatives suspected, such morbid and unswerving attention to social reality often led to the most subversive consequences. For the world to remain at rest, it is best that it not be thought about too much, certainly not studied with any rigor. This is not to ignore the importance of abstraction in reform thought itself. It is important that the progressives also served abstractions and that they were new ones—justice rather than the Constitution or property rights. But what gave progressive ideals an upper hand so often was the progressive mastery of the facts and relations of actual life. With these in hand their ideals—which were after all ancient ideals, but not heretofore much threat to the going arrangement of things—could no longer be domesticated to the primers of school children and the Sunday school lessons of victorian ladies. True, conservatives were able to block most of the agitation arising out of realist thought, but they were not able to exorcise realism itself, which went on working its corrosive way through the fabric of received ideas and habits.

Things-as-they-are were also protected at the turn of the century by the notion that freedom was a condition of being let alone, and especially let alone by the state, the form of power most suspected despite its relative puniness. Progressive intellectuals argued that freedom had a positive dimension and that the prerequisites for freedom included at the very least the presence of public institutions strong enough to intervene to secure economic opportunity. Some even went so far as to suggest that there was no freedom without good housing, health, and economic security in illness and old age. Such notions as these suggested that the way to freedom might lie in a measure of coercion—a complicated, paradoxical, troubling thought destined to grow in influence because it was increasingly true.

Equally disturbing was the redefinition of justice that certain progressive thinkers accomplished. Herbert Croly, for instance, went so far as to argue that merely seeing that all men started with the same political rights and the same economic opportunities (access to credit, markets, transportation, and inventions), as hard as they might be to achieve, would still constitute no guarantee of an even start. Even if equal access to profit-making opportunities were realized, only certain individuals could take advantage of it. "Those who have enjoyed the benefits of wealth and thorough education," Croly wrote in *The Promise of American Life,* "start with an advantage which can be overcome only by very exceptional men. . .; the average competitor without such benefits feels himself disqualified for the contest." The social environment from birth to age twenty-one had filtered out some who were deserving. If we may think of social justice for a moment as, among other things, careers open to talent, Croly saw that it would not be so cheaply bought as his contemporaries hoped. It would require some positive intervention to provide the sort of social environment in which no one of talent was stultified or deprived of the requisite stimulation. Croly did not see how radical such a thought might be. It was not only too radical for his time, but goes down hard in our own. It led to the conclusion that for careers to be truly open to talent there could be no real difference, around the nation and from class to class and race to race, in the factors that awaken and nurture talent from birth—nutrition, health care, exposure to intellectual and aesthetic stimulation, formal education, peer group aspirations. This suggests stunning alterations in our institutions and habits, and one can hardly claim the progressives had this fully in mind. Men such as Wilson aimed at justice only for young white males of good family, but there were men and women of his generation who saw that real justice would require more than he thought in the way of reforms and had in mind a broader range of social groups to whom it might reasonably be owed—to women, for example, and to recent immigrants. Yet if no one of that era followed the idea of social justice as far as it led, did not in any numbers and in any serious way extend it to Negroes and American Indians, for example, it is still to them we owe the reactivation—after a lapse of forty years and the death of men like Lincoln and Wendell Phillips—of one of the most disruptive, creative ideas of our time.

Another requirement of conservatism was that the existing legal and moral definitions of crime and good conduct remain unchallenged, since fortunes had been made and deviants had been jailed by men working on these assumptions. Some civic reformers thought it earthshaking to enforce rigorously the existing standards, punishing public officials for familiar crimes such as graft, and the outcry from threatened people encouraged the Goo Goo's image of himself as an advanced thinker. But what was really radical were ideas such as that popularized by E. A. Ross in *Sin and Society* (1907), that the modern age of social interdependence requires a new, social definition of sin. This meant less concentration on behavior affecting only oneself (drunkenness, reading pornography, lack of ambition), and identified as sinful any act that had deleterious social consequences (watering of stock or strip mining). Such a shift in values could not be accomplished in one generation no matter how many books were written, but it began to work its way into the leading minds, and today we see its growing influence. While some among us would still enforce the moral code of Anthony Comstock, many are coming to condemn more severely the man who drives "his" car with oily exhaust, operates "his" transistor radio on a bus, or carelessly lumbers "his" forest than we do the users of alcohol or hallucinogens or the committers of fornication.

Thought and practice in the realm of crime and punishment was vital to conservatives, whose lives had been built upon scrupulous moral rectitude in the familiar moral categories (in most cases), but whose fortunes had been built upon environmental pollution, exhaustion of resources, and health-breaking working conditions. And if it were not enough to suggest that the "best people" might in fact be criminals, some leading progressive thinkers were beginning to argue that the worst people were not at fault for their behavior. Reformer after reformer began by wishing to jail the municipal bosses. "Their motto," said Mr. Dooley, "was—'Arrest that man!'." These reformers ended up convinced that "the system" corrupted men and that it was neither humanly defensible nor socially efficacious to pillory the criminal. One sees Lincoln Steffens come to this in his autobiography, and Fred Howe in his *Confessions of a Reformer*. But the best example is surely California's crusading editor Fremont Older, who helped jail San Francisco's Boss Ruef; then, after reflecting upon the real sources of municipal corruption, Older worked as hard to get Ruef out of jail as he had to put him in. What was most significant in Older's action was not his sympathy for Ruef but the fact that he had shifted the blame from Ruef's character to the existing social arrangements.

These were some of the ideas let loose by progressive thinkers to discredit and disturb the status quo. The net effect of their thinking was to strengthen the social as against the private focus in American life. After the First World War the individualistic orientation reasserted itself, and the country (and many reformers) shrugged off such collectivist patterns of thought and action as had been foisted on it. As in the days when progressives began their uprising, the dominant current after the war was again toward those uncoordinated, egoistic strivings that had "built this country." But no postwar reaction could entirely erase the collectivized perspective. When the individualistic culture botched its best and in some ways its final opportunity, it would be somewhat easier to move toward collective solutions because of progressivism.

In rating the few intellectual steps toward collectivism as the most substantial accomplishment of progressivism, one would not wish to dismiss the institutional framework progressives erected. Through progressive reform there was established effective supervision of railroad rates, a central bank to begin mastering the art and science of monetary manipulation, innumerable well-staffed bureaus at all governmental levels where the public's interest in insurance funds, securities issues, sewage disposal, patent medicine, and public health might conceivably be protected. Progressivism revitalized the presidency. Progressivism spurred the organization of hundreds of interest groups, from architects to mayors to teachers, and even a few general interest groups for the few altruists and consumers who wished to work for broad public goals. These institutions and organizations are the scaffolding of a more rational, efficient, and possibly even a more liberal social order. We must not confuse this scaffolding with the actual achievement of such a social order, for it was far from that. But it was a beginning.

Impatient men in the troubled 1970s will not highly estimate this accomplishment—a few dangerous ideas, a few organizations, a few governmental agencies that might or might not serve their best implied ends. The study of progressivism does to some extent support the crushing judgment of some contemporaries, but those who incline to such a critical stance might gain a useful perspective by attempting to name the generation that accomplished more.

Fortunately for a movement with so much unfinished business, progressivism in all its forms would be given other chances. After

1929 the country would stand in especial need of the best qualities of those earlier reformers—an activist and hopeful spirit, a faith in human reason, a resourceful humanitarianism. It would need more than these qualities, but they were something, and they were vital. It would need above all their conviction that the forces loose in the "private" world must somehow be brought to public account, so that America could preserve her society in its precious, fragile inheritance: neighborliness, security, moral purpose, meaningful freedom.

No man better embodies all that was generous and sane in progressivism, along with much that was narrow and parochial, than William Jennings Bryan. Surely he spoke for progressivism at its best when, in 1912 with the movement at its apogee and another man selected to lead, he reaffirmed their commitment to an unwearying struggle for a better democracy with a ringing quotation from Byron:

> *The dead have been awakened—shall I sleep?*
> *The World's at war with Tyrants—shall I crouch?*
> *The Harvest's ripe and shall I pause to reap?*
> *I slumber not; the thorn is in my couch.*
> *Each day a trumpet soundeth in mine ear—*
> *It's echo in my heart.*

BIBLIOGRAPHIC ESSAY

A comprehensive essay citing the basic primary sources, syntheses, and monographs appropriate to the period discussed in this book would be as long as the book itself. This essay will identify those secondary sources that were most important in helping me make up my mind—or change it—on these matters. The top of the iceberg of primary materials— memoirs, manuscript collections, newspapers, diplomatic dispatches—are identified from time to time in the text and included among the accompanying documents. Many invaluable secondary sources will not even be cited, but the sort of reader who gets as far as this bibliographic essay will not need to be reminded of all the standard works. He will know this literature generally and wonder what material had a special weight in shaping this book. A few of my important debts to other historians are acknowledged below. The essay follows the text, and the source of direct quotations are identified sequentially. The search for the mood of turn-of-the-century America involves a research effort of some complexity, but it leads one to some absorbing books. Henry Adams' *The Education of Henry Adams* (Boston, 1918) was first privately printed in 1906. Among the recollections of life before the war, two of the most intelligent and literate are Dean Acheson, *Morning and Noon* (New York, 1965), and Henry Seidel Canby, *American Memoir: The Age of Confidence* (New York, 1947). Walter Lord, *The Good Years* (New York, 1960), is an impressionistic study where I found (pp. 2–3), among other things, the quotation from Reverend Hillis. Frederick Lewis Allen's *The Big Change* (New York, 1952) contains (p. 4) the quotation from Morgan's biographer. Other attempts to catch the mood of the period are Paul Angle, *Crossroads: 1913* (Chicago, 1963), Thomas Beer, *The Mauve Decade* (New York, 1926), and Albert Britt, *Turn of the Century* (New York, 1966). Journalist Mark Sullivan's *Our Times: The Turn of the Century,* Vol. 1 (New York, 1934), is a combination of history and recollection; his estimation of the mood in 1900, which I have partially quoted, is on p. 499. Van Wyck Brooks, *The Confident Years: 1885–1915* (New York, 1953) and Alfred Kazin, *On Native Grounds* (New York, 1942), are good studies of the literature of the era. Roderick Nash, "The American Cult of the Primitive," *American Quarterly* 18 (Fall, 1966), offers an important insight into the glorification of the primitive that characterized so much contemporary thought. A brilliant essay by John Higham, "The Reorientation of American Culture in the 1890s," in John Weiss (ed.), *The Origins of Modern Consciousness* (Detroit, 1965), describes the period as one of exuberance and rising vitality, with America largely free of the pessimism that laced European culture. Ray Ginger's *The Age of Excess* (New York, 1965) contains some powerfully evocative passages, although it has deficiencies as a sustained work of synthesis.

Urban history is a difficult genre, but two readable surveys appropriate for this period are Constance M. Green, *The Rise of Urban America* (New York, 1965) and Blake McKelvey, *The Urbanization of America: 1860–1915* (New Brunswick, 1963). Among the many urban biographies the best studies of the largest American cities are Constance M. Green, *Washington: Capital City, 1879–1950* (Princeton, 1963), Gilbert Osofsky, *Harlem: The Making of a Ghetto 1890–1930* (New York, 1966), Bessie L. Pierce, *A History of Chicago,* Vol. 3,

The Rise of a Modern City: 1871–1893 (New York, 1957), and
Moses Rischin, *The Promised City: New York's Jews, 1870–1914*
(Cambridge, Mass., 1962). The explosive growth of these and other
cities created most of the social problems that occupied the progressive
generation, but urbanization was a function of industrialization, another
process that historians rarely describe with stylistic success. Thomas C.
Cochran and William Miller, *The Age of Enterprise* (New York,
1942) and Edward C. Kirkland, *Industry Comes of Age: Business,
Labor, and Public Policy 1860–1897* (New York, 1961) offer good
descriptions of the economic developments that transformed American
society.

On the question of what was bothering the progressives—from
social problems to personal problems—one could cite the entire body
of contemporary media, every autobiography, memoir, and diary. As
for secondary literature, every volume in this bibliography contributes
something, usually indirectly, to our understanding of the social crisis
that produced progressivism. On the general fear of social disintegration, see Rowland T. Berthoff, "The American Social Order: A
Conservative Hypothesis," *American Historical Review* 65 (April,
1960); Wallace D. Farnham, "The Weakened Spring of Government:
A Study in 19th Century American History," *American Historical
Review* 58 (April, 1963); James Willard Hurst, *Law and the Conditions of Freedom in the Nineteenth-Century United States* (Chicago,
1956); Mosei Ostrogorski, *Democracy and the Organization of Political Parties* (London, 1902), from which I have quoted (Vol. 2, p.
550); and Robert Wiebe, *The Search for Order 1877–1920* (New
York, 1967). The quotation from Stephen J. Field is from his con-
curring opinion in the 1895 income tax case, *Pollock* v. *Farmers'
Loan and Trust Co.,* 157 U.S. 607. The quotations from Henry Adams
are from the *Education,* pp. 449 and 505.

Among the many factors accounting for the progressive uprising,
perhaps none was more important than the Christian conscience.
Charles H. Hopkins, *The Rise of the Social Gospel in American Pro-
testantism, 1865–1915* (New Haven, 1940) and Henry May, *The
Protestant Churches and Industrial America* (New York, 1949) are
indispensable on reform sentiment within the churches, and indicate
how deeply involved in reform were Christian ministers and laity. The
importance of the Christian ethic is further illuminated in Carl N.
Degler, *Out of Our Past* (New York, 1959), chapter 12, and Richard

Hofstadter, *The Age of Reform* (New York, 1955), chapter 5. The latter book is, among other things, the most extensive and stimulating discussion of the reformers' motivation. Any number of historians have joined the lively dispute over whether there was, as Hofstadter argued, a "status revolution." The most suggestive sociological evidence is presented in George E. Mowry, *The California Progressives* (Berkeley, 1951), chapter 4; Samuel P. Hays, "The 'Shame of the Cities' Revisited: The Case of Pittsburgh," in Herbert Shapiro (ed.), *The Muckrakers and American Society* (Boston, 1968); Eli D. Potts, "The Progressive Profile in Iowa," *Mid-America* 47 (October, 1965); Richard B. Sherman, "The Status Revolution and Massachusetts Progressive Leadership," *Political Science Quarterly* 78 (March, 1963); Jack Tager, "Progressives, Conservatives, and the Theory of the Status Revolution," *Mid-America* 48 (July, 1966); and Norman Wilensky, *Conservatives in the Progressive Era: The Taft Republicans of 1912* (Jacksonville, 1965).

Much, although not all, of this evidence indicates that conservatives as well as progressives came from the social classes Hofstadter (and Mowry) thought to be heavily progressive, and there have been some recent efforts to identify other social classes and groups as the principal sources of progressivism. J. Joseph Huthmacher made the first of several attempts to locate substantial reformism in the urban lower classes, in his "Urban Liberalism and the Age of Reform," *Mississippi Valley Historical Review,* 49 (September, 1962). More recently, the case for the participation of urban lower-class groups has been taken up by John D. Buenker; see his "The New Stock Politicians of 1912," *Journal of Illinois Historical Society,* 62 (Spring, 1969), and "Cleveland's New Stock Lawmakers and Progressive Reform," *Ohio History,* 25 (Spring, 1969). A contrasting and ultimately more convincing argument that municipal reformers, at least, were from the successful business classes, is made in Samuel P. Hays, "The Politics of Municipal Government in the Progressive Era," *Pacific Northwest Quarterly,* 60 (October, 1964). Also impressive is Robert Wiebe's association of reform with a "new middle class" of upward-mobile professionals, engineers, and businessmen, in *The Search for Order.* The literature on the social class of progressives is large and growing, and Hays's comprehensive summary of 1964 is now somewhat dated, as is my own bibliography on the subject, published in Otis L. Graham, Jr., *An Encore for Reform* (New York, 1967), pp. 229–30. The book that started this argument, Hofstadter's *The Age of Reform,* has had an impressive—and, of course, not always admiring—scholarly reception; see Otis L. Graham, Jr., (ed.), *From Roosevelt to Roosevelt: America, 1901–1941* (New York, 1971).

The quotation from Jane Addams is taken from her *Twenty Years at Hull House* (New York, 1910), p. 109. For an interesting use of the career of Jane Addams in the "status revolution" argument, see Staughton Lynd, "'Jane Addams and the Radical Impulse," *Commentary* 32 (July, 1961).

Conservative ideas at the end of the nineteenth century are ably discussed in Richard Hofstadter, *Social Darwinism in American Thought* (Boston, 1944), Robert G. McCloskey, *American Conservatism in the Age of Enterprise* (Cambridge, Mass., 1951), and Arnold M. Paul, *Conservative Crisis and the Rule of Law* (Ithaca, 1960). Reform thought has attracted a swarm of historians, some of the most perceptive being Henry Steele Commager, *The American Mind* (New Haven, 1950), Sidney Fine, *Laissez-Faire and the General Welfare State (Ann Arbor,* 1956), Morton D. White, *Social Thought in America* (New York, 1949), and Eric Goldman, *Rendezvous with Destiny* (New York, 1952), where I found the quotation from Justice Holmes (p. 105).

The best study of the settlement movement is Allen F. Davis, *Spearheads for Reform: The Social Settlements and the Progressive Movement 1890–1914* (New York, 1967). The centrality of the urge to functional organization was perceived by Hofstadter in *The Age of Reform,* and by Samuel P. Hays, *The Response to Industrialism 1885–1914* (Chicago, 1957). Two studies of engineers, Monte A. Calvert, *The Mechanical Engineer in America: 1830–1910* (Baltimore, 1967) and Edwin T. Layton, "The American Engineering Profession and the Idea of Social Responsibility," unpublished doctoral dissertation, University of California at Los Angeles, 1956, demonstrate that the progressive period was a spawning ground for professional organization, and that these organizations were not only chronologically but in spirit a part of the reform era. Lawrence Cremin has given us an invaluable book in *The Transformation of the School: Progressivism in American Education, 1876–1957* (New York, 1961), and the broader importance of public education to the progressive mind is examined in Rush Welter, *Popular Education and Democratic Thought in America* (New York, 1962).

There are many urban biographies, but only recently have we begun to have an adequate shelf of monographs on the progressive movement in the cities. Some of the more interesting studies are James Crooks, *Politics and Progress: The Rise of Urban Progressivism in Baltimore 1895–1911* (Baton Rouge, 1968), Melvin Holli, *Reform in Detroit: Hazen S. Pingree and Urban Politics* (New York, 1969), Arthur Mann, *Yankee Reformers in the Urban Era* (Cambridge, Mass., 1954), William D. Miller, *Memphis During the Progressive Era, 1900–1917* (Memphis, 1957), and Zane Miller, *Boss Cox's Cincinnati: Urban Politics in the Progressive Era* (New York, 1968). An interesting critical perspective on reform is found in Theodore Lowi, "Machine Politics—Old and New," *The Public Interest* 9 (Fall, 1967). Some of the more valuable state studies are Mowry's *The California Progressives,* Spencer Olin, *California's Prodigal Sons: Hiram Johnson and the Progressives 1911–1917* (Berkeley, 1968), Hoyt L. Warner, *Progressivism in Ohio, 1897–1917* (Columbus, Ohio, 1964), and the broader surveys of state politics in Russel B. Nye, *Midwestern Progressive Politics* (East Lansing, 1951) and C. Vann Woodward, *Origins of the New South 1877–1913* (Baton Rouge, 1951). I was also much enlightened by the treatment of middle-class reformers and their relations with urban labor in Irwin Yellowitz, *Labor and the Progressive Movement in New York State, 1897–1916* (Ithaca, 1965), and by a recent book on one of the more conservative state reform movements, Raymond Pulley, *Old Virginia Restored: An Interpretation of the Progressive Impulse 1870–1930* (Charlottesville, 1968). The sizable role of business groups is especially clear in California; see, for example, Olin's *California's Prodigal Sons,* and Gerald D. Nash, *State Government and Economic Development: A History of Admininistrative Policies in California, 1859–1933* (Berkeley, 1964). Roy Lubove, in "Workmen's Compensation and the Prerogatives of Voluntarism," *Labor History* 8 (Fall, 1967), and in *The Struggle for Social Security 1900–1935* (Cambridge, Mass., 1968) chapter 3, shows that businessmen were interested not only in the right kind of regulatory legislation but in some cases worked also for portions of the "social welfare legislation" agenda. The quotation above on p. 32 is from Lubove's article, p. 259.

There is a mountain of literature on national progressivism, and some of the best of it deals in one way or another with the career of Theodore Roosevelt. William H. Harbaugh, *Power and Responsibility:*

The Life and Times of Theodore Roosevelt (New York, 1961) and George E. Mowry, *The Era of Theodore Roosevelt: 1900–1912* (New York, 1958) are reasonably favorable to T.R. (both contain splendid bibliographies). More critical treatment may be found in Richard Hofstadter, *The American Political Tradition* (New York, 1948), chapter 9; Henry Pringle, *Theodore Roosevelt* (New York, 1931); John Blum, *The Republican Roosevelt* (Cambridge, Mass., 1954); Gabriel Kolko, *The Triumph of Conservatism: A Reinterpretation of American History, 1900–1916* (New York, 1963), chapters 3–5; and Samuel P. Hays, *Conservation and the Gospel of Efficiency: The Progressive Conservation Movement 1890–1920* (Cambridge, Mass., 1959), especially pp. 266–72. Contrasting accounts of the struggle over meat-packing legislation are given in John Braeman, "The Square Deal in Action," in John Braeman, Robert Bremner, and Everett Walters (eds.), *Change and Continuity in Twentieth-Century America* (Columbus, Ohio, 1964), and Kolko, *The Triumph of Conservatism*, chapter 4. On the Pure Food and Drug Act and its administration, see Oscar E. Anderson, *The Health of a Nation: Harvey Wiley and the Fight for Pure Food* (Chicago, 1958), a useful book that is flawed by the uncritical adoption of Wiley's view of who was for and against regulation; Thomas A. Bailey, "Congressional Opposition to Pure Food and Drug Legislation, 1879–1906," *American Journal of Sociology* 36 (July, 1930); the entire December, 1933 issue of *Law and Contemporary Problems,* especially the articles by C. C. Regier, "The Struggle for Pure Food and Drugs," and by L. T. Hayes and F. J. Ruff, "The Administration of the Federal Food and Drug Act." James Harvey Young has written two splendid and often hilarious books on food and drug adulteration and patent medicines in American history and the efforts to protect the consumer—*The Toadstool Millionaires: A Social History of Patent Medicines in America Before Federal Regulation* (Princeton, 1961), and *The Medical Messiahs: A Social History of Health Quackery in Twentieth-Century America* (Princeton, 1967). A gloomy view of the accomplishments of progressive efforts in this area will be visited upon anyone who reads Arthur Kallet and F. J. Schlink, *100,000,000 Guinea Pigs* (New York, 1932) or Ruth DeForest Lamb, *American Chamber of Horrors* (New York, 1936).

On railroad regulation under Roosevelt, see Blum, *The Republican Roosevelt,* Gabriel Kolko, *Railroads and Regulation* (Princeton, 1965), and William Z. Ripley, *Railroads: Rates and Regulation* (New York, 1912). By far the best book on progressive conservation is Samuel P. Hays, *Conservation and the Gospel of Efficiency,* and Hays's general interpretation is shared by James Penick, *Progressive Politics and Conservation: The Ballinger-Pinchot Affair* (Chicago, 1968). The People vs. The Interests interpretation may be found in an unconvincing form in Judson King, *The Conservation Fight: From Theodore Roosevelt to the Tennessee Valley Authority* (Washington, D.C., 1945), and more formidably in J. Leonard Bates, *The Origins of Teapot Dome: Progressives, Parties, and Petroleum, 1909–1921* (Urbana, Ill., 1963), and in Richard Lowitt, "A Neglected Aspect of the Progressive Movement: George W. Norris and Public Control of Hydro-Electric Power, 1913–1919," *The Historian* 27 (1965). A valuable survey with little interpretation is Elmo Richardson, *The Politics of Conservation: Crusaders and Controversies, 1897–1913* (Berkeley, 1962).

The indispensable source on Wilson is the multivolume biography by Arthur Link. Most important for the first administration are *Wilson: The New Freedom* (Princeton, 1965), Vol. 2 in the series, and Vol. 5, *Wilson: Campaigns for Progressivism and Peace* (Princeton, 1965). Arthur Walworth's *Woodrow Wilson* (New York, 1958) is uncritical but valuable as a detailed narrative. More critical treatment may be found in John Blum, *Woodrow Wilson and the Politics of Morality* (Boston, 1956), James Kerney, *The Political Education of Woodrow Wilson* (New York, 1926), and William Diamond, *The Economic Thought of Woodrow Wilson* (Baltimore, 1943). One ought not to ignore the view from the New Left, well stated in Martin J. Sklar, "Woodrow Wilson and the Political Economy of Modern United States Liberalism," *Studies on the Left* 1 (1960). On the Federal Reserve Act, in addition to Link, see Kolko, *The Triumph of Conservatism,* chapter 9, and J. Laurence Laughlin, *The Federal Reserve Act: Its Origin and Problems* (New York, 1933). On the trust issue, see James E. Anderson, *The Emergence of the Modern Regulatory State* (Washington, D.C., 1962), a clear if unoriginal survey, William Letwin, *Law and Economic Policy: The Evolution of the Sherman Anti-Trust Act* (New York, 1965), and Melvin Urofsky, "Wilson, Brandeis, and the Trust Issue, 1912–1914," *Mid-America* 49 (1967). New Freedom tax measures are reviewed in Sidney Ratner, *American Taxation* (New York, 1942). Alpheus T. Mason's Brandeis: *A Free*

Man's Life (New York, 1946) is a good biography of this very important ally and mentor of Wilson. A valuable article on the pressures behind Wilsonian policy is Richard Abrams, "Woodrow Wilson and the Southern Congressmen, 1913–1916," *Journal of Southern History* 22 (November, 1956).

Many good books have been written on the entire diplomatic record of the 1914–17 period. To my mind the best single volume is now Ernest R. May, *The World War and American Isolation* (Cambridge, Mass., 1959). Link's volumes 3 and 4, *Wilson: The Struggle for Neutrality, 1914–1915* (Princeton, 1960), and *Wilson: Confusions and Crises, 1915–1916* (Princeton, 1964), and volume 5, already cited, require a stronger word than invaluable. The most readable and plausible of the revisionist volumes are Charles C. Tansill, *America Goes to War* (New York, 1938), Walter Millis, *Road to War: America, 1914–1917* (Boston, 1935), and the otherwise sympathetic Ray Stannard Baker, *Woodrow Wilson: Life and Letters* (New York, 1927–39, 8 vols), especially volumes 5 and 6. Edwin Borchard and William P. Lage, *Neutrality for the United States* (New Haven, 1940), is more intemperate than most revisionist studies—and that requires a good deal of spleen—but contains a great deal of useful information on the difficult technical issues of neutrality. I found valuable information and invaluable correctives for the revisionist argument in Charles Seymour, *American Neutrality: 1914–1917* (New Haven, 1935), Daniel Smith, *Robert Lansing and American Neutrality: 1914–1917* (Berkeley, 1958), and Edward H. Buehrig, *Woodrow Wilson and the Balance of Power* (Bloomington, Ill., 1955). Paul Birdsall, in "Neutrality and Economic Pressures, 1914–1917," *Science and Society* 3 (Spring, 1939), provides an economic setting that clarifies a great deal, without utilizing any conspiracy theories.

For the policy-making process within Germany, and a firm grasp of German political pressures, see May, *The World War and American Isolation,* Karl E. Birnbaum, *Peace Moves and U-Boat Warfare* (Stockholm, 1958), and Arno J. Mayer, *Political Origins of the New Diplomacy, 1917–1918* (New Haven, 1959). Fritz Fischer's epochal book, *Germany's Aims in the First World War* (New York, 1967—a translation of *Griff nach der Weltmach*) was followed by a sizable critical literature. For the highlights of the argument, see Wolfgang J. Mommsen, "The Debate on German War Aims," in Walter Laquer and George L. Mosse, (eds.) *1914: The Coming of the First World*

War (New York, 1966). On the Allies, I found most useful Lord Beaverbrook, *Politicians and the War 1914–1916* (London, 1928), Viscount Grey of Fallodon, *Twenty-Five Years, 1892–1916* (London, 1925), Marion C. Siney, *The Allied Blockade of Germany, 1914–1916* (Ann Arbor, 1957), Gerda Crosby, *Disarmament and Peace in British Politics 1914–1919* (Cambridge, Mass., 1957), Kent Forster, *The Failures of Peace: The Search for a Negotiated Peace During the First World War* (Philadelphia, 1941), and Laurence W. Martin, *Peace Without Victory: Woodrow Wilson and the British Liberals* (New Haven, 1958). On Allied war aims, one must make do with A. J. P. Taylor, "The War Aims of the Allies in the First World War," in *Essays Presented to Sir Lewis Namier* (London, 1956), and Pierre Renouvin, "Les Buts de Guerre du Gouvernement Français (1914–1918)," *Revue Historique* (March, 1966).

Robert E. Osgood has nicely summarized the arguments that Wilson was primarily (and regrettably) an idealist, in *Ideals and Self-Interest in America's Foreign Relations* (Chicago, 1953). But the other side of the argument, that the president and his advisors had a firm grasp on reality and pursued the national interest as they saw it rather than the abstractions their language usually suggested, has recently gained authority with the publication of books like those of Buehrig, Link (see a brief statement of his view in "The Higher Realism of Woodrow Wilson," *Journal of Presbyterian History* 41 [March, 1963]), and May. A valuable summary of the argument for Wilson's realism is Daniel M. Smith, "National Interest and American Intervention, 1917: An Historiographical Appraisal," *Journal of American History* 53 (June, 1965). But Osgood's argument, especially as stated in "Woodrow Wilson, Collective Security, and the Lessons of History," *Confluence* (January, 1957), is still persuasive. The studies of Wilson's wartime and postwar diplomacy by Arno J. Mayer, *Politics and Diplomacy of Peacemaking* (Princeton, 1967), and N. Gordon Levin, *Woodrow Wilson and World Politics* (New York, 1968), depict Wilson, at least in the years after 1917, as a hard-headed American nationalist whose international commitments owed little to abstract and unrealizable ideals. In view of these apparently conflicting scholarly efforts, the surest ground seems to be that taken by Edward Buehrig in "Idealism and Statecraft," *Confluence* (October, 1956), where Wilson is presented as a man who mixed realism and idealism in a most unsettling way.

Useful monographs on some of the more important and difficult questions concerning the 1914–17 period are C.R.M.F. Cruttwell, *A History of the Great War* (London, 1936) and Cryril Falls, *The First World War* (New York, 1960) for military events; Ralph Nafziger, "The American Press and Public Opinion During World War I, 1914–1917," unpublished doctoral dissertation, University of Wisconsin, 1936, and Harold Syrett, "The Business Press and American Neutrality, 1914–1917," *Mississippi Valley Historical Review* 32 (September, 1945), on public opinion and the press; Samuel R. Spencer, *Decision for War: 1917* (Rindge, New Hampshire, 1953), for the tides of opinion in the weeks before intervention; Warren I. Cohen, *The American Revisionists and the Lessons of World War I* (Chicago, 1966), on revisionist historiography and its influence; and Charles Warren, "Troubles of a Neutral," *Foreign Affairs* (April, 1934), a lawyer's distillation of the lessons of the neutrality period as they might be (and virtually were) applied to prevent a second World War.

Historiographical surveys are numerous, the best recent ones being the article by Daniel M. Smith in *The Journal of American History,* Richard Leopold's "The Emergence of America as a World Power," in John Braeman, *et al.* (eds.) *Change and Continuity in Twentieth-Century America,* and Ernest R. May, *American Intervention: 1917 and 1941* (Washington, D.C., 1960). An admirable effort to sketch the costs of the war is John M. Clark, *The Costs of the World War to the American People* (New Haven, 1931), which may be supplemented by *The Annual Report of the Secretary of the Treasury: 1919* (Washington, D.C., 1920), for financial costs; Kevin McShane, "The 1918 Kansas City Influenza Epidemic," *Missouri Historical Review* 63 (October, 1968), for some of the noncombatant fatalities; and U. S. Senate Document 248, *Report of Federal Trade Commission Regarding Profiteering* (65th Cong., 2d sess., June 29, 1918), for one of the war's effects on the distribution of income.

The affinity of progressivism for an aggressive foreign policy was first suggested by Randolph Bourne and was given its best scholarly expression in William E. Leuchtenburg, "Progressivism and Imperialism: The Progressive Movement and American Foreign Policy, 1898–1916," *Mississippi Valley Historical Review,* 39 (December, 1952). A number of careful surveys of progressive opinion, especially in the Congress, have failed to substantiate this argument. The most important of these, by professors Allen, Sutton, and Bernstein and

Lieb, are summarized in John M. Cooper, Jr., "Progressivism and American Foreign Policy: A Reconsideration," *Mid-America,* 51 (October, 1969).

The Lansing quotation on p. 65 is from Robert Lansing, *War Memoirs of Robert Lansing, Secretary of State* (Indianapolis, 1935), p. 129. The quotation from Count Westarp on p. 81 is from May, *American Isolation,* p. 103. The quotations from *The American Banker* and *The Economist* on p. 89 are from the article by Harold Syrett, already cited. The quotation from Wilson on p. 82 is from Tansill, *America Goes to War,* p. 639. The Wilson quotation on p. 85 is from Walter Millis, *Road to War,* p. 443. The quotation from Andrew Carnegie on p. 93 is from Tansill, *America Goes to War,* p. 54. The *New York Times* quotation on p. 93 is from Millis, *Road to War,* p. 124. The quotation from Spring-Rice on p. 93 is from Millis, p. 115.

The domestic implications of the war, especially on the various segments of the prewar reform movement, are not yet thoroughly charted. Pioneering work has been done by Samuel Haber, *Efficiency and Uplift* (Chicago, 1964), Charles Hirschfeld, "Nationalist Progressivism and World War I," *Mid-America* 45 (July, 1963), Sidney Kaplan, "Social Engineers as Saviors: World War I and American Liberals," *Journal of the History of Ideas* (June, 1956), Walter Trattner, "Progressivism and World War I," *Mid-America* (July, 1962), and Allen F. Davis, "Welfare, Reform, and World War I," *American Quarterly* 19 (Fall, 1967). All of these articles emphasize the ways in which the war effort harmonized with certain strains in progressive thought and assisted certain reform efforts toward fruition, and all—especially the article by Kaplan—reveal how the war came to undermine the reform movement—intellectually, emotionally, politically. The latter development was confessed by a prointervention liberal, Herbert Croly, in his "Liberalism vs. the War," *New Republic* (8 December, 1920), and predicted in Randolph Bourne, *Untimely Papers* (New York, 1919). The conclusions of the Yoakum and Yerkes study, *Army Mental Tests,* are critically reviewed in Daniel J. Kevles, "Testing the Army's Intelligence: Psychologists and the Military in World War I," *Journal of American History* 55 (December, 1968).

A less pessimistic view of the war's impact may be found in George Mowry, "The First World War and American Democracy," in Jesse

D. Clarkson and Thomas C. Cochran (eds.), *War as a Social Institution* (New York, 1941). Other beneficial effects are outlined in Roy Lubove, "Homes and 'A Few Well-Placed Fruit Trees': An Object Lesson in Federal Housing," *Social Research* 27 (Winter, 1960), as well as in the pages of the *Proceedings of the National Conference of Social Work,* especially pp. 674–77 of the 1918 number of the *Proceedings,* where one finds a discussion entitled "The Future Prospects of Leading Wartime Efforts and Movements," and in the essay by Arthur J. Todd in the same number, entitled "New Social Data Growing Out of the War," pp. 683–86.

For evidence that there was great support for a conscription of wealth in April, 1917, see A. Russell Buchanan, "American Editors Examine American War Aims and Plans in April, 1917," *Pacific Historical Review* 9 (September, 1940). The history of the Left in the war period has not been written; for the Congressional Left, one may begin with Alex Arnet, *Claude Kitchin and the Wilson War Policies* (Boston, 1937), Seward Livermore, *Politics is Adjourned: Woodrow Wilson and the War Congresses, 1916–1918* (Middletown, Conn., 1966), the older survey by Frederic C. Paxson, *American Democracy and the World War* (Boston, 1936–45), and the relevant parts of Arno J. Mayer, *Political Origins of the New Diplomacy, 1917–1918* (New Haven, 1959). Scholars have recently developed a strong interest in the nature of business-government relations during the war. Without agreeing with them, I was particularly stimulated by James Weinstein's *The Corporate Ideal in the Liberal State, 1900–1918* (Boston, 1968), and Paul A. C. Koistinen, "The 'Industrial-Military Complex' in Historical Perspective: World War I," *Business History Review,* 41 (Winter, 1967). Melvin Urofsky describes the shaky entente between the steel industry, and especially U. S. Steel's Judge Gary, and the government, in *Big Steel and the Wilson Administration* (Columbus, Ohio, 1969).

The quotation from the *General Federation of Women's Clubs Magazine* on p. 98 is from William O'Neill, *Everyone Was Brave: The History of Social Feminism in America* (Chicago, 1969), p. 34. The quotations from social workers Woods and Devine on p. 99 are from Allen F. Davis, *Spearheads for Reform,* p. 222. The quotation from Robert Woods on p. 99 is from Robert Woods, "The Regimentation of the Free," *The Survey* 40 (6 July, 1918). The quotation from Frances Kellor on p. 100 is from John Higham,

Strangers in the Land (New Brunswick, 1955), p. 234. The quotation from Arthur Link on p. 101 is from Link, *Woodrow Wilson and the Progressive Era* (New York, 1954), pp. 192–93. The quotation from Josephus Daniels on p. 103 is from a letter to Ray Stannard Baker, in Baker, Woodrow Wilson: *Life and Letters,* Vol. 6, p. 506. Jerold Auerbach's "Woodrow Wilson's 'Prediction' to Frank Cobb: Words Historians Should Doubt Ever Got Spoken," *Journal of American History* 54 (December, 1967), convinced me that I can no longer quote this apocryphal story. In the exchange of letters between Wilson's biographer, Arthur S. Link, and Auerbach (see the *Journal of American History* 55 [June, 1968]), Link convinces me that Wilson uttered roughly similar prophecies if not this particular one, and Auerbach convinces me not only that Cobb's story ought to be retired, but that neither in this nor in any other 'prophecy' did Wilson show noticeable concern for the effect of the war on civil liberties. The quotation from Frederic Howe on p. 108 is from Howe, *The Confessions of a Reformer* (New York, 1925), p. 279. The quotation from Mencken on p. 109 is from Gerald Rabkin, *Drama and Commitment* (Indianapolis, 1964), p. 23. The quotation from the Southern Sociological Conference convention in 1919 at Knoxville is from E. Charles Chatfield, "The Southern Sociological Congress: Organization of Uplift," *Tennessee Historical Quarterly* (December, 1960).

The repressive atmosphere of 1919 is seen as largely the administration's fault in Harry N. Scheiber, *The Wilson Administration and Civil Liberties, 1917–1921* (Ithaca, 1960), and receives a more subtle explanation in Stanley Coben, "A Study in Nativism: The American Red Scare of 1919–20," *Political Science Quarterly* 79 (March, 1964); see also John Blum, "Nativism, Anti-Radicalism, and the Foreign Scare, 1917–1920," *Midwest Journal* 3 (1950–51). For a neglected side of the red scare, see William Tuttle, "Views of a Negro During 'The Red Summer of 1919,'" *Journal of Negro History* 51 (July, 1966). The legal issues are clarified in Zechariah Chafee, *Free Speech in the United States* (Cambridge, Mass., 1941). In *The Challenge to American Freedoms: World War I and the Rise of the American Civil Liberties Union* (Lexington, Ky., 1963), Donald D. Johnson describes the response of some intellectuals to the repression of the war period.

The best general analysis of the fate of reform in the 1920s is still Arthur S. Link, "What Happened to the Progressive Movement in the 1920s?" *American Historical Review* 64 (July, 1959). Richard

Hofstadter's *The Age of Reform,* pp. 282–301, contains insights that Link developed and that will probably be read with profit fifty years from now. Although many monographs have appeared since they were published, no one has yet written a better political history than William E. Leuchtenburg's *The Perils of Prosperity* (Chicago, 1958), or a more penetrating "social" history than Frederick Lewis Allen's *Only Yesterday* (New York, 1931).

Several studies reveal a persistence of progressive impulses in the 1920s. For the efficiency thrust, see George Tindall, "Business Progressivism: Southern Politics in the 1920s," *South Atlantic Quarterly* (Winter, 1963); James Weinstein, "Organized Business and the City Commission and Manager Movements," *Journal of Southern History* 28 (May, 1962), Donald Swain, *Federal Conservation Policy, 1921– 1933* (Berkeley, 1963), and the contemporary view of Morris L. Cooke, "The Influence of Scientific Management on Government—Federal, State, and Municipal," *Bulletin of the Taylor Society* 9 (1924). An indispensable source in this connection is *Recent Social Trends in the United States* (New York: 1934). Attention is called to postwar social legislation in Elizabeth Brandeis, "Labor Legislation," in John R. Commons, *et al., History of Labor in the United States, 1896– 1932,* Vol. 2 (New York, 1935), and Henry Seager, "Progress of Labor Legislation, 1900–1925," *American Labor Legislation Review* 20 (December, 1925). Both are forced to admit that the "gains" of the 1920s in such areas as state minimum wage or child labor legislation were very skimpy. Clarke Chambers' *Seedtime of Reform: Social Service and Social Action, 1918–1933* (Minneapolis, 1963), reinforces the impression of liberal discouragement, although the book was written to call attention to the survival of the social welfare wing of progressivism in the 1920s. The regulatory agencies established during the progressive era of course survived in the 1920s, but each in its turn was used by the interests it was designed to regulate or, if they had no work for it, was allowed to stagnate: see G. Cullum Davis, "The Transformation of the FTC, 1914–1929," *Mississippi Valley Historical Review* 49 (December, 1962), and E. Pendleton Herring, *Public Administration and the Public Interest* (New York, 1936). Another progressive reform turned to conservative uses is discussed in V. O. Key and Winston Crouch, *The Initiative and Referendum in California* (Berkeley, 1939).

The political activities of reform groups whose goals were primarily economic may be follo wed in Kenneth McKay, *The Progressive Move-*

ment of 1924 (New York, 1947), and James Shideler, "The Disintegration of the Progressive Party Movement of 1924," *Historian* (Spring,
1951), and James Weinstein, "Radicalism in the Midst of Normalcy,"
Journal of American History (March, 1966)—the latter discovering
more discontent than is usually depicted, but nonetheless leaving
intact the meager summary of results. David Burner's *The Politics of
Provincialism: The Democratic Party in Transition 1918–1932* (New
York, 1968) is a very important study of the party, which somewhat
by accident came to harbor the many conflicting impulses of modern
reform. Burner's book, and Lawrence Levine, *Defender of the Faith:
William Jennings Bryan: The Last Decade 1915–1925* (New York,
1965), are superb introductions to the effect of cultural tensions on the
politics of the 1920s.

Historians have from the beginning recognized that "efficiency"
was one of the guiding ideas of the progressive movement, but most
of the writing on this aspect of the reform impulse has come in the
last few years. An early study was Benjamin P. DeWitt, *The Progressive Movement* (New York, 1915), chapter 15, "The Efficiency
Movement." More recent books include Samuel P. Hays' volume on
conservation, Raymond E. Callahan, *Education and the Cult of Efficiency* (Chicago, 1962), and Samuel Haber, *Efficiency and Uplift:
Scientific Management in the Progressive Era, 1890–1920* (Chicago,
1964). Efficiency invariably meant the application of scientific modes
of thought to traditional processes, and it usually seemed to require
centralization of authority under scientifically or at least technically
minded people. The impact of this part of the progressive movement
upon the size and functions of the federal government may be followed
in A. Hunter Dupree, *Science in the Federal Government: A History
to 1940* (Cambridge, Mass., 1957), and in Arthur Johnson's shrewd
analysis of T.R.'s approach to industrial problems, "Antitrust Policy
in Transition, 1908: Ideal and Reality," *Mississippi Valley Historical
Review* 48 (December, 1961). A good example of this sort of activity
at the local level is the subject of James H. Cassedy's *Charles V.
Chapin and the Public Health Movement* (Cambridge, 1962).

Men of conservative instincts and much to conserve often found it
possible or even imperative to become progressives because of the
emphasis placed on predictability and social control in some parts of
the movement. Their influence, of course, increased the chances that
reform would have a conservative outcome. Gabriel Kolko, in his *The*

Triumph of Conservatism, has gathered together all the evidence he could find (at the federal level) where this was the case. James Weinstein describes the conversion of some businessmen to a mild form of progressivism in his *The Corporate Ideal in the Liberal State: 1900–1918* (Boston, 1968). A pioneering study of businessmen as reformers is Marguerite Green, *The National Civic Federation and the American Labor Movement 1900–1925* (Washington, D.C., 1956). Robert Wiebe's *Businessmen and Reform* (Cambridge, Mass., 1962) does not have the clear thesis of the Kolko and Weinstein books, but it is more plausible. Wiebe finds businessmen favoring certain "reforms," hostile to others, and in general divided and uncertain when it came to utilizing the state.

Samuel P. Hays applied the "community-society" theory to turn of the century America in "Political Parties and the Community-Society Continuum," in W. N. Chambers and W. D. Burnham (eds.), *The American Party Systems* (New York, 1967). Robert Wiebe's *The Search for Order* is the first book-length synthesis for this period which utilizes this concept. The scholarly reception of this book, among others, is the subject of Otis L. Graham, Jr., *From Roosevelt to Roosevelt: 1901–1941* (New York, 1971).

The social justice impulse is the subject of Robert Bremner, *From the Depths: The Discovery of Poverty in the United States* (New York, 1956), Jeremy Felt, *Hostages of Fortune: Child Labor Reform in New York State* (Syracuse, 1965), Clarke Chambers, *Seedtime of Reform,* Allen F. Davis, *Spearheads for Reform,* Roy Lubove, *The Progressives and the Slums: Tenement House Reform in New York City, 1897–1917* (Pittsburgh, 1962), and Henry May, *The Protestant Churches and Industrial America* (New York, 1949). Two of the most consistent champions of the underdog in the progressive era and for years thereafter are the subject of Carl H. Voss, *Rabbi and Minister: The Friendship of Stephen S. Wise and John Haynes Holmes* (Cleveland, 1964). The quotation from George Alger on p. 141 is from Felt, *Hostages of Fortune,* p. 222. The New Dealer who complained of the inefficacy of housing reform, quoted on p. 142, was brought to my attention by John P. Dean, "The Myths of Housing Reform," *American Sociological Review* (1949), p. 106. The quotation from Roy Lubove on p. 143 is drawn from his *The Struggle for Social Security 1900–1935* (Cambridge, Mass., 1968), p. 45. The quotation on p. 143 is from Herbert Croly's *The Promise of American*

Life (New York, 1909), p. 23. The quotation on p. 144 is from Will-ford I. King, *The Wealth and Income of the People of the United States* (New York, 1917), p. 231. Another valuable study of income and its distribution is Simon Kuznets, *National Income: A Summary of Findings* (New York, 1946).

On the attitude of reformers toward blacks, see Dewey Grantham, Jr., "The Progressive Movement and the Negro," *South Atlantic Quarterly* 54 (October, 1955), who finds little sensitivity to racial injustice among reformers, and Gilbert Osofsky, "Progressivism and the Negro: New York, 1900–1915," *American Quarterly* 16 (Summer, 1964), who shows that New York reformers in this area, as in many others, were quite advanced for their time. Charles F. Kellogg's *The NAACP: A History of the National Association for the Advancement of Colored People, 1909–1920* (Baltimore, 1957), describes the organizational efforts of blacks. For something of the lives of blacks in this period, see Rayford Logan, *The Negro in American Life and Thought: The Nadir, 1877–1901* (New York, 1954). The best studies of the two progressive presidents are Seth M. Scheiner, "President Theodore Roosevelt and the Negro, 1901–1908," *Journal of Negro History* 47 (July, 1962), and Henry Blumenthal, "Woodrow Wilson and the Race Question," *Journal of Negro History* 48 (January, 1963). Other useful treatments of this problem are Allen F. Davis, *Spearheads for Reform*, chapter 5; Louis Filler, *Crusaders for American Liberalism* (New York, 1939), chapter 21; C. Vann Woodward, *The Origins of the New South, 1877–1913* (Baton Rouge, 1951), chapters 12 and 13; and a recent brief study by David Southern, *The Malignant Heritage: Yankee Progressives and the Negro Question, 1901–1914* (Chicago, 1968). Two studies of the southern penal system are Jane Zimmerman, "The Penal Reform Movement in the South During the Progressive Era," *Journal of Southern History,* 17 (November, 1951), and Fletcher M. Green, "Some Aspects of the Convict Lease System in the Southern States," in Green (ed.), *Essays in Southern History* (Chapel Hill, 1949). The statement by Homer Folks quoted on p. 148 appeared in *National Conference of Charities and Corrections Proceedings* (Fort Wayne, 1911), p. 8. The remark by Wilson quoted on p. 149 was called to my attention by Southern, *The Malignant Heritage,* on p. 78. The comment of Walter Weyl on p. 152 is from Weyl, *The New Democracy* (New York, 1912), p. 342.

Reformers who were primarily interested in defending the culture of the native white middle classes are the subject of James Timberlake's *Prohibition and the Progressive Movement: 1900–1925* (Cambridge, Mass., 1963), Joseph Gusfield, *Symbolic Crusade: Status Politics and the American Temperance Movement* (Urbana, Ill., 1963), and Norman H. Clark, *The Dry Years: Prohibition and Social Change in Washington* (Seattle, 1965). On the Klan, see the readable survey by David M. Chalmers, *Hooded Americanism: The History of the Ku Klux Klan* (New York, 1965), and the penetrating scholarly analysis of Charles C. Alexander, *The Ku Klux Klan in the Southwest* (Lexington, Ky., 1965). In Alexander's book, and to an ever greater extent in Kenneth T. Jackson, *The Ku Klux Klan in the City, 1915–1930* (New York, 1967), one sees that the Klan attracted many people who sought better schools and law enforcement and a stronger sense of community. The concentration on racial and religious persecution was a decision of the Klan leadership and obscured the similarities between the Klan and parts of prewar progressivism. On woman suffrage, in addition to Alan Grimes, see Eleanor Flexner's survey, *Century of Struggle: The Woman's Rights Movement in the United States* (Cambridge, Mass., 1959), and the thoughtful interpretation by Aileen Kraditor, *The Ideas of the Woman Suffrage Movement, 1890–1920* (New York, 1965).

The overlap between some forms of progressivism and turn-of-the-century nativism is illuminated in John Higham, *Strangers in the Land: Patterns of American Nativism 1860–1925* (New Brunswick, 1955), Roy Lubove, "The Progressives and the Prostitute," *The Historian* 24 (May, 1962), and in Egal Feldman, "Prostitution, The Alien Woman, and the Progressive Imagination: 1900–1915," *American Quarterly* (Summer, 1967). This article called my attention to the passage from Abraham Flexner's *Prostitution in Europe* (New York, 1914), p. 395, which is quoted on p. 155 above.

Crystal Eastman's argument for workmen's compensation is found in her book *Work-Accidents and the Law* (New York, 1910), a volume in the Pittsburgh survey. For Brandeis' argument that social insurance is mandated by the wastefulness and inefficiency of the present remorseless industrial system, as well as by human compassion, see his "Workingmen's Insurance—The Road to Social Efficiency," in *Proceedings of the National Conference of Charities and Corrections* (New York, 1911). Charles Edward Russell, in *The Uprising of the Masses* (New York, 1910), described poverty as social inefficiency.

Irving Fisher, in his "The Significance of the Anti-Alcohol Movement," *Proceedings of the National Conference on Social Welfare* (1919), summarized the reasons for prohibiting alcoholic beverages: "the ideals of work, the requirements of modern industrial competition, the findings of modern science, and the ideals of morality." Like most progressives, Fisher assumed that science, morality, and self-interest all directed the same reforms. All interests were ultimately harmonious. The quotation on p. 155 is from Frederick W. Taylor's *The Principles of Scientific Management* (New York, 1911), p. 8.

Some of the progressive campaigns that combined the social control, nativist, and social justice elements were woman suffrage, the La-Follette Seaman's Act, and the drive against prostitution. See Aileen Kraditor, *The Ideas of the Woman Suffrage Movement,* Jerold Auerbach, "Progressivism at Sea: The LaFollette Act of 1915," *Labor History* (Fall, 1961), and the article by Feldman on prostitution, cited above. A similar blend may be seen in the eugenics movement, which attracted many progressives: see Mark Haller, "Heredity in Progressive Thought," *Social Service Review* 37 (June, 1963). For an example of how the diverse strains of progressivism could combine in a political movement, see Albert D. Kirwan's study of Mississippi reform, *Revolt of the Rednecks: Mississippi Politics 1876–1925* (Lexington, Ky., 1951); for their combination in a single individual, see E. A. Ross, *Seventy Years of It* (New York, 1936), or Paul W. Glad, *The Trumpet Soundeth: William Jennings Bryan and His Democracy 1896–1912* (Lincoln, Neb., 1960). A very perceptive essay on the contradictions so often found in the progressive collective mentality is John Braeman's "Seven Progressives," *Business History Review* 35 (Winter, 1961). The remark by William S. U'Ren on p. 158 is taken from Earl Pomeroy's introduction to Lincoln Steffens, *The Upbuilders* (Seattle, 1968; originally published in 1909 by Doubleday, Page), p. xxxv. The quotation from John Gordon Ross on p. 158 is from Ross, "Ladies in Politics," Forum 95 (November, 1936). The Taft quotation on p. 161 is from Henry Pringle, *The Life and Times of William Howard Taft* (New York, 1939) Vol. 2, p. 967. The quotation from William Olney on p. 163 is from a letter to Charles E. Perkins, president of the Chicago, Burlington, and Quincy Railroad, dated sometime in 1892, and quoted in James R. Smith and Paul L. Murphy (eds.), *Liberty and Justice: A Historical Record of American Constitutional Development* (New York, 1958), pp. 292–293. William

McAdoo's autobiography is *Crowded Years: The Reminiscences of William Gibbs McAdoo* (New York, 1931). On the strain of realism in progressive thought, see Bremner, *From the Depths,* and Richard Hofstadter, "Charles Beard and the Constitution," *American Quarterly* (Fall, 1950). Those who enjoy the sayings of "Mr. Dooley" might begin with Louis Filler (ed.), *The World of Mr. Dooley* (New York, 1962).

Mrs. George Gould

Courtesy of Brown Brothers, New York

Photograph by Lewis W. Hine. Used with permission of the George Eastman House, Rochester, New York

Italian immigrant carrying home materials for the entire family to process at starvation pay, 1909

Courtesy of Brown Brothers, New York

Hester Street, New York City

Teddy Roosevelt

Courtesy of Brown Brothers, New York

Courtesy of Underwood & Underwood, New York

Woodrow Wilson speaking from observation platform of car, 1912

A United Press International Photo
German troops on the attack at Villers-Bretonneaux, April 1, 1918.

Courtesy of Brown Brothers, New York
Returning troops marching on Fifth Ave., New York City

U.S. Signal Corps. Courtesy of the National Archives

President Wilson and the Duke of Connaught being greeted by
children, Dover, England, 1919

A glimpse of the female ankle boarding trolley step entrances, 1908

DOCUMENTS

The documents included here have been chosen because, in addition to their intrinsic importance and influence upon contemporaries, they seem to me to present particularly well a leading progressive idea or conjunction of ideas. Thus, I have omitted books such as William Allen White's *The Old Order Changeth* or Jacob Riis' *How the Other Half Lived,* which embodied the progressive qualities of indignation, factual exposure, and optimism but which made no important intellectual contribution, and have included instead a selection from John Spargo's *The Bitter Cry of the Children,* which advanced a distinctly progressive idea about the relation of environment to justice.

Primary materials selected according to such tastes, it may be said, run the risk of presenting an unrepresentative picture of reform. One overlooks speeches heard by thousands, party platforms, bromidic but hugely popular reform novels, and a wide range of periodical literature because such items were banal and ephemeral; yet they bespoke the progressive mind in its typical forms. But the important ideas of the progressive generation were not all impounded in difficult books by Croly, Dewey, or Holmes. One can find expression that by form and occasion was clearly typical but that embodied some seminal idea or set of ideas in subtle, complex, and sometimes logic-defying combination. The primary materials reprinted here have the common touch because they were designed to persuade masses of voters, readers of popular magazines, fellow professionals, and citizens in large conventions and meetings. But they also display the progressive mind as it reached beyond emotions and formulas to achieve some penetrating insight into modern society, or as it combined several ideas in those breathtakingly implausible combinations that reveal for us as only primary materials can the *zeitgeist* of the era. Possibly the most interesting of such unlikely combinations, to our own generation at least, is the conjunction of racism with progressive idealism. Several selections blend such apparently irreconcilable sentiments. I chose them not to imply that the reformers were unusually racist for their day, since the muddle of evidence on this seems to suggest that most of them were typical of their day in their racial attitudes, and some were far better. The note of racism is deliberately included here because it was a part of their thought, and because an awareness of its pervasiveness helps us to understand the fate of reform in the 1920s.

For the period of diplomatic difficulties and war, 1914–18, I have reprinted documents that seem to demonstrate a peculiarly progressive way of looking at these questions. Thus, one will not find below the *Lusitania* or *Sussex* notes, but I have tried to present the evolving Wilsonian position, along with that of the liberal opposition. For the postwar years I have selected documents that reveal the reform mind as it groped for reorientation. The last five selections are assessments of the reform record by authorities with good but varying credentials.

index